CW00202106

THE ANTICHRIST

The malevolent figure of the Antichrist endures in modern culture, whether religious or secular; and the spectral shadow he has cast over the ages continues to exert a strong and powerful fascination. Philip C. Almond tells the story of the son of Satan from his early beginnings to the present day, and explores this false Messiah in theology, literature, and the history of ideas. Discussing the origins of the malign being who at different times was cursed as Belial, Nero, or Damien, the author reveals how Christianity in both East and West has imagined this incarnation of absolute evil destined to appear at the end of time. For the better part of the last 2,000 years, Almond suggests, the human battle between right and wrong has been envisaged as a mighty cosmic duel between good and its opposite, culminating in an epic final showdown between Christ and his deadly arch-nemesis.

PHILIP C. ALMOND is Professorial Research Fellow at the Institute for Advanced Studies in the Humanities at the University of Queensland. His many books in the fields of religion and intellectual history include *God: A New Biography* (2018), *Afterlife: A History of Life after Death* (2016), *The Devil: A New Biography* (2014), *The Lancashire Witches* (2012), *England's First Demonologist* (2011), *Demonic Possession and Exorcism in Early Modern England* (Cambridge University Press, 2004), *Adam and Eve in Seventeenth-Century Thought* (Cambridge University Press, 1999), and *Heaven and Hell in Enlightenment England* (Cambridge University Press, 1994). Among other languages, his work has been translated into Catalan, Dutch, German, Hungarian, and Polish.

'An ambitious untangling of a host of different traditions and stories – all super-heated by religious controversy – *The Antichrist* succeeds triumphantly in reducing them to calm intelligibility. This is a major feat, not only of scholarship, but also of reflection, planning and writing. I was not previously aware of many of the complexities of the story, or that so much intellectual activity had been devoted to defining and elaborating upon the characteristics and "life" of the Antichrist specifically. The biography format is a good way to explore this tradition. An accessible account will be very valuable to scholars who want to know more about the Antichrist, as well as to students and the general reader. Almond's book combines solid research with a readable and lively account.'

Marion Gibson, Professor of Renaissance and Magical Literatures, University of Exeter, author of *Rediscovering Renaissance Witchcraft* and of *Witchcraft: The Basics*

'Philip Almond's remarkable new book – a companion piece to his earlier work on the Devil – is clearly and vividly written. Giving full attention to previous ideas about the Antichrist, especially those of Bernard McGinn, the author looks at the subject differently and originally in a way that meshes the topical and the chronological. He clearly sets forth the fundamental dichotomy between the Antichrist as a real, historical person and the Antichrist as a metaphor for human evil. Both these interpretations appear in different forms throughout the history of Christianity; and although the metaphorical dominates contemporary theology, even today there are many for whom the metaphorical is not the only view. The fuzziness of the concept makes it particularly hard to trace historically, but Almond has done a fine job here. He also successfully relates his topic to broader intellectual and social changes. In all, the book is an advance in both theological and popular understanding, and I recommend it warmly.'

Jeffrey Burton Russell, Professor Emeritus of History, University of California, Santa Barbara; author of *Lucifer: The Devil in the Middle Ages* and of *A History of Heaven: The Singing Silence*

THE
ANTICHRIST

A NEW BIOGRAPHY

PHILIP C. ALMOND
University of Queensland

CAMBRIDGE
UNIVERSITY PRESS

CAMBRIDGE
UNIVERSITY PRESS

University Printing House, Cambridge CB2 8BS, United Kingdom

One Liberty Plaza, 20th Floor, New York, NY 10006, USA

477 Williamstown Road, Port Melbourne, VIC 3207, Australia

314–321, 3rd Floor, Plot 3, Splendor Forum, Jasola District Centre,
New Delhi – 110025, India

79 Anson Road, #06–04/06, Singapore 079906

Cambridge University Press is part of the University of Cambridge.

It furthers the University's mission by disseminating knowledge in the
pursuit of education, learning, and research at the highest international
levels of excellence.

www.cambridge.org
Information on this title: www.cambridge.org/9781108479653
DOI: 10.1017/9781108855945

First published 2020

Printed in the United Kingdom by TJ International Ltd, Padstow Cornwall

A catalogue record for this publication is available from the British Library.

Library of Congress Cataloging-in-Publication Data
NAMES: Almond, Philip C., author.
TITLE: The antichrist : a new biography / Philip C. Almond,
University of Queensland.
DESCRIPTION: Cambridge, United Kingdom ; New York, NY, USA :
Cambridge University Press, 2020. | Includes bibliographical
references and index.
IDENTIFIERS: LCCN 2020018172 (print) | LCCN 2020018173 (ebook) |
ISBN 9781108479653 (hardback) | ISBN 9781108855945 (ebook)
SUBJECTS: LCSH: Antichrist.
CLASSIFICATION: LCC BT985 .A39 2020 (print) | LCC BT985 (ebook) |
DDC 236–dc23
LC record available at https://lccn.loc.gov/2020018172
LC ebook record available at https://lccn.loc.gov/2020018173

ISBN 978-1-108-47965-3 Hardback

To Jenna

CONTENTS

List of Plates   *page x*
Acknowledgements   *xv*

Prologue   **1**

1 The Origins of the Antichrist
Tradition   **7**
Millennial Moments   7
The Life of the Antichrist   11
'The Antichrist' Arrives   15
Eschatology and the Antichrist   19
The Man of Lawlessness and the Son of Perdition 23
The Dragon and the Beasts   25
False Prophets, Messiahs, and a World Deceiver 31
The Eschatological Tyrant   36

2 The Story Begins   **41**
Irenaean Innovations   41
Variations on an Irenaean Theme   47
Nero and the Double Antichrists   56
The Son of Satan?   67
To See Him Was to Know Him   72

3 The Antichrist, East and West **77**
The Antichrist Within   77
The Antichrist, Then and Now!   85

Contents

The Antichrist, Immanent and Imminent   91
Simon, the Magical Antichrist   100
The Last World Emperor   104
Gog and Magog   112
In the Meantime!   120

4 Antichrists, Present and Future   **126**
Muhammad the Antichrist   126
Al-Dajjal, the Deceiver   132
Armilus, the Jewish Antichrist   139
The Antichrist of Roger de Hoveden   142
Apocalypse Maybe?   145
Sexy Beast   153
Magnus Antichristus   159

5 Of Prophets, Priests, and Kings   **165**
Antichrists, Regal and Papal   165
The Antichrist Mysticus   174
Mystical Prophets and an Angelic Pope   183
The Radical Antichrist   190

6 The Antichrist Divided   **201**
The Return of Adso's Antichrist   201
The Magisterial Antichrist   208
Revisiting the Book of Revelation   219
The Empire Strikes Back   224
The Antichrist of the Radical Reformation   229

7 Antichrists – Papal, Philosophical, Imperial   **236**
The 'Scientific' Antichrist   236
Sceptics and Believers   244

Contents

French Antichrists 252

Back to the Futurists 264

Deconstructing the Antichrist 270

The Floating Signifier 274

Epilogue A Brief Meditation on History **285**

Bibliography *291*

Index *309*

The colour plate section can be found between pp. 144 and 145

PLATES

1   *Elijah and Enoch murdered by the Antichrist* (mid
    eleventh century, France), Beatus of Liebana,
    Commentary on the Apocalypse, fol. 55. Alamy
    (HN2N4B).
2   *St Michael killing the dragon*, Lieferinxe, Josse
    (Master of St Sebastian) (fl. 1493–1508) / Musée du
    Petit Palais, Avignon, France / Bridgeman Images
    (XIR167578).
3   *Seven-headed serpent from the Book of Revelation*,
    from the Luther Bible, c. 1530 (coloured woodcut),
    German School (sixteenth century) / Bible Society,
    London, UK / Bridgeman Images (BAL34274).
4   *The martyrdom of Isaiah.* Miniature, Musée Condé,
    Chantilly, France / Alamy (P9EPKY).
5   *The Antichrist at the gates of Jerusalem.* The History
    Collection / Alamy (J4T2HD).
6   *Antiochus Epiphanes IV and his army before Jerusalem.*
    Ms 728/312 fol. 301 v, Antiochus Epiphanes IV
    Seleucid king of Syria (175–163 BC) and his army
    before Jerusalem, and the pillage of the Jewish
    temple, French edition of original written by
    Jean de Courcy (c. 1350–1431) (vellum) (detail of
    71878), French School (fifteenth century) / Musée
    Condé, Chantilly, France / Bridgeman Images
    (CND291656).

7 *The fall of Simon Magus*, from 'La Chronique de Nuremberg' by Hartmann Schedel, Nürnberg, 1492 (colour woodcut), German School (fifteenth century) / Bibliothèque Mazarine, Paris, France / Archives Charmet / Bridgeman Images (BMR163356).

8 *Saint Peter and Simon Magus*, by Benozzo Gozzoli (1420–1497) / Alamy (CTWW5E).

9 *Antichrist riding Leviathan*, Cod. Guelf. 1 Gud. lat. 42 r, from 'Liber Floridus' by Lambert de Saint-Omer c. 1120 (vellum), French School (twelfth century) / Herzog August Bibliothek, Wolfenbüttel, Germany / Prismatic Pictures / Bridgeman Images (DGC954839).

10 *Alexander building a wall to enclose the people of 'Gog and Magog'*, from Wauquelin's story of Alexander. Bruges, Belgium fifteenth century [1] (fifteenth century). Jean Wauquelin (d. 1452) / Alamy (PO28HK).

11 *St Michael vanquishes the Antichrist*, Church of Santa Maria del Pi, Barcelona, 1455, Jaume Huguet (1412–92) / Alamy (EBAE73).

12 *Birth of the Antichrist*, Hildegard, *Scivias*, 3.11, Eibingen, MS 1, fol. 214 v (copy of Wiesbaden, Hessische Landesbibliothek, MS 1), Vision of the Last Days (photo: after *Scivias*, CCCM 43A, by permission of Brepols Publishers).

13 *The fall of the Antichrist*, Retablo de la Leyenda de San Miguel – Detalle de la Caida del Anticristo – Hacia 1440 – Temple/Tabla – NP 1332 – Gotico español – Conjunto 10139 y 10146. Author: Master

of Arguis (fifteenth century). Location: Museo del
Prado – Pintura, Madrid, Spain / Alamy (P2Y3TG).

14 *The birth of the Antichrist from a dying woman via
    a Caesarean operation*, reproduction, 1933, of a
    woodcut, 1475 / Wellcome Library (no. 16938i).

15 *On the birth of the Antichrist*, 1498 / Wellcome
    Collection (CC BY).

16 *The seven-headed-beast coming from the sea*, 1360–70
    (fresco), Menabuoi, Giusto di Giovanni de'
    (d. 1393) / Padua baptistery, Padua, Italy / Alinari /
    Bridgeman Images (ALI208415).

17 *Miniature of Pope John XXII*, Vaticinia de
    Pontificibus. Italy, Central (Florence); second
    quarter of the fifteenth century. Source: Harley
    1340, f. 5. / Alamy (J8GO4A).

18 *Piramide papistique. Satiric representation* of the *Roman
    Church hierarchy* as the *Serpent* of *Hell*. Protestant
    anti-papist flyer, Holland, sixteenth century / Alamy
    (JKTY3X).

19 *Sermon and deeds of the Antichrist from Last Judgment
    cycle*, 1499–1504 (fresco), Signorelli, Luca
    (c. 1450–1523) / Orvieto cathedral, Italy /
    De Agostini Picture Library / S. Vannini /
    Bridgeman Images (DGA911867).

20 *Sermon and deeds of the Antichrist from Last Judgment
    cycle* (detail), 1499–1504 (fresco), Signorelli, Luca
    (c. 1450–1523) / Orvieto cathedral, Italy /
    De Agostini Picture Library / S. Vannini /
    Bridgeman Images (DGA911868).

21 *Sermon and deeds of the Antichrist from Last Judgment
    cycle* (detail), 1499–1504 (fresco), Signorelli, Luca
    (c. 1450–1523) / Orvieto cathedral, Italy /

De Agostini Picture Library / S. Vannini / Bridgeman Images (DGA911881).

22 *Sermon and deeds of the Antichrist from Last Judgment cycle* (detail), 1499–1504 (fresco), Signorelli, Luca (c. 1450–1523) / Orvieto cathedral, Italy / De Agostini Picture Library / S. Vannini / Bridgeman Images (DGA911867).

23 *Sermon and deeds of the Antichrist from Last Judgment cycle* (detail), 1499–1504 (fresco), Signorelli, Luca (c. 1450–1523) / Orvieto cathedral, Italy / De Agostini Picture Library / S. Vannini / Bridgeman Images (DGA911867).

24 *Sermon and deeds of the Antichrist from Last Judgment cycle* (detail), 1499–1504 (fresco), Signorelli, Luca (c. 1450–1523) / Orvieto cathedral, Italy / De Agostini Picture Library / S. Vannini / Bridgeman Images (DGA911867).

25 *Sermon and deeds of the Antichrist from Last Judgment cycle* (detail), 1499–1504 (fresco), Signorelli, Luca (c. 1450–1523) / Orvieto cathedral, Italy / De Agostini Picture Library / S. Vannini / Bridgeman Images (DGA911867).

26 *Thomas Murner as cat, Emser as goat, Pope Leo X as antichrist, Johannes Eck as dog, Lempp as pig*, woodcut, Nuremberg, c. 1520, private collection / Alamy (A7WBBP).

27 *The Whore of Babylon*, from the Luther Bible, c. 1530 (coloured woodcut), German School (sixteenth century) / Bible Society, London, UK / Bridgeman Images (BAL 12732).

28 'The Beast as described in the Revelations', hand-coloured etching by Thomas Rowlandson

(1757–1827). English artist and caricaturist. Dated 1808 / Alamy (F7P672).

29 *Rosemary's Baby*, USA, 1968. Director: Roman Polanski. Actors/stars: Mia Farrow, John Cassavetes, Ruth Gordon / Alamy (HM8JYF).

30 *The Final Conflict (aka Omen III)*, 1981. Director: Graham Baker. Actor/star: Rossano Brazzi (Father DeCarlo) / Alamy (HCTY56).

ACKNOWLEDGEMENTS

This book was written in the Institute for Advanced Studies in the Humanities at the University of Queensland in Australia. For the past decade, this institute and its predecessor, the Centre for the History of European Discourses, have provided a congenial, stimulating, and, more often than one can hope to expect, an exciting context in which to work. For this I am indebted in particular to my friends and colleagues Professor Peter Harrison, the Director of the Institute, Emeritus Professor Peter Cryle, Emeritus Professor Ian Hunter, and Emeritus Professor Fred D'Agostino. They have all given of their time to talk with me on many occasions. I am grateful also to the many postdoctoral fellows and other research fellows of the Institute, all of whose dedication to their work has provided so much encouragement to my own.

A wide-ranging book such as this is inevitably indebted to those scholars who have previously done the hard yards in this intellectual domain. Without their often ground-breaking work, this book would not have been possible. I have expressed my debt to many of these in the course of this study. But I am particularly indebted to many of the works of Bernard McGinn, and particularly to his seminal study *Antichrist*. He ends this work with a passage from Denis the Carthusian: 'Have we not worn ourselves out with that accursed Antichrist?' Well, that is now three of us, at least.

I take the opportunity once again to thank Alex Wright, my editor at Cambridge, for his support and encouragement of this work. I thank him too for the friendship we have forged over many years on the eight projects we have worked on together.

I am grateful again to my partner, Patricia Lee. Yet again, she has listened day by day to this text as it progressed, and has offered much helpful advice. This work is dedicated to my stepdaughter, Jenna.

PROLOGUE

~

*It is therefore necessary for us to mark diligently, and to espy
out this fellow: and it is convenient for us also, to give the eyes
of our hearts attentively unto this purpose (especially the world
that now is) to the intent we may be able to know (out of the
scriptures) both him and all his wiles, and to beware of him,
that he beguile us not.*

Rudolph Walther, *Antichrist* (1556)

For the better part of the last 2,000 years, Christians
have followed the advice of the Swiss theologian Rudolph
Walther (1519–86). They have devoted themselves to
espying out the Antichrist. Christians lived in expectation that the end of history was at hand. And the
Antichrist was the most conspicuous sign that its end was
nigh. Thus, to discern, or at least to estimate, the arrival
time of the Antichrist was in everyone's present, future,
and eternal interest.

The Antichrist would be the archetypal evil human
being, ultimate evil in human form. He would come at
the end of the world to persecute the Christian faithful. Finally, however, he would be defeated by Christ or
by the archangel Michael. The Bible, and particularly
the prophetic books of Daniel and Revelation, it was
believed, enabled biblical readers to pursue him through
its pages. Consequently, searching the biblical books for
knowledge of him was an obligation laid upon believers
by God. As Isaac Newton (1642–1727) told his readers, 'If
God was so angry with the Jews for not searching more
diligently into the Prophecies which he had given them

1

to know Christ by, why should we think he will excuse us for not searching the Prophecies which he hath given us to know Antichrist by?"[1]

This book tells the story of the Antichrist from his beginnings in the New Testament up to the present time. Far from being a fully developed figure within the Christian tradition from an early period, it was only at the end of the first millennium that a biography of the birth, life, and death of the Antichrist was written by Adso (d. 992), a Benedictine monk of Montier-en-Der in north-eastern France. Adso brought together the key features of the life of the Antichrist as it had developed over the first millennium of the common era. His was the tyrannical Antichrist outside the Christian church. But within 200 years of Adso's biography, his tyrannical Antichrist would be set over against another story of a papal Antichrist – a deceiver and hypocrite within the church – initiated by Joachim (c. 1135–1202), a monk of the Cistercian tradition, in Fiore in southern Italy. From the year 1200, and for the next 800 years, these two competing visions of the Antichrist – the Adsonian imperial tyrant outside the church and the Joachite papal deceiver within it – would constitute two competing narratives of the life of the Antichrist.

The figure of the Antichrist was the final result of a double dilemma within early Christianity. First, theologically, through his life, death, and resurrection, Jesus had overcome evil. Yet evil continued. Second, eschatologically, early Christianity expected Christ's second

---

[1] Frank E. Manuel, *The Religion of Isaac Newton* (Oxford: Clarendon Press, 1974), appendix A, p. 109.

coming imminently. Yet he failed to return. The failure of Christ to return made possible, and the apparent failure of his victory over evil made necessary, the creation of a future end to the world when evil would be decisively defeated. In short, the Antichrist became, along with the Devil, a key component of a Christian providentialism that demanded, in spite of the redemption by Christ already effected, a final resolution of cosmic and human evil.[2]

'The Antichrist' was, from the beginning, a fluid and unstable idea. This was the result of an array of tensions within the concept of the Antichrist that developed over the first twelve centuries of the common era. The first of these arose from the question of whether the Antichrist would be an eschatological tyrant outside the church or a deceiver within it, later to be formalised in the contrast between Adso and Joachim. This issue was present within Christianity as early as the second century. Second, imbedded within the biblical accounts was the tension between the Antichrist who is to come and the many Antichrists already present. Third, there was the discord between the Antichrist to come and the Antichrist already present within every individual. Fourth, there was the tension between the Antichrist outside the church and the Antichrists within it. Fifth, granted the distinction between a literal and a mystical or hidden meaning to the Scriptures, there was the interplay between the 'real' Antichrist who was to come and the 'spiritual' Antichrist already present. These tensions

---

[2] See Philip C. Almond, *The Devil: A New Biography* (London and Ithaca: I. B. Tauris and Cornell University Press, 2014), ch. 3.

were all in play when eschatological anxieties surged at the end of the first millennium.

Sixth, with the stories of Adso and Joachim in place by the year 1200, there developed the conflict over the eschatological tyrant *who was to come* (exemplified in the Adsonian tradition) and the papal deceiver *who was already present* (exemplified in the Joachite tradition), whether as an individual or as a collective. The story of the Antichrist then became one of identifying figures or institutions outside (emperors and empires) or inside the church (popes and papacy) in the present time as the Antichrist. This was often allied with a new reading of history (especially via the books of Revelation and Daniel) that would see the end times as having already begun. This would climax in the Reformation's identification of the Antichrist with the pope and the papacy.

Finally, alongside these literal readings of the Antichrist, heavily dependent on prophetic interpretations of Scripture, a 'rhetorical' Antichrist came into being. 'The Antichrist' became 'popularised'. It was more a matter of 'demonising' opponents in the present than speculating about evil incarnate in the future. This was a use of 'the Antichrist' that was to become increasingly common after the middle of the nineteenth century, when apocalypticism and biblical prophecy became marginalised among Western intellectual elites. Freed from reliance upon biblical categories, the Antichrist was then free to roam across landscapes, both religious and secular, fictional and non-fictional.

To explore the life of the Antichrist is also to engage with a large set of related stories. In part, these are the result of the Antichrist absorbing a significant number of biblical figures – Gog and Magog, Behemoth and Leviathan, the beasts from the earth and from the sea, the mark of the beast and his number, the false prophet, and the destroyer. But the story of the Antichrist was enhanced and enriched as it incorporated the legends of Alexander the Great, of the two witnesses of the book of Revelation, of Simon Magus, of Antiochus Epiphanes and the emperor Nero, of Muhammad the prophet, of the Last World Emperor, and of Angelic Popes. The Antichrist tradition was enriched when, influenced by the Christian stories of the Antichrist, Islam and Judaism constructed their own Antichrists – al-Dajjal, the Antichrist of the Muslims, and Armilus, the Antichrist of the Jews.

The Antichrist still 'lives' on in modern popular culture, both secular and religious. Yet, for the past 150 years, he has become marginal to the dominant concerns of Western intellectual life. That life could not once have been thought or imagined without the Antichrist looming on the horizon of the everyday has been all but forgotten. The aim of this book is to bring to the modern reader a deeper appreciation and understanding of how, from the earliest centuries of the Christian period to the present day, an awareness of who we are as human beings included the story of who we could be at our worst. With that comes the deeper recognition that, for the better part of the last 2,000 years, the battle between good and evil within each of us was imagined as part of a battle between good and evil at the depth of things. At the cosmic level, it was envisaged as a battle between God and Satan; at the human level, it was seen as a battle between

Christ, the son of God, and the Antichrist, the son of Satan. Thus, the battle between good and evil was at the heart of history itself. As we will see in the course of this book, it was a battle that could and would only be resolved at the end of history.

I

The Origins of the Antichrist Tradition

~

Then I saw an angel coming down from heaven, holding in his
hand the key to the bottomless pit and a great chain. He seized
the dragon, that ancient serpent, who is the Devil and Satan, and
bound him for a thousand years, and threw him into the pit, and
locked and sealed it over him, so that he would deceive the nations
no more, until the thousand years were ended. After that he must
be let out for a little while.

Revelation 20.1–3

Millennial Moments

The end of the first millennium was at hand. For some,
so was the end of the world. That Satan would be bound
for a thousand years prior to his release and eventual
confinement in hell for an eternity was a certainty. That
Satan was already bound was a reading of Revelation
20.1–3 (above) that resonated throughout the medieval
period. It had the authority of Saint Augustine (354–430).
According to Augustine, the binding of Satan had already
happened as a result of the victory won over him by the
life, death, and resurrection of Jesus the Christ. It was
then that he had been thrown into the bottomless pit. The
Devil, Augustine declared, 'is prohibited and restrained
from seducing those nations which belong to Christ, but
which he formerly seduced or held in subjection'.[1]

---

[1] Marcus Dods (trans.), *The City of God*, 20.7, in *NPNF, first series*, vol. II,
    p. 427.

According to Augustine, at the end of time and history, Satan would be loosed again. Revelation 13.5 had prophesied that the beast that arose out of the sea would exercise authority for forty-two months. Augustine identified the beast with Satan. The Devil, he wrote, would then 'rage with the whole force of himself and his angels for three years and six months'.[2] Then, there would occur the final battle between God and Satan, Christ would come in judgement, and the Devil and his angels, together with the wicked in their resurrected bodies, would be consigned to everlasting punishment in the fires of hell. The time of Satan's release was also the time of the Antichrist, evil incarnate. As Augustine had put it, 'Christ will not come to judge quick and dead unless Antichrist, His adversary, first come to seduce those who are dead in soul ... then shall Satan be loosed, and by means of that Antichrist shall work with all power in a lying though a wonderful manner.'[3]

Although Augustine was committed to a real end of history at some time or other, he read metaphorically rather than literally the 'one thousand years' before Satan was loosed. But many did read it quite literally. Consequently, there was the expectation that Christ would return, Satan would be loosed, and the Antichrist would arise somewhere between the year 979 (a millennium from the then supposed date of Christ's birth) and the year 1033 (a millennium from the then presumed date of his death and resurrection).

Thus, there were many of the ecclesiastical elite and, no doubt, many among the populace at large who, while

---

[2] *Ibid.*, 20.8, vol. II, p. 428.   [3] *Ibid.*, 20.19, vol. II, p. 438.

taking their basic eschatological or apocalyptic soundings from Augustine, nevertheless saw the end of the world as happening more or less in the immediate future.[4] In a letter to the kings of France just before the end of the tenth century, Abbo, abbot of Saint-Benoît-sur-Loire (c. 945–1004), recalled that 'as a youth I heard a sermon preached to the people in the Paris church to the effect that as the number of 1000 years was completed, Antichrist would arrive, and not long after, the Last Judgment would follow'.[5] He went on to say that he resisted this as vigorously as he could in his preaching, using the books of Revelation and Daniel in rebuttal. But he had also to respond to 'another error which grew about the End of the World', and one which had 'filled almost the entire world'.[6] This was to the effect that, whenever the commemoration of the Annunciation fell on a Good Friday, the world would end.

It is reasonable to assume that Queen Gerberga, sister of the German ruler Otto I and wife of the French king Louis IV d'Outremer, shared in the apocalyptic anxieties of her subjects. With the battle to be joined between God and the Antichrist in the near future, and with her husband's kingdom under threat as a result, it was even

---

[4] Although the term 'apocalyptic' refers to prophetic revelations generally, in this book I take the terms 'apocalyptic' and 'eschatological' to refer to the events surrounding the cataclysmic end of history embedded within the Christian tradition.

[5] Quoted in Richard Landes, 'The Fear of an Apocalyptic Year 1000: Augustinian Historiography, Medieval and Modern', in Richard Landes, Andrew Gow, and David C. van Meter (eds.), *The Apocalyptic Year 1000: Religious Expectation and Social Change, 950–1050* (New York: Oxford University Press, 2003), p. 250.

[6] *Ibid.*

more reasonable that she should wish to get details on the origin, career, and signs of the Antichrist's arrival. Thus, somewhere around the year 950, she wrote to Adso, a Benedictine monk (later abbot) of Montier-en-Der in north-eastern France, to learn, as Adso put it, 'about the wickedness and persecution of the Antichrist, as well as of his power and origin'.[7]

His response to Queen Gerberga was contained in a letter entitled *On the Origin and the Time of the Antichrist* (*De ortu et tempore Antichristi*). It was the first biography of the Antichrist or, perhaps better, since it mimicked the genre of 'the lives of the saints', it was the first life of an anti-saint.[8] Adso knew this genre, for he was himself the author of five lives of saints. His originality lay, not so much in any original additions to the Antichrist traditions, but rather in synthesising many of them into a coherent 'Life of the Antichrist' from his birth to his death. As Richard K. Emmerson remarks, in giving the numerous discussions of Antichrist the form of the lives of the saints, Adso's biography contributed 'to the establishing of the Antichrist tradition as a major part of the religious consciousness of the later Middle Ages'.[9] The text survives in 9 versions and in 171 manuscripts. Along with the original Latin version, there were numerous

---

[7] Bernard McGinn (trans.), 'Adso of Montier-en-Der: Letter on the Origin and the Time of the Antichrist', in Bernard McGinn (trans. and ed.), *Apocalyptic Spirituality* (London: SPCK, 1979), p. 89. This remains the most accessible 'critical' translation.

[8] It was also known as the *Libellus de Antichristo* (*Little Book about the Antichrist*).

[9] Richard K. Emmerson, 'Antichrist as Anti-saint: The Significance of Abbot Adso's *Libellus de Antichristo*', *The American Benedictine Review* 30 (1979), 190.

translations into vernacular languages. It was, in short, an apocalyptic bestseller.

To Queen Gerberga, at least, Adso's life of the Antichrist contained a message of hope. For he had declared that the Antichrist would not come so long as the power of the Roman Empire survived, and, at the present, that power resided in the French monarchy, embodied in Gerberga's husband. For the moment, at least, Gerberga's anxieties could be calmed.

The Life of the Antichrist

The Antichrist was, according to Adso, quite simply contrary to Christ in all things. He would do everything against Christ. Thus, where Christ came as a humble man, the Antichrist would come as a proud one. He would exalt the wicked and revive the worship of demons in the world. Seeking his own glory, he 'will call himself Almighty God'.[10] Many of the 'ministers of his malice' have already existed, such as the Greek king Antiochus Epiphanes (c. 215–164 BCE) and the Roman emperors Nero (37–68 CE) and Domitian (51–96 CE). Indeed, there had always been many Antichrists, for anyone 'who lives contrary to justice and attacks the rule of his [Christ's] way of life and blasphemes what is good is an Antichrist, the minister of Satan'.[11]

The Antichrist that is to come would be a Jew from the tribe of Dan. Like other men, but unlike Christ who was born of a virgin, he would be born from the union of a man and a woman. Moreover, like other men, but

---

[10] McGinn (trans.), 'Adso of Montier-en-Der', p. 90.   [11] *Ibid.*, p. 90.

unlike Christ who was born without sin, he would be conceived, generated, and born in sin. At the moment of conception, the Devil would enter his mother's womb. In the case of Mary the mother of Jesus, the Holy Spirit so entered into her that what was born of her was divine and holy; 'so too the devil will descend into the Antichrist's mother, will completely fill her, completely encompass her, completely master her, completely possess her within and without, so that with the devil's cooperation she will conceive through a man and what will be born from her will be totally wicked, totally evil, totally lost'.[12] Although not literally the son of the Devil in the way that Christ was the son of God, 'the fullness of diabolical power and of the whole character of evil will dwell in him in bodily fashion'.[13]

As Christ knew Jerusalem as the best place for him to assume humanity, so too the Devil knew a place most fit for the Antichrist – Babylon, a city that was the root of all evil. However, although he would be born in Babylon, he would be brought up in the cities of Beth-saida and Corozain, the two cities that Christ reproached (Matthew 11.21). He would be reared in all forms of wickedness by magicians, enchanters, diviners, and wizards. Evil spirits would be his instructors and his constant companions.

Eventually, he would arrive in Jerusalem. There, he would circumcise himself and say to the Jews, 'I am the Christ promised to you who has come to save you, so that I can gather together and defend you.'[14] The Jews would flock to him, unaware that they were receiving the Antichrist. He would torture and kill all those Christians

[12] *Ibid.*, pp. 90–1.   [13] *Ibid.*, p. 93.   [14] *Ibid.*, p. 94.

that did not convert to his cause. He would then erect his throne in the temple, raising up the temple of Solomon to its former state. Kings and princes would be converted to his cause and, through them, their subjects. He would then send messengers and preachers through the whole world. He would also work many prodigies and miracles:

He will make fire come down from earth in a terrifying way, trees suddenly blossom and wither, the sea become stormy and unexpectedly calm. He will make the elements change into differing forms, divert the order and flow of bodies of water, disturb the air with winds and all sorts of commotions, and perform countless other wondrous acts. He will raise the dead.[15]

His power would be so great that even many of the faithful would wonder if he was, in reality, *Christ* returning.

They would not, however, wonder for very long. For the Antichrist would persecute faithful Christians in three ways. He would corrupt those he could by giving them gold and silver. Those whose faith was beyond such corruption, he would overpower with terror. He would attempt to seduce those that remained with signs and wonders. Those who were still continuing in their faith, unimpressed by his powers, would be tortured and put to death in the sight of all.

Then Adso invoked the authority of the New Testament that there would come a time of tribulation unlike anything experienced before (Matthew 24.21). Every Christian who was discovered would 'either deny God, or, if he will remain faithful, will perish, whether

---

[15] *Ibid.*, p. 92.

through sword, or fiery furnace, or serpents or beasts, or through some other kind of torture'.[16] This tribulation would last throughout the world for some three and a half years. The Antichrist would not, however, come without warning. Before his arrival, the two great prophets, Enoch and Elijah, would be sent into the world. They would defend the faithful against the Antichrist and prepare the elect for battle with three and a half years of preaching and teaching during the time of tribulation. They would convert the Jews to Christianity.

The Antichrist, having taken up arms against Enoch and Elijah, would kill them. Then the judgement of God would come upon the Antichrist. He would be killed by Jesus or by the archangel Michael, albeit through the power of Christ. God would then grant the elect forty days to do penance for having been led astray by the Antichrist. Adso was uncertain how long, after this forty days, it would be before the final judgement. It remained, concluded Adso, 'in the providence of God who will judge the world in that hour in which for all eternity he predetermined it was to be judged'.[17]

How then did the traditions of the Antichrist that came together in Adso's *On the Origin and the Time of the Antichrist* develop over the first millennium of the Common Era?[18]

---

[16] *Ibid.*, p. 92.   [17] *Ibid.*, p. 96.

[18] On the origins of the Antichrist and the legend more generally, see Wilhelm Bousset, *The Antichrist Legend; A Chapter in Christian and Jewish Folklore, Englished from the German of W. Bousset* (London: Hutchinson and Co., 1896); Bernard McGinn, *Antichrist: Two Thousand Years of Fascination with Evil* (San Francisco: Harper, 1994); Gregory C. Jenks, *The Origins and Early Development of the Antichrist Myth* (Berlin: Walter de Gruyter, 1991); L. J. Lietaert Peerbolte, *The*

'The Antichrist' Arrives

In the history of Christian thought, Jesus the Christ was goodness in human form. The Antichrist, by contrast, was evil incarnate. And yet the New Testament is remarkably silent about the Antichrist. There are only three passages in the New Testament that refer to the Antichrist, all of which occur in the letters of John. The first appearance of the term 'Antichrist' in Christian literature occurs in 1 John 2.18–27. It declares that the Antichrist is both one *and* many. It declares too that there are already many Antichrists in the world, and that their presence is a sign that the end of the world is at hand: 'Children, it is the last hour! As you have heard that antichrist is coming, so now many antichrists have come. From this we know that it is the last hour' (1 John 2.18). There was, in short, an expectation that, before Christ came again, the Antichrist himself would come. The text was a key one in the history of the Antichrist. For it set up the tension between the Antichrist of the future yet to come and the many Antichrists already present.

Who were these many Antichrists? The context of this verse makes it clear that they were, at least, Christians who had left the community to which the author was writing. It is clear too that they had left because they denied that Jesus was the son of God: 'This is the antichrist, the

Antecedents of Antichrist: A Traditio-Historical Study of the Earliest Christian Views on Eschatological Opponents (Leiden: Brill, 1996); Richard K. Emmerson, *Antichrist in the Middle Ages: A Study of Medieval Apocalypticism, Art, and Literature* (Seattle: University of Washington Press, 1981). McGinn's *Antichrist* remains the key text on the history of the Antichrist more generally, with a wealth of bibliographical data. I am especially indebted to it.

one who denies the Father and the Son' (1 John 2.22).
We get a further clarification of who these Antichrists
were in the second passage that deals with the Antichrist
(1 John 4.1–6). Again, the author refers to opponents who
are designated this time as 'false prophets' (1 John 4.1).
These too seem to have denied the divinity of Christ.
Every spirit that confesses, we read, that Jesus Christ has
come in the flesh is from God, while 'every spirit that
does not confess Jesus is not from God. And this is the
spirit of the antichrist of which you have heard that it
is coming' (1 John 4.3). Here, the Antichrist is already
present as the spiritual power behind those who deny the
truth of the Christian confession. The Antichrist that is
to come is 'in spirit' already present.

Like the term 'the Antichrist', the term 'false prophet'
is also one that refers to the end times. Thus, for example,
in the first of the New Testament gospels, the appearance
of false prophets and false Christs was one of the signs
of the Last Days (Mark 13.22). And in the last book of
the New Testament, the book of Revelation, the second
beast of the apocalypse was also identified with 'the false
prophet'. The false prophets of the first letter of John
were the deceivers of his second letter. Where in the first
letter many false prophets were said to have gone out into
the world, here 'many deceivers' were said to have gone
out. Again, these were unbelievers who did not confess
that Jesus Christ had come in the flesh. Any such person,
we read, 'is the deceiver and the antichrist!' (2 John 7).
In sum, the Antichrist of the two letters of John referred
to opponents of Christ who foreshadowed the coming of
the Antichrist or already embodied his activity as false
prophets and deceivers. In each case, they appear to have

denied the supernatural origin of Christ. And, in each case, 'the Antichrist' functioned to indicate that the end of the world was at hand.

The three letters of John in the New Testament can be probably dated to around the end of the first century.[19] It is clear, not only from the references to the Antichrist but from the more general theology of the first two letters, that they were written in the general expectation of the end of the age, the passing away of the world, the return of Jesus, and the Day of Judgement. Thus, the legend of the Antichrist was grounded in Christian expectation of the 'last things' (death, judgement, heaven, and hell). For its part, within the Christian tradition, the doctrine of the last things (eschatology) was set within the broader framework of a four-act historical drama. It began with God's creation of the world and the creation of Adam and Eve. It then proceeded, in the second act, to their fall into sin and their expulsion from the Garden of Eden. In the third and central act, God became man and redeemed humankind from the sin of Adam and Eve through the life, death, and resurrection of Jesus Christ. In the final act, at the end of history, the Antichrist would arise, Christ would return, Satan and the Antichrist would be defeated, the dead would arise, and God would judge the living and the dead, some for the joys of eternal life in heaven, others for the sufferings of an eternity in hell.

---

[19] The question of whether these letters were all written by the same author, together with the question of their relationship to the gospel of John, remains a matter of debate. See John Painter, 'Johannine Literature: The Gospel and Letters of John', in David E. Aune, *The Blackwell Companion to the New Testament* (Oxford: Blackwell, 2010), ch. 20.

If the first appearance of the term 'the Antichrist' was some seventy years after the death of Jesus Christ, some forty or fifty years more were to pass before its next appearance. This was around the middle of the second century in a letter of Polycarp, the bishop of Smyrna (c. 69–c. 155), to the Philippians. As with the community referred to in the letters of John, the Philippian community too was split into theological factions focused around the supernatural origin of Christ. So Polycarp quoted 1 John 4.3 against the dissenters:

'For whosoever does not confess that Jesus Christ has come in the flesh, is antichrist'; and whosoever does not confess the testimony of the cross, is of the devil; and whosoever perverts the oracles of the Lord to his own lusts, and says that there is neither a resurrection nor a judgement, he is the first-born of Satan.[20]

It was to be another thirty or so years, around 180, before Irenaeus, the bishop of Lyons (c. 130–c. 200), invoked 'the Antichrist' again in his *Against Heresies*. As a youth he had heard Polycarp preach. But unlike Polycarp, for whom 'Antichrist' referred only to contemporary heretics and not to an individual to arrive at the end of history, the Antichrist of Irenaeus was clearly an eschatological figure. More importantly, Irenaeus brought together a number of traditions within early Christianity that had been developing since the middle of the first century around Antichrist-like figures that would arise at the end of days. With Irenaeus, as we will later see, the legend of the Antichrist begins.

[20] A. Cleveland Coxe (ed.), *The Epistle of Polycarp to the Philippians*, 7, in *ANF*, vol. I, p. 34.

Eschatology and the Antichrist

Christianity was, from its beginnings, an apocalyptic tradition. Jesus was an eschatological preacher who proclaimed that the last times had begun, that the end of the world was at hand, and that the resurrection of the dead was to be succeeded by God's judgement upon those who rejected the teachings of Jesus.[21] The eschatology of Jesus was itself part and parcel of the eschatology of the Judaism within which Jesus' own teaching was imbedded. A core part of the Jewish eschatology of this time was its expectation of the coming of the Messiah or Christ. The most common belief was that the Messiah would be a descendant of King David, that he would appear at the end of history as a warrior who would defeat the enemies of the people of Israel, and that he would judge the wicked and usher in God's kingdom over which he would rule.[22]

It is impossible to tell whether Jesus thought of himself as the Messiah who was to come in the Last Days. If he did so think, it was certainly not as the expected warrior-Messiah who would militarily overthrow the foreign rulers from Rome. We can say, however, that he probably did see himself as an eschatological prophet appointed by God and sent to announce the imminent catastrophe about to fall upon the people of Israel. So it is perhaps not

[21] On the eschatology of Jesus, see Dale C. Allison, Jr, 'The Eschatology of Jesus', in John J. Collins, *The Encyclopedia of Apocalypticism: Vol. I, The Origins of Apocalypticism in Judaism and Christianity* (New York: Continuum, 1998), pp. 267–302.

[22] See John J. Collins, 'From Prophecy to Apocalypticism: The Expectation of the End', in John J. Collins (ed.), *The Encyclopedia of Apocalypticism: Vol. I, The Origins of Apocalypticism in Judaism and Christianity* (New York: Continuum, 1998), pp. 129–61.

surprising that, after his death, his followers came to see him not merely as an eschatological prophet in the style of John the Baptist, but as *the* eschatological prophet – the Messiah or the Christ of the Last Days.

The writings of the New Testament were composed between the time of the death of Jesus somewhere between 30 and 36 CE and the end of the first century. They were composed in an eschatological setting in the belief that Jesus was the Messiah who was to usher in the end of history. That the end did not come as soon as many early followers of Jesus initially expected entailed the necessity of the development of a narrative of what was to happen between the death and resurrection of Jesus and his return to judge the living and the dead. The Jesus of the first three gospels – Mark, Matthew, and Luke, all of which were written in the second half of the first century – was clearly presented as an eschatological prophet. 'Truly I tell you,' declared the Jesus of Mark's gospel, 'there are some standing here who will not taste death until they see that the Kingdom of God has come with power' (Mark 9.1). Each of these three gospels contained parallel teachings by Jesus on eschatological themes (Mark 13.1–37, Matthew 24.1–51, and Luke 21.1–36) that are known as the Little or Synoptic Apocalypse.[23]

The gospel of Mark contains the earliest version of Jesus' eschatological teachings. According to this, as Jesus was leaving the temple in Jerusalem, one of his disciples expressed his admiration for the size of the stones and buildings. Jesus replied that eventually not one stone

---

[23] The differences between the three accounts are of no matter for our purposes.

would be left standing on another. In short, the temple would be destroyed. The context then shifted to the Mount of Olives, where Jesus delivered an eschatological narrative that connected the destruction of the temple to the end of the world.

Although the Antichrist was not mentioned, there was a number of features of the later Antichrist tradition that appeared in Jesus' eschatological teachings. The first of these was his warning to beware of those who would later come in the name of Jesus saying, 'I am he' (Mark 13.6) and who would lead many astray. Later in the narrative, Jesus warned of those who would say, 'Look! Here is the Messiah' or 'Look! There he is.' 'False messiahs [christs] and false prophets will appear', he declared, 'and produce signs and omens [wonders/miracles] to lead astray, if possible, the elect' (Mark 13.22–3).

The second feature of Jesus' eschatological discourse that was to feature in the later Antichrist tradition was the appearance of the 'abomination of desolation' or the 'desolating sacrilege':

But when you see the desolating sacrilege set up where it ought not to be … then those in Judea must flee to the mountains; the one on the housetop must not go down or enter the house to take anything away; the one in the field must not turn back to get a coat … For in those days there will be suffering such as has not been from the beginning of creation that God created until now, no, and never will be (Mark 13.14–19).

This notion of the 'abomination of desolation' was drawn from the Old Testament book of Daniel (9.27, 11.31, 12.11) and the first book of the Maccabees (1.54 KJV). In the latter of these (c. 100 BCE), we read that 'the abomination of desolation' was set up upon the altar of the temple. In both Daniel and 1 Maccabees, 'the abomination of desolation' referred to the profanation of the temple that would precede the end of days. The villain of the piece in both was the Hellenistic king Antiochus IV Epiphanes. In 169 BCE, Antiochus had captured Jerusalem. Two years later, he had banned the practice of the Jewish religion and set up a pagan altar in the temple in Jerusalem.

The book of Daniel (168–164 BCE) presented Antiochus as the final tyrant who would suddenly appear at the end of history. He would be a person of unparalleled wickedness and sinful pride who would consider himself greater than any god and would blaspheme the true God. He would profane and desecrate the temple, and set up the abomination of desolation. He would seduce by deceit and persecute the people for the three and a half years of his reign. This would end suddenly as a result of divine intervention, when there would be 'a time of anguish, such as has never occurred since nations first came into existence' (Daniel 12.1). Then would follow a final judgement, when 'Many of those who sleep in the dust of the earth shall awake, some to everlasting life and some to everlasting shame and contempt' (Daniel 12.2). The final eschatological tyrant will become a core component of the story of the Antichrist, and these features of the final tyrant will all be incorporated into the Antichrist tradition.

The third feature of Jesus' eschatological discourse in the Little Apocalypse was its general view of the Last Days and of the events that would precede them. There would be wars and rumours of wars, earthquakes, and famines. These would be 'the beginnings of the birth-pangs' (Mark 13.8). During this time, Christians would be persecuted, brother would betray brother to death, and fathers their children. Children would rise up against their parents and have them put to death. However, those who endured to the end in the faith would be saved. After all this tribulation, the end would come. There would be cosmological signs: '[T]he sun will be darkened, and the moon will not give its light, and the stars will be falling from heaven, and the powers [supernatural beings] in the heavens will be shaken' (Mark 13.24–5). Then the Son of Man [the Christ] would come in the clouds with great power and glory. He would send out the angels to collect the elect from the ends of the earth to the ends of heaven. That all said, the date of the end could not be predicted. This uncertainty will become a common feature of the final Antichrist tradition: 'But about that day or hour, no one knows, neither the angels in heaven, nor the Son, but only the Father. Beware, keep alert; for you do not know when the time will come' (Mark 13.33).

The Man of Lawlessness and the Son of Perdition

In the later Antichrist tradition, the 'abomination of desolation' was to become personalised as the Antichrist. That possibility was already present in the New Testament in Paul's second letter to the Thessalonians.[24] There it is 'the man of sin, the son of perdition' (2 Thessalonians 2.3 KJV) himself who 'takes his seat in the temple of

---

[24] I refer to the author as Paul even though the authorship of 2 Thessalonians by the apostle Paul remains a matter of scholarly contention. See K. L. Hughes, *Constructing Antichrist: Paul, Biblical Commentary, and the Development of Doctrine in the Early Middle Ages* (Washington, DC: The Catholic University of America Press, 2012).

God declaring himself to be God' (2 Thessalonians
2.4). 'The Man of Sin [Lawlessness, ἀνομίας], the Son of
Perdition' appears in the first two chapters of this letter as part of a more general discussion of Christian
eschatology.

It is clear from the first chapter of this letter that
the audience to whom Paul was writing were remaining
steadfast in their faith in spite of the persecution that
they were suffering. The thrust of Paul's argument was
that, in spite of their suffering now, they would be vindicated in the future when Christ returned. Those who
persecuted them would then receive their eschatological
comeuppance:

[W]hen the Lord Jesus is revealed from heaven with his mighty
angels, in flaming fire, inflicting vengeance on those who do
not know God and on those who do not obey the gospel of
our Lord Jesus. These will suffer the punishment of eternal
destruction, separated from the presence of the Lord and from
the glory of his might.

(2 Thessalonians 1.7–9)

Then Christ would be glorified in the midst of his saints
and marvelled at by all those who have believed.

That said, Paul was quick to point out in the next
chapter that his addressees should not be afraid that this
was to happen imminently. Rather, an array of events was
to occur before the Day of the Lord began. In the first
place, the Man of Sin who was also the Son of Perdition
was yet to come. Empowered by Satan, the wickedness of
the world would reach its climax in him. There remained
the question of why he had not yet come. Although 'the

mystery of lawlessness is already at work', the ungodly one was currently being held back by a restraining power until his time came.

Who or what this restraining power was would long remain a matter of debate. Paul probably left it deliberately ambiguous. Rhetorically, he was quite simply buying time. His addressees could expect neither the lawlessness to end nor the Son of Perdition to arrive any time soon. That said, when the Son of Perdition did come, then the Lord Jesus would 'destroy him with the breath of his mouth, annihilating him by the manifestation of his coming' (2 Thessalonians 2.8). When the Man of Sin, the Son of Perdition who proclaimed himself a god, came, he would deceive the people through signs and wonders before being defeated in a final eschatological battle with Christ. Most significantly, Paul has moved him to centre stage in the unfolding of the final events in the history of the world.

Later, he will be identified as the Antichrist.

The Dragon and the Beasts

The Antichrist will also come to be identified with the beast(s) in the last book of the New Testament, the book of Revelation (c. 70–c. 95), written by a 'John of Patmos' (Revelation 1.9). It is, to say the least, a complex and obtuse book, with features that allowed for a large variety of equally complex and obtuse readings. But with respect to the Antichrist, we can pick up the story in the eleventh chapter of this work. According to this, there would come a time when 'the nations' had been tramping over Jerusalem (or the world more generally) for forty-two months, or three and a half years. During this time, there would arise two witnesses – eschatological prophets dressed in sackcloth who called for repentance.

These two prophets would overcome all opposition, for fire comes forth from their mouths and their foes are consumed by it. During the 1,260 days of their prophesying, they would also have authority to shut the sky, so that no rain would fall, along with authority over the waters to turn them into blood and to strike the earth with any kind of plague they desired. The prophets that the author intends to describe are, fairly clearly, Elijah and Moses. For the former had punished King Ahab by withholding rain (1 Kings 17) and the latter was reminiscent of Moses inflicting plagues upon the Egyptians when the Pharaoh refused to allow the people of Israel to leave Egypt.

At the end of their period of prophesying, the first beast would arise: 'the beast that comes up from the bottomless pit will make war on them and conquer them and kill them, and their dead bodies will lie in the street of the great city that is prophetically called Sodom and Egypt, where also their Lord was crucified' (Revelation 11.7–8) (see Plate 1). People from different tribes and nations would come and gaze at their dead bodies, gloating over them and celebrating their deaths, refusing to allow them to be placed in a tomb. But then, after three and a half days, the breath of life from God would enter them, and they would stand on their feet. Those who were to see them would be terrified, all the more so when they heard a voice from heaven saying to the resurrected witnesses, 'Come up here!' And, while their enemies watched them, they would ascend to heaven in a cloud. At that same moment, there would be a great earthquake, and one-tenth of the city would collapse, and 7,000 people would be killed. The remainder would be terrified. As we will shortly see, although the author of Revelation intended the two witnesses to be read as Elijah and Moses, the Christian eschatological tradition will interpret them as Elijah and Enoch, the two Old Testament worthies who were thought never to have died but to have ascended into heaven.

This is the first time in the book of Revelation that we hear of the beast from the abyss who is introduced only to kill the two witnesses. This beast is not to be heard of again until chapter 13. In the meantime, the author tells us, in chapter 12, the story of the dragon, the woman, and her child. This story is prefaced by the appearance in the heavens of two portents. The first was a woman, in the process of giving birth, 'clothed with the sun, with the moon under her feet, and on her head a crown of twelve stars' (Revelation 12.1). The woman was later to be identified with the church, the Virgin Mary, and the divine Wisdom. The moon under her feet and the stars in her crown became part of traditional Marian iconography. Then there appeared a great, red dragon 'with seven heads and ten horns, and seven diadems on his heads' (Revelation 12.3). The dragon stood before the woman ready to eat the child as soon as it was born. She gave birth to a male child who was immediately snatched away and taken to God. The woman then fled into the wilderness to a place prepared by God, there to be nurtured for 1,260 days.

As a result of the dragon's attempt to consume the child, war broke out in heaven between Michael and his angels and the dragon and his. Although the dragon and his angels fought back, they were defeated and thrown out of heaven (see Plate 2). Then we learn the identity of the dragon. It was he 'who is called the Devil and Satan, the deceiver of the whole world' (Revelation 12.9). Unable to further damage the woman, the dragon went on to make war against the rest of her children. In this, he was assisted by his partners, the two beasts, the one from the sea and the other from the land. They evoke the tradition of Leviathan and Behemoth, the two primeval monsters who live on the sea and land respectively (see Job 40–1).

Like the dragon in the previous chapter, the beast that arose from the sea in chapter 13 had ten horns and seven heads. There is little doubt that the author had the four beasts of the Old Testament book of Daniel in mind. In chapter 7 of that work, Daniel told of his vision of four beasts that came up out of the sea – a first that was like a lion and had eagle's wings, a second that was like a bear with three tusks in its mouth, another like a leopard with four bird-like wings on its back and four heads, and a fourth with great iron teeth and claws of bronze. This last beast was different from the rest, not least because it had ten horns. While Daniel was looking at this fourth beast, a little horn appeared among the other ten that had eyes like human eyes and spoke arrogantly. Three of the earlier horns were plucked up by the roots.

Within the book of Daniel the beasts and the horns served as part of a philosophy of history explaining the inevitability of a succession of empires. The empire of the fourth beast would succeed the previous three until there came 'an Ancient One' who put the fourth beast to death and destroyed its body with fire. The 'Ancient One' then gave eternal dominion over all things to 'one like a human being coming with the clouds of heaven' (Daniel 7.13).

The fourth empire of the 'little horn' would succeed the three empires of the uprooted horns. The fourth king would reign for a 'time, two times, and half a time' (Daniel 7.25) before he too was consumed and destroyed. The fourth monarchy would be followed by the Kingdom of God – the 'fifth monarchy'.[25]

In the book of Revelation, the four beasts that arose from the sea in Daniel are merged into one. The beast from the sea in Revelation 13 combined features from each of Daniel's beasts (Daniel 7). Like the first beast in Daniel, the beast in Revelation arose from the sea. Like the fourth beast in Daniel, the beast that arose from the sea in Revelation had ten horns, although a further little one came up among them (Daniel 7.7–8). Like the second and third beasts in Daniel, the beast from the sea in Revelation was like a leopard and had feet like a bear. And Revelation's beast from the sea, like the first beast in Daniel, had a mouth like a lion.

The dragon gave the beast from the sea power and authority for forty-two months. For this period, the whole earth followed the beast in amazement and worshipped the dragon. One of its heads was to receive a mortal wound, but it was one from which the beast would recover. Like the little horn in Daniel (Daniel 7.20), the beast was also given a mouth to speak arrogantly and to utter blasphemies against God. It was also allowed to make war on the saints and to conquer them.

[25] On the complexities of Daniel 7, see Carol A. Newsom with Brennan W. Breed, *Daniel: A Commentary* (Louisville, Kentucky: Westminster John Knox Press, 2014).

Along with the worship of the beast from the sea, its followers are said to bear a mysterious mark, either the name of the beast or the number of its name, which signified who was a follower of the beast. Small or great, rich or poor, free or slave were marked on the right hand or forehead. '[L]et anyone with understanding', we read, 'calculate the number of the beast, for it is the number of a person. Its number is six hundred sixty-six' (Revelation 13.18). The beast that arose from the sea was later to be read as a prophecy of the Antichrist that was to come.

The task of marking the hands or foreheads of the followers of the beast that arose from the sea was assigned to the other beast, the one that arose out of the earth. This beast had two horns like a lamb and it spoke like a dragon. Later in the book of Revelation it was to be called 'the false prophet' (Revelation 16.13, 19.20, 20.10). Its primary role was to exercise authority on behalf of the first beast. It forced the earth and its inhabitants to worship the first beast. It performed great signs and wonders, even, like the prophet Elijah, bringing fire down from heaven in the sight of all, thus deceiving the inhabitants of the earth. It was able to animate the image of the beast so that 'it could even speak, and cause those who would not worship the image of the beast to be killed' (Revelation 13.15). It was, on occasion, read as an Antichrist succeeding the first beast (see Plate 3).

The beast from the sea and the beast from the land reappear in chapter 19 of the book of Revelation, where they are players in the final eschatological battle. Then the heavens were said to have opened, and a rider on a white horse – Christ – accompanied by his heavenly armies appeared to judge and to make war. The beast from the sea and the kings of the earth gathered for battle at a place called Harmagedon. Christ destroyed their armies, and the beast was captured, along with the beast from the land – the false prophet. These two 'were thrown alive into the lake of fire that burns with sulphur' (Revelation 19.20). The rest were killed with the sword by the rider on the white horse, and their remains eaten by birds.

An angel that came down from heaven seized Satan the dragon, bound him, and threw him into the pit for a thousand years. When the thousand years were ended, Satan was released to gather the nations of the earth – Gog and Magog – together for battle. They surrounded the camp of the saints and the city of Jerusalem. But fire came down from heaven, and they were consumed. Satan was defeated for the second time and thrown into the lake of fire and sulphur, there to rejoin the beast and the false prophet.

In the thousand-year period between the first and second defeats of Satan, those who had died for their faith would reign with Christ. The rest of the dead would come to life at the end of this millennial time, 'when Death and Hades gave up the dead that were in them, and all were judged according to what they had done' (Revelation 20.13). Then there was a new heaven, a new earth, and a new Jerusalem, 'coming down out of heaven from God, prepared as a bride adorned for her husband' (Revelation 21.2).

False Prophets, Messiahs, and a World Deceiver

By the end of the New Testament period, around the beginning of the second century, expectations of the imminent end of the world were no doubt receding. But those traditions that were to make up the story of the Antichrist continued to develop, not least that of the false prophets and the world deceiver who would appear in the Last Days. Thus, for example, *The Didache* or *The Teaching of the Apostles* (c. 120) warned its readers to be prepared for the end. Even though no one knew when the Lord would return, its author did not expect it imminently, since there was yet time for his readers to perfect themselves in their faith.

In *The Didache*, the Last Days were a drama in five acts. In the first, the world was turned upside down. False prophets and seducers would increase, sheep would be turned into wolves, love would turn into hate. Men would hate, persecute, and betray each other. In the second act, 'the Deceiver of the world' would appear 'as though he were the Son of God'.[26] So, as an imitator of Christ, he would need to present like the son of God. In the tradition of false prophets generally, he would work signs and wonders. Like the beast from the sea in Revelation, the world would be delivered into his hands. And, like the Son of Perdition in 2 Thessalonians, he would do 'horrible things', unparalleled in their wickedness since the world began.

Third, when the Deceiver of the world came, all mankind would be tested by fire. Many would perish, but those who were strong in their faith would survive. Fourth, the three signs of the Truth would appear. There would be the sign of the opening of the heavens. This would be followed by the sound of a trumpet. Then there would

---

[26] Francis X. Glimm et al. (trans.), *Didache or Teaching of the Apostles*, 16, in his *The Apostolic Fathers* (Washington, DC: The Catholic University of America Press, 2010), p. 184.

follow the resurrection of the dead – not of all men, as the tradition would eventually have it, but only of the believers. Finally, as in the Little Apocalypse of the gospel of Matthew (24), Christ would come 'on the clouds of heaven'. There the story of *The Didache* abruptly ends. The Deceiver of the world plays no elaborate role in *The Didache*. He appears there as a sign of the end. There is no mention of a final eschatological battle, or of his defeat. But what we can say is that by the time of *The Didache*, at its earliest around 120, the notion of a final and future cosmic eschatological opponent was gaining a permanent place within the Christian tradition. The key tension within the history of the Antichrist, that between the eschatological tyrant and the final deceiver, was now in place.

Like *The Didache, The Apocalypse of Peter* (100–150) drew upon the Little Apocalypse of Matthew 24. It was written as a discourse of the risen Christ to the faithful. Although it is now mostly remembered for its early descriptions of the punishments and joys of the damned and the saved, it played a significant role in the development of the Antichrist tradition through its evocation of an *individual* false Christ that was to come at the end of the world. The story began with Christ seated on the Mount of Olives, when his disciples came to him and asked what the signs of his return and of the end of the world would be. Christ told them the parable of the fig tree. According to this, when the fig tree had sprouted, the end of the world would come. He then elaborated on what the end of the world would be like. In those days, false Christs would come, claiming 'I am the Christ who has now come into the world'.

The text now shifts from plural false Christs to a single false Messiah. 'But this deceiver is not the Christ.'[27] The false Christ would slay the many who rejected him. Those who died would be reckoned among the good and righteous martyrs who had pleased God in their lives. The two witnesses of the book of Revelation (whom *its* author intended to be Elijah and Moses) now become, perhaps for the first time, Enoch and Elijah. They were sent to teach the believers that the one who claimed to be Christ was the Deceiver who had to come into the world and do signs and wonders in order to deceive.

It was the Greek theologian Justin (c. 100–c. 165), later beheaded in the reign of the emperor Marcus Aurelius, who continued the tradition of the Man of Sin or Lawlessness that we have already encountered in 2 Thessalonians above. Justin is most remembered for his attempts to demonstrate that Christianity was in alignment with Greek philosophy. But he was also a staunch defender of the developing Christian apocalyptic tradition. His account of the eschatological Man of Sin occurred in a discussion that he had with the Jew Trypho in Ephesus around 135. Justin was clearly referencing a tradition about the eschatological tyrant similar to that in 2 Thessalonians. But Justin's final enemy, 'The Man of Sin' (ἀνομίας), was read in terms of the book of Daniel. According to this, the one who was coming, the little horn that arose from the head of the fourth beast that had ten horns (Daniel 7.20, 24), would speak blasphemous words against God (Daniel 11.36) and would reign 'for

[27] J. K. Elliott, *The Apocalypse of Peter*, 2, in J. K. Elliott (ed.), *The Apocryphal New Testament* (Oxford: Clarendon Press, 1993), p. 601.

a time, times, and half a time (Daniel 7.25). The debate within the *Dialogue with Trypho* concerned the meaning of this last phrase. 'Thus were the times being fulfilled', declared Justin,

[A]nd he whom Daniel foretold would reign for a time, times, and a half, is now at the doors, ready to utter bold and blasphemous words against the Most High. In ignorance of how long he will reign, you hold a different opinion, based on your misinterpretation of the word 'time' as meaning one hundred years. If this is so, the man of sin must reign at least three hundred and fifty years, computing the holy Daniel's expression of 'times' to mean two times only.[28]

This discussion of the Man of Sin in Justin's *Dialogue with Trypho* took place within an account of the 'two comings' of Christ – the first when Christ had come and been crucified, the second when he would come again in glory accompanied by his angels. Justin was to discuss the Man of Sin in a later chapter of the *Dialogue with Trypho*, again in the context of the two comings of Christ. The first coming, Justin reminded his readers, was when Christ suffered and was crucified without glory or honour; the second was when he would come from the heavens in glory. Again referencing the book of Daniel (11.36), that would be the time when '*the man of apostasy* who utters extraordinary things against the Most High, will boldly attempt to perpetrate unlawful deeds on earth against us Christians'.[29]

---

[28] Thomas B. Falls (trans.), *Dialogue with Trypho*, 32, in Thomas B. Falls (trans.), *Saint Justin Martyr* (Washington, DC: The Catholic University of America Press, 2008), pp. 195–6.

[29] *Ibid.*, 110, p. 317.

Justin, like the author of the book of Revelation, was no doubt drawing upon a tradition within early Christianity of a blasphemous eschatological tyrant who would reign for a period of time shortly before Christ came in glory. This was a tradition that was reliant on the book of Daniel. But Justin was also drawing on an early Christian tradition in which the evil tyrant who was to come and persecute those of the faith was known as 'the Man of Sin', 'the Son of Perdition', and 'the Man of Apostasy'.

The Eschatological Tyrant

Like Justin's *Dialogue with Trypho*, the *Epistle of Barnabas* (70–150) looked to the book of Daniel for its understanding of the final opponent. The eschatological section in this work takes the form of a moral exhortation to Christians to be as perfect as possible when the end comes. Above all, they have to beware 'the final trap'. This had to do with the appearance of the eschatological tyrant described in Danielic terms as the evil king or little horn that had sprung from the head of the fourth beast who would humble three of the ten kings or great horns in the last times (Daniel 7.19–21, 24). His readers were warned even now to beware of 'the Black One' (Satan) and to flee all vanity, to hate evil deeds, and to seek the common good. Eventually, we read, the Lord would judge the world, and each would receive according to his deeds. Finally, Christians were exhorted never to become complacent about their sins 'lest the Prince of evil [Satan] gain power over us and cast us out from the

Kingdom of God'.[30] Satan was clearly active in the present times, but, down the line, the eschatological tyrant of Daniel would appear.

The *Epistle of Barnabas* gives us an early indication of just when the tyrant might appear. It contains a very early reference to the tradition that the time from the creation of the world until its end would be 6,000 years:

Concerning the Sabbath He Speaks at the beginning of Creation: 'And God made in six days the work of His hands, and on the seventh day He ended, and rested on it and sanctified it.' Note, children, what 'He ended in six days' means. It means this: that the Lord will make an end of everything in six thousand years, for a day with Him means a thousand years ... So, then, children, in six days everything will be ended. 'And he rested on the seventh day.' This means: when His Son will come and destroy the time of the lawless one and judge the godless, and change the sun and the moon and the stars – then He shall indeed rest on the seventh day.[31]

It is reasonably clear that the *Epistle of Barnabas* did not make a strong distinction between Satan as a supernatural figure engaged both in the present and the future and the future eschatological tyrant, from the Danielic tradition, as a human being. The boundaries were similarly blurred in a Christian text known as the *Testament of Hezekiah* (early second century) that forms part (3.13–4.22) of a larger work of both Jewish and Christian origin known as *The Ascension of Isaiah*. In this story, the false

---

[30] Francis X. Glimm et al. (trans.), *Epistle of Barnabas*, 4.13, in his *The Apostolic Fathers*, p. 184.

[31] *Ibid.*, 15.3–5, pp. 215–16.

prophet Belkira brought charges of sedition and treason against Isaiah. King Manasseh had Isaiah arrested.
Isaiah was imprisoned and then executed by being sawn
in two with a wood saw (see Plate 4). At the time, King
Manasseh was under the influence of the demonic figure
called Beliar who was especially angry at Isaiah for having had a vision of Beliar (Sammael, Satan) descending
from the vault of heaven and having prophesied the coming of Christ as a man, his earthly ministry, crucifixion,
resurrection, ascension, and second coming.

For the author of the *Testament of Hezekiah*, his own
times were deeply corrupt. As the end of the world
approached, the disciples would abandon the teaching of
Christ, Christian leaders would love office, money, and
worldly things, and lack wisdom. This was the world of
corruption, strife, and dissent into which Beliar, the great
angel, the king of this world, would ultimately descend.
He would have power over the sun and the moon. He
would come down 'from his firmament in the form of a
man, a king of iniquity, a murderer of his mother – this is
the king of this world – and will persecute the plant which
the twelve apostles of the Beloved will have planted'.[32]
He would be both tyrant and deceiver, for he would
act and speak like Christ, saying, 'I am the Lord, and
before me there was no one.'[33] Many would believe that
he was Christ come again. Most Christians would follow
him. He would show his miraculous power in every city
and district and, like the 'abomination of desolation' in

---

[32] M. A. Knibb (trans.), *Martyrdom and Ascension of Isaiah*, 4.3, in James
H. Charlesworth (ed.), *The Old Testament Pseudepigrapha, Vol. II* (New
York: Doubleday, 1985), p. 161.
[33] *Ibid.*, 4.6, p. 161.

Revelation, would set up his image everywhere. He would rule for three years, seven months, and twenty-two days. The few Christians who remained faithful would await the coming of their Beloved. This was Daniel's 'time, times and half a time' revisited but computed differently.

The *Testament of Hezekiah* then presented a quite distinctive eschatology. It is in fact a complex interweaving of two early Christian traditions about the afterlife. The first of these was that the dead would go to Abraham's bosom (heaven) or Hades (hell) directly after death, the other, that life after death would not commence until Christ comes in judgement at the end of the world.[34] According to the *Testament of Hezekiah*, there would be no final eschatological battle. Rather, when Christ did come with his angels and saints, he would simply drag Beliar and his hosts into Gehenna.

There would also be no final judgement for both the living and the dead, the faithful and the faithless. Rather, in the *Testament of Hezekiah*, the faithful who have died were already in heaven, and those still alive would ascend into heaven before the final judgement. So the saints already in heaven would bring heavenly robes for those on the earth. All of them would then ascend into heaven, the faithful leaving their bodies behind on the earth. Only then would a judgement occur, and only upon the wicked. The heavens and the earth and everything in it would be reproved by an angry Christ. The wicked would then be raised from the dead. Christ would cause fire to come forth from him and consume all the impious.

---

[34] See Philip C. Almond, *Afterlife: A History of Life after Death* (London and Ithaca: I. B. Tauris and Cornell University Press, 2016).

Thus, by the early second century, we can say that the belief that, before Christ finally comes in judgement, there would arise a powerful eschatological opponent who would mercilessly persecute the Christian faithful was firmly in place. He would be a false prophet and a false messiah. He would be both an eschatological tyrant and a world deceiver, the Man of Sin and the Son of Perdition. He would be Daniel's abomination of desolation and the little horn of the fourth beast, along with one or more of Revelation's beasts. He would be the demonic Beliar, both identical with and distinct from Satan. He was a creature not so much of the present as of the (not too distant) future.

Ironically, it was the failure of the end of the world to arrive that made possible, and perhaps necessary, an historical narrative of the interim period between the ascension of Jesus and his return to judge the living and the dead. The task was to explain the failure of the end to come as expected as part of the unfolding of God's overall plan for the Last Days. The opposition that the followers of Jesus were encountering made necessary an account of the end times that included powerful opponents within and without the faith, together with the expectation of a final eschatological enemy. By the end of the second century, as we will see in the next chapter, these different traditions of the final eschatological opponent were to come together in the figure of the Antichrist.

2

The Story Begins

~

Children, it is the last hour! As you have heard that antichrist is
coming, so now many antichrists have come. From this we know
that it is the last hour.

1 John 2.18

Irenaean Innovations

Irenaeus, bishop of Lyons, was the first Christian theologian to bring the various traditions of the final eschatological enemy into a cohesive narrative whole. He did
so within the context of a more general Christian eschatology.[1] Thus, in his work *Against the Heresies* (*Adversus
Haereses*), he combined the abomination of desolation,
the little horn, the fourth beast, and the fourth king from
the book of Daniel with the Man of Sin and the Son of
Perdition from 2 Thessalonians and the beast that rose
up from the sea from Revelation.

Irenaeus was also the first to unite all these figures as
manifestations of the one future Antichrist. Surprisingly
perhaps, Irenaeus did not reference those texts in John's
two letters that refer specifically to the Antichrist
(1 John 2.18–27, 2 John 7). By the time of Irenaeus, 'the
Antichrist' was probably sufficiently common a term for
the final eschatological opponent that Irenaeus did not to
need to do so. Be that as it may, the Antichrist, he wrote,

---

[1] On Irenaeus, see Denis Minns, *Irenaeus: An Introduction* (London:
Bloomsbury, 2010).

[B]eing an apostate and a robber, is anxious to be adored as God; and that, although a mere slave, he wishes himself to be proclaimed as a king. For he [Antichrist] being endued with all the power of the devil, shall come, not as a righteous king, nor as a legitimate king, [i.e., one] in subjection to God, but an impious, unjust, and lawless one; as an apostate, iniquitous and murderous; as a robber, concentrating in himself [all] satanic apostasy, and setting aside idols to persuade [men] that he himself is God, raising up himself as the only idol, having in himself the multifarious errors of the other idols.[2]

At the centre of Irenaeus' account of the Antichrist was the doctrine of recapitulation. The Antichrist would sum up or 'recapitulate' all the evil that was Satan together with all the evil that had occurred in the history of mankind since the Fall. This was a recognition that the redemption in Christ was not yet complete and that a further event of cosmic significance needed to occur before human evil could be finally and definitively overcome. This would happen when the Antichrist was finally defeated and all evil was destroyed along with him:

For when he (Antichrist) is come, and of his own accord concentrates in his own person the apostasy, and accomplishes whatever he shall do according to his own will and choice, sitting also in the temple of God, so that his dupes may adore him as the Christ; wherefore also shall he deservedly 'be cast into the lake of fire'.[3]

Irenaeus was also the first to connect the Antichrist to the tribe of Dan, one of the twelve tribes of Israel.

[2] A. Cleveland Cox (ed.), *Irenaeus Against Heresies*, 5.25.1, in *ANF*, vol. I, p. 553.
[3] *Ibid.*, 5.28.2, vol. I, p. 557.

Dan, the patriarch of the tribe, was the son of Jacob and Bilhah, the handmaid of Jacob's wife, Rachel (Genesis 30.1–7).[4] Irenaeus' reasons for this were twofold. First, he cited the Old Testament book of Jeremiah 8.16 as evidence for this connection. For Irenaeus, this text showed not only that the Antichrist would come suddenly, but also that 'We shall hear the voice of his swift horses from Dan; the whole earth shall be moved by the voice of the neighing of his galloping horses: he shall also come and devour the earth, and the fullness thereof, the city also, and they that dwell therein.'[5] This was something of an interpretative stretch, not least because the referent in the Jeremiah passage was clearly the city of Dan in the north of the land of Canaan rather than the tribe of Dan.[6]

That said, however, and second, Irenaeus assumed that the author of Revelation was himself convinced that the Antichrist would be a Jew who would come from the tribe of Dan. It was for this reason, Irenaeus believed, that the book of Revelation had omitted the tribe of Dan from its list of the twelve tribes that would make up the 144,000 who were marked by God with a seal on their foreheads (Revelation 7.3–18).[7] It is unlikely that the author of Revelation excluded Dan from his list of tribes on account of his believing that the final enemy would

---

[4] *Ibid.*, 5.30.2, vol. I, p. 559. Thanks to Margaret Attwood's *The Handmaid's Tale*, the story is better-known than most in Genesis.

[5] *Ibid.*, 5.30.2, vol. I, p. 559.

[6] On Dan, see Mark W. Bartusch, *Understanding Dan: An Exegetical Study of a Biblical City, Tribe and Ancestor* (London: Sheffield Academic Press, 2003).

[7] Cox (ed.), *Irenaeus Against Heresies*, 5.30.2, in *ANF*, vol. I, p. 559.

come from the tribe of Dan. More likely, the author of Revelation simply drew from one of a number of lists of the twelve tribes in the Jewish literature of the New Testament period.[8] So, like his use of Jeremiah 8.16, we can take this as another piece of theological inventiveness on Irenaeus' part. Most importantly, in his identification of the Antichrist as a Jew, Irenaeus was building anti-Judaism into Christian eschatology. Anti-Judaism had been built into the Christian history of salvation from its beginnings. It was now also a part of Christian eschatology. The Jews had been crucial opponents of Christ. They would now become the staunch supporters of the Antichrist.

Equally innovative was Irenaeus' explanation of the number of the beast (for him, the Antichrist) as six hundred and sixty-six. It formed part of his doctrine of recapitulation. Thus, the 'six hundred' referred to all the wickedness that took place prior to the flood that destroyed the world when Noah was 600 years of age (Genesis 7.6). The 'sixty-six' referred to all the errors of idolatry since the time of the flood, exemplified by the golden statue set up by King Nebuchadnezzar that had a height of 60 cubits and a breadth of 6 cubits (Daniel 3.1). The refusal of Shadrach, Meshach, and Abednego to worship the idol led to their being thrown into a furnace of blazing fire. Thus, Irenaeus concluded,

[T]he six hundred years of Noah, in whose time the deluge occurred because of the apostasy, and the number of the cubits of the image for which these just men were sent into the fiery

---

[8] See Richard Bauckham, 'The List of Tribes in Revelation Again', *Journal for the Study of the New Testament* 42 (1991), 99–115.

furnace, do indicate the name of that man in whom is concentrated the whole apostasy of six thousand years, and unrighteousness, and wickedness, and false prophecy, and deception.[9]

Irenaeus had no doubt that the number of the Antichrist was six hundred and sixty-six. But the convoluted proof that he offered was perhaps necessitated by their being an alternative reading of the number of the beast, namely 'six hundred and sixteen'. Irenaeus himself knew that there were manuscript copies of the book of Revelation that had six hundred and sixteen as the number of the beast. He believed, however, that six hundred and sixty-six was both the more approved and the more ancient, explaining 'six hundred and sixteen' as the result of a scribal error.[10] To us, it may hardly seem to matter. But it mattered to Irenaeus because there were, he declared, those who on the basis of this number, six hundred and sixteen, had sought to identify the person whose name corresponded to that number. This was theologically dangerous, he believed, for 'if these men assume one [number], when this [Antichrist] shall come having another, they will be easily led away by him, as supposing him not to be the expected one, who must be guarded against'.[11]

Irenaeus was not opposed to number symbolism – witness his reading of the meaning of six hundred and

---

[9] Cox (ed.), *Irenaeus Against Heresies*, 5.29.2, in *ANF*, vol. I, p. 558.

[10] On the textual history of these variants, see J. N. Birdsall, 'Irenaeus and the Number of the Beast: Revelation 13.18', in A. Denaux (ed.), *New Testament Textual Criticism and Exegesis* (Leuven University Press, 2002), pp. 349–59. Birdsall suggests that six hundred and sixteen might have been the earlier of the two traditions.

[11] Cox (ed.), *Irenaeus Against Heresies*, 5.30.1, in *ANF*, vol. I, p. 559.

sixty-six above. Nor was he opposed in principle to the system known as isopsephy, by which Greek letters were assigned numbers so that words might be generated from a numerical sequence. Thus, he recognised several possible names for the number six hundred and sixty-six, namely, Euanthas, Lateinos, and Teitan. Still, at the end of the day, he thought it better to await the end of the world. Had it been necessary for the name to be known in the present, the author of Revelation would have announced it. Better therefore, he believed, 'to await the fulfilment of the prophecy, than to be making surmises and casting about for any names that may present themselves, inasmuch as many names can be found possessing the number mentioned; and the same question will, after all, remain unsolved'.[12]

Like the *Epistle of Barnabas*, Irenaeus believed that the time from the creation until the return of Christ would be 6,000 years. Three and a half years before this, having devastated everything, the Antichrist would begin his reign, sitting like the abomination of desolation in the temple in Jerusalem (see Plate 5). Only then would Christ return and the Antichrist be destroyed: 'and then the Lord will come from heaven in the clouds, in the glory of the Father, sending this man and those who follow him into the lake of fire'.[13] The righteous would then arise from the dead. Irenaeus was a millenarian in the strict sense. Thus, the righteous who rose from the dead, along with those who had resisted the Antichrist and suffered tribulation and those who had escaped him, would dwell for a thousand years (the seventh 'day') in a renewed

[12] *Ibid.*, 5.30.3, vol. I, p. 559.   [13] *Ibid.*, 5.30.4, vol. I, p. 560.

earthly Jerusalem. These would gradually become accustomed to partake of the divine nature.

At the end of the thousand years, the wicked too would rise from the dead and the final judgement would begin. Then Christ would 'order the reapers to collect first the tares together, and bind them in bundles, and burn them with unquenchable fire, but to gather up the wheat into the barn; and to call the lambs into the kingdom prepared for them, but to send the goats into everlasting fire, which has been prepared by his Father for the devil and his angels'.[14] There would then be a new heaven and a new earth, and the heavenly Jerusalem would come down to earth. According to their merits, some would go to heaven, others would enjoy the delights of Paradise, while still others would possess the splendours of the city.[15]

Variations on an Irenaean Theme

Hippolytus of Rome (c. 130–c. 236) was traditionally said to have been a disciple of Irenaeus. This is unlikely. But his eschatology was certainly influenced by that of Irenaeus. Irenaeus had not predicted any time for the return of Christ, although he nonetheless gave the sense that it would be sooner rather than later. For his part, Hippolytus postponed it to around 300 years into the future. Hippolytus accepted, like Irenaeus, that the length of time from creation until the return of Christ would be 6,000 years. And, like Irenaeus, he accepted that, after the end of the sixth millennium, there would be a 1,000-year reign of Christ on earth along with his saints

---

[14] *Ibid.*, 5.27.1, vol. I, p. 556.   [15] *Ibid.*, 5.36.1, vol. I, p. 567.

before the final judgement. But, within this chronology, he went several steps further, both in his commentary on the book of Daniel and in his *Treatise on Christ and the Antichrist* – the first Christian work to have the name 'Antichrist' in its title.

First, he gave a date for the birth of Christ, namely, 5,500 years after creation:

For the first appearance of our Lord in the flesh took place in Bethlehem, under Augustus, in the year 5500; and he suffered in the thirty-third year. And 6,000 years must needs be accomplished, in order that the Sabbath may come, the rest, the holy day 'on which God rested from all his works'. For the Sabbath is the type and emblem of the future kingdom of the saints, when they 'shall reign with Christ', when He comes from heaven, as John says in his Apocalypse: for 'a day with the Lord is as a thousand years'.[16]

Second, and most importantly, this dating of the birth of Christ allowed him to specify when Christ would return. Thus, he declared, 'From the birth of Christ, then, we must reckon the 500 years that remain to make up the 6,000, and thus the end shall be.'[17] Hippolytus thus became not only the first Christian theologian to give a date for the return of Christ, but also 'the first Christian writer to reject explicitly the hope of an imminent

---

[16] A. Cleveland Coxe (ed.), *The Extant Works and Fragments of Hippolytus, On Daniel*, 4, in *ANF*, vol. V, p. 179. For the importance of Hippolytus in Western chronography, see Richard Landes, 'Lest the Millennium Be Fulfilled: Apocalyptic Expectations and the Pattern of Western Chronography 100–800 CE', in Werner Verbeke et al., *The Use and Abuse of Eschatology in the Middle Ages* (Leuven University Press, 1988), pp. 137–211.

[17] Coxe (ed.), *The Extant Works and Fragments of Hippolytus, On Daniel*, 4, in *ANF*, vol. V, p. 179.

Parousia [of Christ]'.[18] It meant too that the time of the Antichrist was postponed well into the future. Any enthusiastic expectations that his readers might have had about the imminent return of Christ were dampened. Hippolytus was encouraging Christians to settle in for the reasonably long haul.

This millennial eschatology of Hippolytus was combined with another chronology, namely that of the seventy weeks of years of Daniel 9.24–7. According to this, there were seventy weeks allocated 'to finish the transgression, to put an end to sin, and to atone for iniquity, to bring in everlasting righteousness, to seal both vision and prophet, and to anoint a most holy place' (Daniel 9.24). In the last week, wrote Daniel, the prince who is to come will 'make a strong covenant with many for one week, and for half of the week he shall make sacrifice and offering cease; and in their place shall be an abomination that desolates, until the decreed end is poured out upon the desolator' (Daniel 9.27).

This last week of years was read eschatologically by Hippolytus as a final seven-year period. He also calculated each half of the last week as consisting of 1,260 days, bringing the three and a half years of the first half-week of Daniel 9.27 into line with the 1,260 days of the two witnesses of the book of Revelation (Revelation 11.3) and with the 'time, two times, and half a time' of Daniel 7.25.[19] Like

---

[18] David Dunbar, 'The Delay of the Parousia in Hippolytus', *Vigiliae Christianae* 37 (1983), 313. See also David Dunbar, 'The Eschatology of Hippolytus of Rome', PhD dissertation, Drew University, 1979. I am particularly indebted to Dunbar for this account of the eschatology of Hippolytus.

[19] A. Cleveland Coxe (ed.), *The Extant Works and Fragments of Hippolytus, Treatise on Christ and Antichrist*, 43, 47, in *ANF*, vol. V, p. 213.

many chronologies yet to come, that of Hippolytus is like playing three-dimensional chess. But what matters (or in this case, counts) is that Hippolytus was synthesising a number of different biblical chronologies to enable him to get an accurate fix on the arrival of the Antichrist. Thus, according to Hippolytus, we might expect the Antichrist to be active in the decade before 500.

Like Irenaeus, Hippolytus looked to the tribe of Dan as the source of the Antichrist. Drawing on the fact that both the tribe of Judah and the tribe of Dan are described as a 'lion's whelp' (in Genesis 49.9 and Deuteronomy 33.22), he was able to parallel the descent of Christ from the tribe of Judah and that of the Antichrist from the tribe of Dan:

[B]y thus naming the tribe of Dan as the one whence the accuser is destined to spring, he made the matter in hand quite clear. For as Christ is born of the tribe of Judah, so Antichrist shall be born of the tribe of Dan. And as our Lord and Saviour Jesus Christ, the Son of God, was spoken of in prophecy as a *lion*, on account of his royalty and glory, in the same manner also has the Scripture prophetically described the accuser as a lion, on account of his tyranny and violence.[20]

All this was perhaps stretching the eschatological friendship a bit too far. But it did allow Hippolytus elsewhere to extend this fundamental imitation of Christ by the Antichrist. In so doing, he brought into the centre of the Antichrist story, over against the notion of the Antichrist as the eschatological tyrant, the notion

---

[20] A. Cleveland Coxe (ed.), *The Extant Works and Fragments of Hippolytus, Appendix to the Works of Hippolytus*, 19, in *ANF*, vol. V, pp. 246–7.

of the Antichrist as *the Great Deceiver* who mimicked Christ. The Deceiver, he declared, 'seeks to liken himself in all things to the Son of God. Christ is a lion, so Antichrist is also a lion; Christ is a king, so Antichrist is also a king; The Saviour was manifested as a lamb; so he too, in like manner, will appear as a lamb, though within he is a wolf'.[21] Like Christ, he continued, the Antichrist will be Jewish in origin (in the circumcision), he will send out apostles (although his followers will be false), he will bring together people who are scattered abroad, he will give a seal to those who believe in him, he will appear in the form of a man, and he will raise a temple of stone in Jerusalem (as Christ in his resurrection raised up a temple of flesh). As Christ was the son of God, so the Antichrist will be 'son of the devil'.[22]

During the first half of Daniel's last week, the Antichrist will establish himself as a messianic saviour-figure to the Jews. Rather puzzlingly, Hippolytus also seems to expect that, as a political tyrant, the Antichrist will be Roman. Thus, he follows Irenaeus in identifying Teitan, Evanthus, and Latinus as possible names for the Antichrist before settling on the last as most likely:

But, as we have already said, the wound of the first beast was healed, and he (the second beast) was to make the image speak, that is to say, he should be powerful [Revelation 13.11–16]; and it is manifest to all that those who at present still hold the power are Latins. If, then, we take the name as the name of a single man, it becomes *Latinus*.[23]

---

[21] Coxe (ed.), *The Extant Works and Fragments of Hippolytus, Treatise on Christ and Antichrist*, 6 in *ANF*, vol. V, p. 206.

[22] *Ibid.*, 15, vol. V, p. 207.   [23] *Ibid.*, 50, vol. V, p. 215.

In short, the Antichrist (Revelation's 'beast from the earth'), paradoxically both Jewish and Roman, restores and rebuilds the wounded Roman Empire (Revelation's 'wounded beast from the sea'). In the first half-week, the Antichrist will conquer all:

He will gather together all his strength, from the east even to the west. They whom he calls and they whom he calls not, shall go with him. He shall make the sea white with the sails of his ships, and the plain black with the shields of his armaments. And whosoever shall oppose him in war shall fall by the sword.[24]

During this same half-week, there will also be an increasing conflict between the Antichrist and the church. This was exemplified for Hippolytus in the careers of the two witnesses of the book of Revelation 11.3. They are now identified as Elijah and Enoch. They were to preach for 1,260 days 'clothed in sackcloth, proclaiming repentance to the nations'.[25] As John the Baptist was the forerunner of the first coming of Christ, so Elijah and Enoch would be the forerunners of his second coming: 'These, then, shall come and proclaim the manifestation of Christ that is to be from heaven; and they shall also perform signs and wonders, in order that men may be put to shame and turned to repentance for their surpassing wickedness and piety.'[26] Because they will not give glory to the Antichrist, they will be slaughtered by the Antichrist. Subsequently they will be resurrected and ascend into heaven. Their martyrdom signalled the end of the first half-week.

---

[24] *Ibid.*, 15, vol. V, p. 207.   [25] *Ibid.*, 43, vol. V, p. 213.
[26] *Ibid.*, 46, vol. V, p. 213.

The second half-week of Daniel began with the Antichrist at the height of his powers as the abomination of desolation. Proclaimed as king, he 'shall prove himself an abomination of desolation to the world'.[27] During the next three and a half years of the Antichrist's reign, the saints would be persecuted, not least because they would refuse to worship him. Hippolytus' is a description of the persecution of Christians reflective of the persecutions by the Romans of the early Christians:

Such trouble, such distress, will then occur in all the world! All believers everywhere carried away and slaughtered in every city and country; the blood of the righteous poured out, men burned alive, and others thrown to the beasts; children murdered in the streets; all left unburied to be eaten by dogs; virgins and wives seduced by impious speech and shamefully deceived and taken by force; the graves of the saints opened, their remains dug up and dispersed over the plains; blasphemies committed.[28]

How long was the reign of Antichrist? It covered the second half-week of Daniel's last week of years. Thus, at the end of forty-two months, the Antichrist would be defeated with the return of Christ, 'who shall bring the conflagration and just judgment upon all those who have refused to believe on him'.[29] But Hippolytus had one final innovation. For he had noticed that Daniel had also spoken of both 1,290 days and 1,335 days (Daniel 12.11–12).

---

[27] Coxe (ed.), *The Extant Works and Fragments of Hippolytus, On Daniel*, 40, in *ANF*, vol. V, p. 185.

[28] Quoted in Dunbar, 'The Eschatology of Hippolytus of Rome', pp. 103–4.

[29] Coxe (ed.), *The Extant Works and Fragments of Hippolytus, Treatise on Christ and Antichrist*, 64 in *ANF*, vol. V, p. 218.

Thus, while the Antichrist would reign 1,290 days, there would be a period of 45 days of happiness for the saints before Christ returned.[30] This period between the defeat of the Antichrist and the return of Christ was to become known as 'the refreshment of the saints'.[31]

As we have seen in the first chapter, the vision of Daniel referred to four beasts arising from the sea, the fourth of which had great iron teeth, claws of bronze, and ten horns (Daniel 7.19–22). Hippolytus understood the first three beasts as the empires of Babylon, Persia, and Greece, and, along with Irenaeus, interpreted the fourth as Rome. Only when the Roman Empire declined could the Antichrist ('the little horn') arise to restore and revive the fourth beast. In a different register, according to Hippolytus, the Antichrist was also the beast that rose from the earth that restored the beast that arose from the sea, that is, Rome:

And the words 'he exercised all the power of the first beast before him, and caused the earth and them which dwell therein to worship the first beast, whose deadly wound was healed' [Revelation 13.12], signify that, after the manner of Augustus, by whom the empire of Rome was established, he too will rule and govern, sanctioning everything by it, and taking greater glory to himself. For this is the fourth beast, whose head was wounded and healed again, in its being broken up or even dishonoured, and partitioned into four crowns; and

[30] Coxe (ed.), *The Extant Works and Fragments of Hippolytus, On Daniel*, 40, in *ANF*, vol. V, pp. 184–5.
[31] See Robert E. Lerner, 'Refreshment of the Saints: The Time after Antichrist as a Station for Earthly Progress in Medieval Thought', *Traditio* 32 (1976), 97–144.

he [Antichrist] then shall with knavish skill heal it, as it were, and restore it.[32]

Like Irenaeus and Hippolytus, the Latin theologian Tertullian (c. 160–c. 220) also identified Rome as the fourth empire. For Tertullian, that the Roman Empire would need to decline before the Antichrist could arise and Christ return was no bad thing. The end of the world was not something to be wished for. As Kevin Hughes remarks, 'the empire is a necessary evil used by God's providential will to forestall the arrival of the Man of Sin himself'.[33] The author of 2 Thessalonians had declared that 'the lawless one' would be revealed only when 'the one who now restrains it is removed' (2 Thessalonians 2.7). Tertullian was the first to identify 'the one who now restrains' with the Roman Empire. 'What obstacle is there', he asked, 'but the Roman state, the falling away of which, by being scattered into ten kingdoms, shall introduce Antichrist upon [its own ruins]?'[34] So he recommended that Christians should pray for the emperors and for the stability of the empire. For we know, he wrote, 'that a mighty shock impending over the whole earth – in fact, the very end of all things threatening dreadful woes – is only retarded by the continued existence of the Roman empire'.[35] As we know, this was an argument later used by Adso to comfort Gerberga.

---

[32] Coxe (ed.), *The Extant Works and Fragments of Hippolytus, Treatise on Christ and Antichrist*, 49 in *ANF*, vol. V, p. 214.

[33] Hughes, *Constructing Antichrist*, p. 32.

[34] A. Cleveland Coxe (ed.), *On the Resurrection of the Flesh*, 24, in *ANF*, vol. III, p. 563.

[35] A. Cleveland Coxe (ed.), *Apology*, 32, in *ANF*, vol. III, pp. 42–3.

Nero and the Double Antichrists

By the end of the second century, then, the basic components of the story of the Antichrist were in place. The Antichrist was both a false Messiah and an eschatological tyrant whose coming would bring about the return of Christ and usher in the end of history. Having rebuilt Jerusalem, he would set himself up as God, demanding the worship of all and persecuting those who refused. After some three and a half years of dominance, he would be defeated by Christ and his angels. Resurrection and judgement would follow.

That said, as we saw in Hippolytus, the story was still unstable, not least over the core issue of whether the Antichrist was Jewish or Roman or from the East more generally. One solution to this problem was to propose two Antichrists, the one Roman and the other Persian. It was a synthesis of the competing traditions first put forward by the mid third-century Latin poet Commodian.[36] The eschatology of Commodian appears in each of his two works – *The Instructions of Commodianus in Favour of Christian Discipline, against the Gods of the Heathens* and *An Apologetic Poem against Jews and Gentiles.* Just to add to the eschatological confusion, the eschatology of these two works differs: there is only one Roman Antichrist in the former work but two Antichrists – a Roman and a Persian – in the latter.

According to the *Apologetic Poem*, the end of the 6,000 years was at hand, a seventh persecution was about to

---

[36] The date and place of Commodian remain much contested, ranging from the mid third to the mid fifth century, and from Syria to North Africa to southern Gaul.

begin, and, thus, the rise of the Antichrist was imminent. His arrival would be preceded by an attack on Rome by an army of Goths who would persecute the Romans but treat the Christians as brethren. The Romans would be liberated by the first Antichrist – a king from the East: '[T]his is Nero, who had flogged Peter and Paul in the city. From hidden places at the very end of the world he shall return, since he was preserved for these things.'[37] In *The Instructions of Commodianus*, Commodian has Nero 'raised up from hell'.[38] Nero as the archetypal evil human has now entered the Christian eschatological tradition.

Commodian was uncertain of the exact time of the return of the resurrected Nero, although it would be in the middle of the final week of years. He would be worshipped by both the Jews and the Romans who would collaborate in the persecution of the Christians. Although prophets would arise to preach against the Antichrist, only the prophet Elijah was named. In a rage, Nero *revivivus* would turn the rivers into blood, drought and famine would ensue, and there would be a worldwide plague. The Jews and Romans would conspire against Elijah and persuade Nero to have him burned, along with the other prophets. The Christians would also then be persecuted. An early intervention by Christ would see him revive those Christians who had been denied graves and take them into heaven. Nero, along with two other Caesars, would continue to persecute the Christians for three and

---

[37] Darius Matthias Klein (trans.), 'Excerpt from Commodianus' *Carmen Apologeticum*', p. 2. Available at http://christianlatin.blogspot.com/2008/08/excerpt-from-commodianus-carmen.html

[38] A. Cleveland Coxe (ed.), *The Instructions of Commodianus*, 41, in *ANF*, vol. V, p. 211.

a half years: 'Blood shall flow everywhere … Fear shall prevail, hands shall fail, and hearts shall tremble: many shall be the deaths fit to impose upon the martyrs.'[39]

The *Apologetic Poem* then predicts the rise of another king from the East, who would cross the dried-up Euphrates, bringing the Persians, Medes, Chaldeans, and Babylonians along with him. He would destroy Nero and his two Caesars, and 'hand them over to the vultures to be eaten'.[40] He would also destroy Rome and then march on to Judea, seducing the Jews with signs. As Nero was the Antichrist for the Romans, so is the one from Persia the Antichrist for the Jews: 'These are the two of whom there have been prophecies throughout the generations, who shall appear in the final age. Nero is the destroyer of the city, but this latter shall lay waste to the whole earth.'[41]

As a result of this second Antichrist's wickedness, God would lead an army of Jews from the far side of the Euphrates, a pious and obedient vegetarian (for some unknown reason) Jewish remnant awaiting the life to come. Eventually, after a series of military victories, they would come to Jerusalem. The Antichrist would flee north to raise another army for the final eschatological battle, in which he and his army would suffer defeat. The wicked king and the false prophets 'shall endure the punishments of Hell while still living', and his commanders and ambassadors would be enslaved.[42] God would then begin to judge the world by fire. Graves would be broken open, 'bodies will rise up from the slime', and 'whatever is marked by corruption will be carried by Hell's

---

[39] Klein (trans.), 'Excerpt from Commodianus' *Carmen Apologeticum*', p. 3.
[40] *Ibid.*, p. 4.   [41] *Ibid.*, p. 4.   [42] *Ibid.*, p. 5.

savage guardians into the abyss'.[43] For those who were not known to Christ, there would be only death-bearing punishments.

The dead who had been faithful to Christ would arise and enjoy immortal life in a Jerusalem that would come down from heaven. Then they would marry and have children for a thousand years, with abundant food, an ideal climate, and perfect health. After the thousand years, a new judgement would begin in which, with the exception of the camp of the saints, the whole earth would be burnt up. The just would arise to meet their Lord in the air, while the wicked who remained would be plunged into hell.

In looking to Nero as one of his two final eschatological tyrants, Commodian was drawing upon a tradition, present since the 'death' of the Emperor Nero in 68 CE, that he had not died at all and would eventually return. After it was no longer feasible to believe that Nero was still alive, this would transform itself in Commodian into the legend that he would rise from the dead or emerge from the underworld as the first of the eschatological tyrants.

As we noted in Chapter 1 above, according to the *Testament of Hezekiah* (early second century), the eschatological tyrant Beliar would manifest himself as a Nero-like figure, 'a king of iniquity', and, like Nero, 'a murderer of his mother'.[44]

---

[43] *Ibid.*, p. 6.
[44] Knibb (trans.), *Martyrdom and Ascension of Isaiah*, 4.3, in Charlesworth (ed.), *The Old Testament Pseudepigrapha, Vol. II*, p. 161. Nero had his mother, Agrippina, murdered in 59 CE.

The *Sibylline Oracles*, a collection of prophetic utterances attributed to the ancient Sibyl of Babylon, similarly foretold the coming of a Nero-like eschatological figure. Thus, book 3 of the *Sibylline Oracles* (mid second century BCE) spoke of Beliar coming from the line of Augustus Caesar, who will perform miracles, raise the dead, and lead many astray before being destroyed by God with fire.[45] Book 5 (late first century CE) informed its readers of a final war in the last time when 'A man who is a matricide will come from the ends of the earth in flight and … destroy every land and conquer all'.[46] He would destroy many men and great rulers, raising up those crouched in fear, before falling in a final battle. Elsewhere, in book 8 (before 180), he is said to ravish the nation of the Hebrews before destroying the 'overbearing threat of the Roman, for the Empire of Rome which then flourished has perished'.[47]

Commodian was, nevertheless, the first explicitly to name Nero as the Antichrist who was to come, and, to my knowledge, the first to say that he would *rise from the dead* to become a final eschatological tyrant. We find the connection between Nero and the Antichrist again in Gaul around the end of the fourth century in the writings of Sulpicius Severus (c. 363–c. 420), the disciple and biographer of Martin of Tours. In his *Sacred History*, he reported on the belief that, even if Nero had attempted to kill himself with a sword, he had survived, his 'mortal wound was cured, and his life preserved [like the beast

---

[45] J. J. Collins (trans.), *Sibylline Oracles* 3.63–74, in James H. Charlesworth (ed.), *The Old Testament Pseudepigrapha, Vol. I* (New York: Doubleday, 1983), p. 363.
[46] *Ibid.*, 5.363–5, p. 402.   [47] *Ibid.*, 8.140–4, p. 421.

from the sea in Revelation 13.3] ... to be sent forth again near the end of the world, in order that he may practise the mystery of iniquity'.[48]

For Severus, the return of Christ was imminent. Thus, in his *Life of St Martin*, on the basis of several reports, one of a young man in Spain declaring himself to be Elijah and later Christ, another of a man who claimed to be John the Baptist, and others of false prophets in general, Severus declared 'that the coming of Antichrist is at hand'.[49] In a passage in Severus' *Dialogues*, the character Gallus tells of Martin's belief that 'Antichrist, having been conceived by an evil spirit, was already born, and had by this time reached the years of boyhood, while he would assume power as soon as he reached the proper age'.[50]

Martin had also declared that, before the end of the world, both Nero *and* the Antichrist had to come. Nero would rule in the Western portion of the world after having subdued ten kings. He would carry out a persecution intended to compel men to worship the idols of the Gentiles. The Jewish Antichrist, on the other hand, would first seize upon the Eastern Empire, restore and rebuild Jerusalem and its temple, and make it his capital. He would then try to compel all to deny Christ as God, maintain that he himself was Christ, and order all men to be circumcised. Martin also declared that Nero would be destroyed by the Antichrist and the whole world would

---

[48] Alexander Roberts (trans.), *The Sacred History*, 2.29, in *NPNF, second series*, vol. XI, p. 111.

[49] Alexander Roberts (trans.), *Life of St. Martin*, 24, in *NPNF, second series*, vol. XI, p. 15.

[50] Alexander Roberts (trans.), *The Dialogues of Sulpicius Severus*, 14, in *NPNF, second series*, vol. XI, p. 45.

come under his control 'until that impious one should be overthrown by the coming of Christ'.[51]

Still, even as Sulpicius Severus was reporting on Martin's belief in the return of Nero, his contemporary Augustine was expressing his reservations about the return of Nero, alive or resurrected, in *The City of God*. The author of 2 Thessalonians, we recall, had written that 'the mystery of lawlessness is already at work, but only until the one who now restrains it is removed' (2 Thessalonians 2.7). Augustine was not alone in confessing that he had no idea what was meant. Still, he did go on to report such conjectures as he had read or heard. 'Some think', he wrote,

[t]hat the apostle Paul referred to the Roman empire, and that he was unwilling to use language more explicit, lest he should incur the calumnious charge of wishing ill to the empire which it was hoped would be eternal; so that in saying, 'For the mystery of iniquity doth already work,' he alluded to Nero, whose deeds already seemed to be as the deeds of Antichrist. And hence some suppose that he shall rise again and be Antichrist. Others, again, suppose that he is not even dead, but that he was concealed that he might be supposed to have been killed, and that he now lives in concealment in the vigor of that same age which he had reached when he was believed to have perished, and will live until he is revealed in his own time and restored to his kingdom. But I wonder that men can be so audacious in their conjectures.[52]

That said, scepticism about the return of Nero had already been expressed a century earlier. Thus, around

---

[51] *Ibid.*, 14, vol. XI, p. 45.
[52] Marcus Dods (trans.), *The City of God*, 20.19, in *NPNF, first series*, vol. II, p. 438 (my italics).

the year 300, the African Lactantius (c. 240–c. 320) converted to Christianity and was to become tutor to the son of the Emperor Constantine. In his *Of the Manner in Which the Persecutors Died*, he set out to demonstrate how God destroyed those who had persecuted the church from its beginnings (of whom Nero was first up) and what the punishments were that God had inflicted upon them. This necessitated his rejecting the possibility that Nero had not died and would return:

God looked on the affliction of His people; and therefore the tyrant, bereaved of authority, and precipitated from the height of empire, suddenly disappeared, and even the burial-place of that noxious wild beast was nowhere to be seen. This has led some persons of extravagant imagination to suppose that, having been conveyed to a distant region, he is still preserved alive; and to him they apply the Sibylline verses concerning 'The fugitive, who slew his own mother, being to come from the uttermost boundaries of the earth'; as if he who was the first should also be the last persecutor and thus prove the forerunner of Antichrist! But we ought not to believe those who, affirming that the two prophets Enoch and Elias have been translated into some remote place that they might attend our Lord when He shall come to judgement, also fancy that Nero is to appear hereafter as the forerunner of the devil, when he shall come to lay waste the earth and overthrow mankind.[53]

Lactantius nevertheless did expect that, before the arrival of the Antichrist, there would be a final eschatological tyrant. We find his developed eschatology

---

[53] A. Cleveland Coxe (ed.), *Of the Manner in Which the Persecutors Died*, 2, in *ANF*, vol. VII, p. 302.

in his *Divine Institutes* and in his *Epitome of the Divine Institutes*, the first complete attempt in Latin to defend Christianity to a cultured Roman audience more at home with classical literature than the Bible. More inclined to quote the Sibyls, the oracles of the mysterious Hystaspes, the Egyptian Hermes Trismegistus, and the Roman poet Virgil than the Bible, his Christian readers (and by now readers of this book) would nonetheless have discerned his biblical allusions, even if his 'pagan' readers didn't.

Like Hippolytus, Lactantius expected that the end of history would come when the world had completed 6,000 years. And, following Hippolytus, he expected it, at the latest, in some 200 years from his time, that is, around 500. As the end of the world approached, Lactantius expected a world in which 'All justice will be confounded and the laws will be destroyed.'[54] This would be caused by the collapse of the Roman Empire, when 'the East will again bear rule, and the West be reduced to servitude'.[55] After the collapse of Rome, ten kings would arise who would consume all things.

A powerful king from the North would then arise who would destroy three of these kings before being recognised as prince of all by the remaining seven. 'Then, in truth', we read,

a detestable and abominable time shall come, in which life shall be pleasant to none of men … Death shall be desired, but it will not come; not even shall night give rest to their fear, nor

---

[54] William Fletcher (trans.), *The Divine Institutes*, 7.15, in *ANF*, vol. VII, p. 212.
[55] *Ibid*.

shall sleep approach to their eyes, but anxiety and watchfulness shall consume the souls of men; they shall deplore and lament, and gnash their teeth; they shall congratulate the dead, and bewail the living.[56]

This eschatological king would be killed by another who 'shall arise out of Syria, born from an evil spirit, the overthrower and destroyer of the human race'.[57] This was the true Antichrist, who would 'falsely call himself Christ'.[58] Lactantius was the first to suggest that the Antichrist would be conceived not by a holy spirit, as was Christ, but by an evil one. In spite of Revelation's expectations of two witnesses who were to come, Lactantius had only one great prophet with great powers 'sent from God to turn men to the knowledge of God'.[59] Antichrist would overcome and kill this great prophet (presumably Elijah) who had come before him. Left unburied, the prophet would come to life on the third day and, watched by all in wonder, would ascend into heaven. The Antichrist would then call himself God and demand to be worshipped as the son of God. He would call fire down from heaven, cause the sun to change its course, and make an image speak such that many, even of the wise, would be drawn to him. He would attempt to destroy the temple of God and would persecute the righteous. Those who joined with him would be marked by him, like sheep. Those who refused would be slain with exquisite tortures. He would be given power to desolate the earth for forty-two months.

---

[56] *Ibid.*, 7.16, vol. VII, pp. 213–14.   [57] *Ibid.*, 7.17, vol. VII, p. 214.
[58] *Ibid.*, 7.19, vol. VII, p. 215.   [59] *Ibid.*, 7.17, vol. VII, p. 214.

The Christians who had fled the persecution would call upon God to save them. Then God would 'hear them and send from heaven a great king to rescue and free them, and destroy all the wicked with fire and sword'.[60] Christ would descend with a company of angels to the middle of the earth, preceded by an unquenchable fire. The forces of the Antichrist would be slaughtered from the third hour until the evening 'and blood shall flow like a torrent'.[61] Only the Antichrist would escape, until he would eventually be captured in a final, fourth battle and be delivered up to be burned. Satan would then also be imprisoned, 'bound with fiery chains'.[62] Those who had remained in the religion of God would then be raised from the dead to reign with God for a thousand years in the rebuilt holy city.

At the end of the thousand years, Satan would be loosed from hell and the nations would attempt to storm the city of the saints. Then God would again 'rain upon the wicked fire with brimstone and hail, and they shall be on fire, and slay each other'.[63] The righteous would for a time be concealed under the earth until, after three days, the rebellious nations were all destroyed. The righteous would then re-emerge to see the corpses of the wicked sink into the bowels of the earth. God would then renew the world, the righteous would receive their garments of immortality, and the wicked would rise from the dead to be condemned to eternal punishment and delivered into eternal fires.

[60] *Ibid.*, 7.17, vol. VII, p. 215.   [61] *Ibid.*, 7.19, vol. VII, p. 215.
[62] William Fletcher (trans.), *The Epitome of the Divine Institutes*, 72, in *ANF*, vol. VII, p. 254.
[63] *Ibid.*, 72, vol. VII, pp. 254–5.

The Son of Satan?

As we noted above, the African theologian Lactantius was the first to suggest that the Antichrist would be conceived not by a holy spirit as was Christ, but by an evil spirit. It was a bit of a throw-away line, and Lactantius did not elaborate. Martin of Tours, we recall, also believed that the Antichrist had been conceived by an evil spirit. In both cases, it is difficult to tell from the Latin original whether 'an evil spirit' or 'the evil spirit' was intended. References to Satan rather than 'an evil spirit' make things clearer. Thus, for example, the so-called Ambrosiaster in his commentary on 2 Thessalonians (366–84) declared, 'As the Son of God in His human birth manifested his divine nature, so also shall Satan appear in human form.'[64] Similarly, Theodoret, bishop of Cyrrhus (c. 393–c. 458/466), if not declaring that the Antichrist was the son of Satan, nonetheless saw him as embodying all the Devil's power: 'For the persecutor of men simulates the incarnation of our God and Saviour; and as He by assuming our human nature accomplished our salvation, so *that one* also by making choice of a man capable of receiving the fullness of his power shall tempt men.'[65]

The belief that the Antichrist was Satan incarnate was undoubtedly widespread. This is demonstrated in the case of the Sicilian Julius Firmicus Maternus, an astrologer by trade and a Christian by conversion. That the Antichrist was Satan was an assumption of his *The Error of Pagan Religions* (c. 347), a work devoted to persuading the Emperors Constantius and Constans to destroy

[64] Quoted in Bousset, *The Antichrist Legend*, p. 142.   [65] *Ibid.*

the pagan idols. In the context of a discussion about the virtue of the Christian anointing of the dead *versus* the pagan tradition of the anointing of the living, he declared, 'who would not despise the folly of this business and hold it in scorn? Therefore the devil has his anointed ones ['Christi'] and because he himself is Antichrist, he reduces unfortunate wretches into an unholy alliance with the infamy of his own name.'[66]

Hippolytus too had implied that the Antichrist and the Devil were one and the same. Hippolytus, we recall, had looked to the tribe of Dan as the source of the Antichrist. Along with that, he invoked the description of Dan in Genesis 49.17 as a serpent lying on the ground. By the time of Hippolytus, the serpent in the book of Genesis had been identified as the Devil.[67] Hippolytus was thus able to align those of the tribe of Dan with the serpentine Devil in the Garden of Eden and the Antichrist. 'What, then', he asked, 'is meant by the serpent but Antichrist, that deceiver who is mentioned in Genesis, who deceived Eve and supplanted Adam?'[68]

But it was an unknown author (known as Pseudo-Hippolytus) somewhere between the fourth and the ninth centuries, in a work entitled *On the End of the World*, who drew out the parallels between the births of Christ and the Antichrist. As Christ was both divine and son of God, so the Antichrist was both demonic and son of Satan:[69]

---

[66] Clarence A. Forbes (trans.), *Firmicus Maternus: The Error of the Pagan Religions* (New York: Newman Press, 1970), 22.4, p. 94.

[67] See Almond, *The Devil*, p. 34.

[68] Coxe (ed.), *The Extant Works and Fragments of Hippolytus, Treatise on Christ and Antichrist*, 14, in *ANF*, vol. V, p. 207.

[69] Traditionally, it has been ascribed to Hippolytus of Rome, not least because it repeats large sections of Hippolytus' *Treatise on Christ*

Since the Saviour of the world, with the purpose of saving the race of men, was born of the immaculate and virgin Mary, and in the form of the flesh trod the enemy under foot, in the exercise of the power of His own proper divinity; in the same manner also will the accuser [diabolus, ὁ διάβολος, the Devil] come forth from an impure woman upon the earth, but shall be born [as if] of a virgin spuriously.[70]

That said, Pseudo-Hippolytus was reluctant *exactly* to mirror the birth of the Antichrist in reverse to that of Christ. The Antichrist was born, he said, not of a virgin but of a woman who only *seemed* virginal. Moreover, while, in the case of Christ, God dwelt with us in *exactly* the same flesh as that which he made for Adam and all those that came after him, the Antichrist would take up flesh '*only in appearance*'.

Pseudo-Hippolytus was to follow Daniel in allowing the Antichrist to reign for three and a half years. Initially at least, he would mimic Christ in order to seduce the faithful from the love of Christ. He began as the Great Deceiver. He would be gentle, loveable, quiet, pious, and pacific. He would hate injustice, detest gifts, and not allow idolatry. He would love the Scriptures, reverence priests, honour his elders, repudiate fornication, detest adultery, and be kind and compassionate to strangers and the poor. However, this was all a deceit to induce people to make him king. The Jews especially would want to make him king, a glory that he would initially refuse but eventually agree to.

---

and the Antichrist. Chapters 12–21 and 36 are largely drawn from the *Treatise on Christ and the Antichrist.*

[70] A. Cleveland Coxe (ed.), *The Extant Works and Fragments of Hippolytus, A Discourse … on the End of the World*, 21, in *ANF*, vol. V, pp. 247–8.

Having been made king, he would rebuild the temple in Jerusalem and give it to the Jews. Then his true nature as the eschatological tyrant would be revealed: 'in all things he will be harsh, severe, passionate, wrathful, terrible, inconstant, dread, morose, hateful, abominable, savage, vengeful, iniquitous'.[71] He would demand that all go to worship him. All who went would receive his mark of six hundred and sixty-six on their right hand and on their forehead. Pseudo-Hippolytus interpreted the number of the Antichrist to mean 'I deny'. 'For even in recent days', he wrote, 'that bitter adversary took up the word *deny*, when the lawless pressed upon the witnesses of Christ, with the adjuration, "Deny thy God, the crucified One."'[72]

The created world would become completely chaotic. The heavens would no longer give their dew, the clouds would not give rain, the earth would not yield its fruit, the seas would stink and the fish would die, the rivers would dry up, and there would be a deadly disease all over the earth. So many would die that there would not be enough left to bury them. The whole earth would be 'filled with the stench arising from the dead bodies'.[73]

Those who refused to worship the Antichrist would flee and hide themselves in the mountains and in caves. On their account, God would shorten the three and a half years of the Antichrist. Christ would come in judgement, and the Antichrist would be destroyed: 'Then shall the son of perdition be brought forward, to wit, the accuser, with his demons and with his servants, by angels

---

[71] *Ibid.*, 26, vol. V, p. 249.   [72] *Ibid.*, 28, vol. V, p. 249.
[73] *Ibid.*, 27, vol. V, p. 249.

stern and inexorable. And they shall be given over to the fire that is never quenched, and to the worm that never sleepeth, and to the outer darkness.'[74]

The tradition that the Antichrist was the Devil was to survive in Eastern Christianity at least until the ninth century. Thus, the Greek *Apocalypse of Daniel* tells of a great king by the name of Dan who would gather the Jews together in Jerusalem and begin to persecute the Christians. In what must be the most extravagant account of the rise of the Antichrist, with Dan reigning, the demonic Antichrist would emerge from the bowels of the earth:

And he will come into a small gardion fish. And he is coming in the broad sea. And he will be caught by twelve fishermen. And the fishermen will become maddened toward each other. One will prevail over them, whose name is Judas. And he takes that fish for his inheritance and comes into a place named Gouzeth and there sells the fish for thirty silver pieces. And a virgin girl will buy the fish. Her name (is) Injustice because the son of injustice will be born from her. And her surname will be Perdition. For by touching the head of the fish she will become pregnant and will conceive the Antichrist himself. And he will be born from her (after) three months. And he will suckle (from) her (for) four months ... And he also has upon his forehead three letters: A, K, T. And the A signifies: 'I deny', the K: 'And I completely reject', the T: 'The befouled dragon'.[75]

As if not sufficiently recognisable by the mark on his forehead, the *Apocalypse of Daniel* gave a description of

---

[74] *Ibid.*, 40, vol. V, p. 252.
[75] G. T. Zervos (trans.), *Apocalypse of Daniel*, 9, in Charlesworth (ed.), *The Old Testament Pseudepigrapha, Vol. I*, p. 767.

the physical attributes of the Antichrist that would have made him instantly recognisable. He would be 15 ft tall, and his hair would reach to his feet. According to one manuscript, his feet would be 3½ ft in length. His right eye would be like that of a lion, while his lower teeth would be made of iron and his lower jaw of diamond.

To See Him Was to Know Him

In the light of the developing interest in the Antichrist in the period from the end of the first century for the next 300 years, it is surprising that none of the mainstream Greek Eastern or Latin Western theologians provided physical descriptions of the Antichrist. It is surprising because, both in the second and in the fourth centuries, there was a flowering of the science of physiognomy, according to which particular human physical features were a certain guide to the nature of the soul.[76] Nevertheless, within Eastern Christianity there are a number of texts composed within the first millennium, of which the *Apocalypse of Daniel* was the last, that do give us descriptions of the Antichrist. These are suggestive of a physiognomic Antichrist tradition within Eastern Christianity, even though it is difficult to map it onto the classical physiognomic tradition.[77] In a sense, this was

[76] See Elizabeth C. Evans, *Physiognomics in the Ancient World* (Philadelphia: The American Philosophical Society, 1969).

[77] Although it has been attempted. See, especially, J. Massyngbaerde Ford, 'The Physical Features of the Antichrist', *Journal for the Study of the Pseudepigrapha* 14 (1996), 23–41. See also Bernard McGinn, 'Portraying Antichrist in the Middle Ages', in Werner Verbeke et al., *The Use and Abuse of Eschatology in the Middle Ages* (Leuven University Press, 1988), pp. 1–48.

physiognomy in reverse for, rather than reading from how someone looked to how he must be, these read from how the Antichrist must be to how he must look. I focus here on four texts in various versions, namely, *The Testament of Our Lord* (in Syriac, Ethiopian, and Latin), *The Apocalypse of Elijah* (Greek and Coptic), *The Apocalypse of Pseudo-John* (Greek), and *The Apocalypse of Ezra* (Greek).[78]

If their physiognomic meaning is less than apparent, their prophetic function is clear. Quite simply, the texts were meant to ensure that, when we saw him, we would know him. The prologue to *The Testament of the Lord* purports to give the words of Jesus Christ to his apostles and to Mary, Martha, and Salome on the evening after his resurrection, and, in particular, the signs of the end. Among these was the appearance of the Antichrist, 'the Son of Perdition, the Adversary, who boasteth and exalteth himself, working many signs and miracles, that he may deceive the whole earth, and overcome the innocent, My holy ones'.[79] Granted the description that followed, he was not likely to be overlooked: 'his head [is] as a fiery flame: his right eye shot with blood, his left [eye] blue-black, and he hath two pupils. His eyelashes [eyebrows] are white; and his lower lip is large; but his right thigh slender; his feet broad; his great toe [or finger] is bruised and flat. This is the sickle of desolation.'[80] The

[78] For the most extensive comparison of physical descriptions of the Antichrist, see J.-M. Rosenstiehl, 'Le Portrait de l'Antichrist', in M. Philonenko et al. (eds.), *Pseudépigraphes de l'Ancien Testament et Manuscrits de la Mer Morte* (Paris: Presses Universitaires de France, 1967), pp. 45–60.

[79] James Cooper and Arthur John Maclean (trans.), *The Testament of Our Lord* (Edinburgh: T. & T. Clark, 1902), 9, p. 56.

[80] *Ibid.*, 11, pp. 57–8.

Latin version added that his eyes were angry and his legs thin.

In its description of the Antichrist, the Greek version of *The Apocalypse of Elijah* mirrored that of *The Testament of Our Lord*. But the Coptic version was quite distinctive. 'For behold', we read,

> I will tell you his signs *so that you might know him*. He is a ... skinny-legged young lad, having a tuft of gray hair at the front of his bald head. His eyebrows will reach to his ears. There is a leprous bare spot on the front of his hands. He will transform himself in the presence of those who see him. He will become a young child. He will become old. He will transform himself in every sign. But the signs of his head will not be able to change. *Therein you will know that he is the son of lawlessness.*[81]

Another tradition of the physical appearance of the Antichrist appeared in the Greek *The Apocalypse of Pseudo-John*. This consisted of a set of questions about the end of the world, asked of the ascended Jesus by a 'John of Patmos'. In response to John's request that Jesus tell him what the Antichrist would be like, Jesus declared,

> His face appears dark as Hell, the hairs of his head sharp as arrows, his brows wild like a field; his right eye is like the star which rises early, his other eye as a lion's; his mouth measures half a yard, and his teeth a span; his fingers resemble sickles; his footprint measures a foot and a half; and on his forehead the name Antichrist is engraved.[82]

---

[81] O. S. Wintermute (trans.), *Apocalypse of Elijah*, 3.14–18, in Charlesworth, *The Old Testament Pseudepigrapha*, *Vol. I*, pp. 745–6 (my italics).

[82] John M. Court, *The Book of Revelation and the Johannine Apocalyptic Tradition* (Sheffield Academic Press, 2000), p. 35.

The narrator of *The Apocalypse of Ezra* desired information on the physical attributes of the Antichrist so that he could 'inform the race of men lest they believe in him'.[83] To all intents and purposes, the description of the Antichrist in *The Apocalypse of Ezra* mirrored that of *The Apocalypse of Pseudo-John*, with the addition that the face of the Antichrist was that of a wild man.[84] While it is difficult to read particular physical attributes in any of these texts as corresponding to especial vices, there is little doubt that readers of these descriptions would have interpreted them as suggestive of monstrosity, evil, and malevolence, a dangerous mixture of the human, the demonic, and the bestial.

The 'logic' of the Antichrist predisposed those who theorised about his nature towards the affirmation that, as Christ was fully both God and man, so the Antichrist was also both Satan and man. However, this assumed a supernatural equivalence between God and the Devil that many mainstream theologians were unwilling to accept. Hippolytus, we recall, had hedged his opinion by saying that, if the Devil took flesh, he did so *only by simulation*.

To some, a different 'logic' predisposed towards the belief that, just as Christ was fully human yet absolutely 'sin-free', so the Antichrist was fully human yet completely 'sin-full'. In this case, he was not so much a supernatural being who became flesh as a natural being who became fully demonised. Thus, for example, for Irenaeus,

---

[83] M. E. Stone (trans.), *Greek Apocalypse of Ezra*, 4.29, in Charlesworth, *The Old Testament Pseudepigrapha, Vol. I*, p. 575.

[84] *Ibid.*, 4.30, p. 575.

the Antichrist was not the Devil incarnate, although he was 'endued with all the power of the devil ... concentrating in himself [all] satanic apostasy'.[85]

But it was Jerome (c. 342–420), the translator of the Bible into Latin (known as the Vulgate), who was to set the pattern for the Western view of the nature of the Antichrist as merely human. Thus, in commenting on 'the little horn' of Daniel 7.8, we read, 'Nor let us think that he [the Antichrist] ... is the devil [diabolum] or a demon, but *one of men* [unum de hominibus] in whom Satan is wholly to dwell bodily'.[86] In short, the Antichrist was the ultimate demoniac. Similarly, it was John Chrysostom (c. 347–407), bishop of Constantinople, who was to establish the Eastern tradition of the Antichrist as the absolutely evil man. Who is the man of sin and the son of perdition, he asked? 'Is it then Satan? By no means; but some man, that admits his fully working in him. For he is a man.'[87]

From this point on, in the main, both in the East and the West, the Antichrist travelled on a path separate from, if parallel to, the Devil. Fully human certainly, the son of Satan probably, but not the Devil incarnate.

---

[85] Cox (ed.), *Irenaeus against Heresies*, 5.25.1, in *ANF*, vol. I, p. 553.

[86] Quoted in Bousset, *The Antichrist Legend*, p. 139. For the Latin original, see p. 272, n. 19.

[87] Gross Alexander (trans.), *Homilies ... on the Second Epistle of St. Paul the Apostle to the Thessalonians, Homily 3*, in *NPNF, first series*, vol. XIII, p. 386. Bousset, *The Antichrist Legend*, p. 139, has this as *Homily 3*.

3

The Antichrist, East and West

~

How long shall it be until the end of these wonders?

Daniel 12.6

The Antichrist Within

The first 300 years of the Christian era were lived in the expectation that the return of Christ was imminent. Within this expectation of a world about to end, the Antichrist came to play a progressively more important role. However, with the conversion of the Emperor Constantine in 312, apocalyptic expectations cooled. They remained so for the rest of the fourth century. When the Emperor Theodosius made Christianity the official religion of the Roman Empire in 380, it looked as if, far from the end of the world being at hand, Christianity was here for the long haul and the arrival of the Antichrist was postponed indefinitely. As Kevin Hughes neatly puts it, 'In the age of Christian empire, the apocalyptic frame of crisis and judgment is passé. In fact, apocalyptic anxiety and hope are transmuted into millennial confidence that the Church is thriving in "Christian Times".'[1] That said, the eschatological understanding of history remained deep within the Christian tradition. Good times still raised eschatological hopes of the return of Christ (with or without a thousand-year reign of Christ on earth), bad

[1] Hughes, *Constructing Antichrist*, p. 32.

77

times led to expectations of worse yet to come when the Antichrist arrived.

If the Antichrist was predominantly a future historical figure, he could also be read as a figure already present – collectively within institutions like the empire or the church, or present within each individual. The Alexandrian Origen (c. 185–c. 254) can lay claim to be the first Christian theologian to have Platonised Christianity and, in so doing, to have read the historical and literal meaning of the Scriptures in terms of their hidden and mystical meaning for the individual soul. Although Origen's writings are often anything but clear, it seems likely that he did accept that the Antichrist would be a future historical figure, not least because he criticised the 'heretic' Celsus' failure to understand the Scriptural references to the future coming of the Antichrist. If so, he was the first inversely to mirror the birth of Christ and the birth of the Antichrist, and the first to suggest that the Antichrist was the son of Satan. It was right, he wrote, 'that one of the extremes, the best, should be called Son of God because of his superiority, and that the one diametrically opposed to him should be called son of the evil daemon, who is Satan and the devil'.[2]

That said, Origen was as interested, if not more so, in the anthropological as the eschatological meaning of the Antichrist. Thus, he reversed the declaration in 1 John 2.18 that there were many Antichrists in the world to assert that there were also many Christs. This enabled him to interpret the mixture of goodness and evil among

---

[2] Henry Chadwick (trans.), *Origen: Contra Celsum*, 6.45 (Cambridge University Press, 1953), p. 362.

men in terms of the hidden presence within them of both Christ and Antichrist. Christ and the Antichrist were thus the limiting human examples of that mixture of both of them present within all of us. 'Why, then', he asked, 'is it absurd that among men there should be two extremities, if I may so say, the one of goodness, the other of its opposite, so that the extremity of goodness exists in the human nature of Jesus ... whereas the opposite extremity exists in him who is called Antichrist?'[3] In short, Origen set up the tension within the Antichrist tradition between the Antichrist to come and the Antichrist within each individual.

Jerome, arguably the most important influence on Western Christian thinking next to Augustine, reflected both tendencies. Under the influence of Origen, he accepted that the Scriptures had both a literal and a spiritual meaning. He embraced an eschatology that referred literally to persons and events in the historical past and future while also reading them spiritually in terms of the individual and the church in the historical present. Thus, for example, in his *Commentary on Matthew* (398), Jerome declared that 'the abomination of desolation' (Matthew 24.15, Daniel 9.27) could be interpreted literally of the Antichrist that was to come, of the image of Caesar that Pilate placed in the temple, and of the equestrian statue of the Emperor Hadrian 'which stands to the present day in the very location of the holy of holies'.[4] It could also 'be understood of all perverted teaching' from which

3 *Ibid.*, 6.45, p. 362.
4 P. Scheck (trans.), *Commentary on Matthew* (Washington, DC: The Catholic University of America Press, 2010), 24.15, 16–18, p. 272.

the true believer should flee to 'the eternal mountains from which God illumines marvellously'.[5] Like Origen, he took a leaf out of the first epistle of John to emphasise that, along with the Antichrist that was yet to come, there were already many Antichrists in the world. 'I am of the opinion', he declared, 'that all heresiarchs are antichrists and teach things in the name of Christ that are contrary to Christ.'[6]

In the late fourth century, Jerome appears to have had no immediate expectations of the return of Christ, or of the rise of the Antichrist. In his Latin translation of the *Chronicle* of Eusebius of Caesarea (c. 260–c. 340), which he completed around 380, he had dated the birth of Christ at 5,199 years after the creation of Adam.[7] So, on the 6,000-years calculation between the creation of the world and its end, he was not expecting the future Antichrist to arrive for some further 800 years. But by the turn of the third century, his apocalyptic antennae were more attuned to an apocalypse sooner rather than later. For Rome was then under attack by the Goths under their leader, Alaric. Rome, the bulwark against the arrival of the Antichrist, was about to fall. Thus, for example, in a letter in 409 to the widow Agerucha, a highborn woman of Gaul, he wrote, 'He that letteth [he that restrains] is taken out of the way [the Roman Empire], and yet we do not realise that Antichrist is near. Yes, Antichrist is near whom the Lord Jesus Christ "shall consume with

[5] *Ibid.*, 24.16–18, p. 272.   [6] *Ibid.*, 24.5, p. 270.

[7] See Roger Pearse (ed.), *The Chronicle of St. Jerome*, in *Early Church Fathers – Additional Texts*. Available at www.tertullian.org/fathers/index .htm#JeromeChronicle

the spirit of his mouth".[8] No need then, or any time for that matter, for the widow to consider remarriage, the married state being one that Jerome thought undesirable at the best of times.[9]

In another letter, c. 405, this time in response to a letter from Algasia, yet another female admirer from Gaul, Jerome had summarised the Antichrist tradition at the time. Among a number of questions, Algasia had asked for the meaning of the passage in 2 Thessalonians 2.3 that Christ would not come 'unless the rebellion comes first and the man of sin is revealed'.[10] In reply, Jerome told her that, for the moment, it was the Roman Empire that was restraining the Antichrist from arriving. The obtuseness of Paul's reference was the consequence, declared Jerome, of Paul's fear of persecution:

He does not want to say 'the destruction of the Roman Empire', because those who rule think that it is eternal. Thus according to the Apocalypse of John, the blasphemous name, 'Romae aeternae', is written on the forehead of the scarlet harlot. If he had said boldly and openly, 'Antichrist will not come until the Roman Empire falters', a just cause of persecution of the Eastern church would then seem to arise.[11]

Jerome followed Hippolytus in imagining the Antichrist as mirroring Christ: 'Just as in Christ the fullness of

---

[8] W. H. Fremantle et al. (trans.), *Letter 123*, 16, in *NPNF, second series*, vol. VI, p. 236.

[9] See J. N. D. Kelly, *Jerome: His Life, Writings, and Controversies* (London: Duckworth, 1975), ch. 17.

[10] Algasia was quoting Jerome's Vulgate Bible: 'nisi discessio uenerit primum et reuelatus fuerit homo peccati'.

[11] Quoted in Hughes, *Constructing Antichrist*, p. 77. I am indebted to Hughes for his discussion of *Letter 121*.

divinity existed corporally, so all the powers, signs, and prodigies will be in Antichrist, but all of them will be false.'[12] At the end of the day, just as the rod of Moses devoured those of the magicians of Pharaoh, so the truth of Christ would devour the lie of Antichrist. At the end of the world, Christ would require no heavenly host to destroy the Antichrist – his own brilliance would suffice.

Anti-Judaism had been implicit in the Christian story of the life, death, and resurrection of Jesus. By the time of Jerome, that the Jews would be supporters of the Antichrist was already a part of his story. That, like Christ, the Antichrist was a Jew was part of this. For Jerome, the Antichrist was a Jew, albeit one from Babylon. Little wonder that the Jews, having rejected Christ, increased and confirmed their perfidy by accepting the Antichrist. They would be condemned for spurning Christ and embracing the Antichrist on the last day. Jerome was to think more 'systematically' about the role of the Jews in the life and death of the Antichrist a few years later in his commentary on the book of Daniel. There too, the Jews 'who did not believe the truth but supported a lie' would be condemned during the last six months of the three-and-a-half-year rule of the Antichrist.[13]

Jerome's primary intention in his commentary on the book of Daniel was to rebut the anti-Christian polemic on this work by the Neoplatonist philosopher Porphyry (c. 232–303). Porphyry had argued, according to Jerome, that the author of Daniel did not so much foretell the

---

[12] *Ibid.*, p. 77.
[13] Gleason L. Archer (trans.), *St. Jerome, Commentary on Daniel*, 7.25, in Roger Pearse (ed.), *Early Church Fathers – Additional Texts*. Available at www.tertullian.org/fathers/index.htm#JeromeChronicle

future as relate the past, the work having been written by someone who was living in Judea during the time of the Hellenistic king Antiochus IV Epiphanes. Jerome, like his predecessors Eusebius of Caesarea (c. 260–c. 340), Apollinarius (c. 310–c. 390), and Methodius (d. c. 311), was having none of this. 'I wish to stress', he declared, 'that none of the prophets has so clearly spoken concerning Christ as has this prophet Daniel.'[14] Making a prophetic virtue out of historical necessity, Jerome argued that the very attack on Daniel was testimony to his accuracy, for 'so striking was the reliability of what the prophet foretold, that he could not appear to unbelievers as a predictor of the future, but rather a narrator of things already past'.[15]

As for the Antichrist, Porphyry had contended that, whatever was 'foretold concerning Antichrist at the end of the world was actually fulfilled in the reign of Antiochus'.[16] Jerome disagreed vehemently. Yet, for all that, he did have to concede that many of the details about the Antichrist were appropriate to Antiochus. After all, in 167 BCE, Antiochus had sacked Jerusalem and erected a statue of himself as Zeus in the Jewish temple (see Plate 6). To square the behaviour of Antiochus with the expected activities of the Antichrist, Jerome's explanation drew on the notion of 'types'. It was the habit of Holy Scripture, he wrote, to set forth by means of types the reality of things to come, shadows and symbols of reality. Thus, 'just as the Savior had Solomon and the other saints as types of His advent, so also we should believe that the Antichrist very properly had as a type of himself

[14] *Ibid.*, Prologue.   [15] *Ibid.*   [16] *Ibid.*

the utterly wicked king, Antiochus, who persecuted the saints and defiled the Temple'.[17] On this principle, Porphyry's claim that Daniel was referring to Antiochus and not the Antichrist mattered little. Daniel was in fact referencing both. Thanks to Jerome, Antiochus (along with a number of others, as we will see) became 'the most widely discussed type of Antichrist in the Middle Ages'.[18]

Jerome was to make yet another contribution to the story of the Antichrist, namely, that the Antichrist would meet his death on the summit of the Mount of Olives, the place from which Christ ascended into heaven.[19] That Christ would return to earth at the same place he had left it in order to destroy the Antichrist has a certain logic to it. Jerome found biblical 'verification' in Isaiah 25.7, which he rendered as: 'The Lord shall in the holy mountain cast down the face of the ruler of darkness which is over all races, and him who rules over all peoples.' This was, even for Jerome, an exegetical bridge too far. His own translation of this passage in the Vulgate bore little resemblance to his 'Antichrist' translation of it in his Daniel commentary.[20]

Jerome was also the populariser of the tradition that there would be a period on earth between the death of the Antichrist and the final judgement. Jerome took the reign of the Antichrist to be three and a half years, or 1,290 days. But he had also noted that Daniel 12.12 suggested that there were another forty-five days before

---

[17] *Ibid.*, 11.24.   [18] Emmerson, *Antichrist in the Middle Ages*, p. 28.

[19] Archer (trans.), *St. Jerome, Commentary on Daniel*, 11.44–5.

[20] *Ibid.* The Vulgate has: 'And he shall destroy in this mountain the face of the bond with which all people were tied, and the web that he began over all nations.'

'our Lord and Savior is to come in his glory'.[21] This was messy, and Jerome knew it. Jerome viewed the idea of a thousand-year reign of the saints on earth as nothing but a fable. Rome was to be the last *earthly* kingdom. But his forty-five days between the death of the Antichrist and the Last Judgement did look like a miniature version of it. God only knows the reason for it, he wrote. Perhaps, he went on, the rule of the saints was delayed 'in order that their patience may be tested'.[22] After three and a half years of the Antichrist, perhaps their patience had been tested enough. Elsewhere, in his commentary on the gospel of Matthew (398), Jerome got himself into another conceptual bind. There, while he promised a brief period of peace before a permanent peace, during which the faithfulness of believers would be tested, he was forced into complete uncertainty about how long this period would be, a consequence of his sticking literally to Matthew 24.42: 'Watch, therefore, for you do not know at what hour your Lord will come.'[23] Adso, we may recall, also had a bet both ways. He reduced the forty-five days to forty but was uncertain as to how long it would be after this until the final judgement.

The Antichrist, Then and Now!

One way to emphasise the Antichrist(s) in the present was to postpone the arrival of the final Antichrist into the distant future. The alternative strategy was to emphasise the imminence of his arrival – the sooner the arrival of

---

[21] *Ibid.*, 12.12.   [22] *Ibid.*
[23] Scheck (trans.), *Commentary on Matthew*, 24.42, p. 280.

the Antichrist, the narrower the gap between any present and future Antichrists. This was the strategy of the North African theologian Tyconius (d. c. 400). Tyconius had been a member of the Donatist party until excommunicated by them in 380. In spite of that, Tyconius refrained from seeking communion with the Catholic church in Africa, retaining his affiliation, at least at a personal level, with the Donatists.[24] The Donatists held that the true church contained only the righteous, and (perhaps not surprisingly) that the Donatists themselves *were* this true church. In contrast, Tyconius maintained that, before the end of the world, the church was a community of *both sinners and saints*. It was a position that significantly influenced his eschatology and his understanding of the Antichrist.

Tyconius' most significant contribution to the Western Christian tradition was his commentary on the book of Revelation (c. 385). As David C. Robinson remarks, it 'shaped the Latin reception of and interpretation of the Apocalypse [Revelation] for the next eight hundred years'.[25] Its genuinely innovative feature was its interpretation of Revelation not primarily as an eschatological work, but rather as one also applicable to the present situation of the church or, perhaps better, one in which present and future were rolled in together.

For Tyconius, the present and the future could be considered together because the book of Revelation had

---

[24] On the Donatists, see David E. Wilhite, *Ancient African Christianity* (London: Routledge, 2017).
[25] Francis X. Gumerlock (trans.) and David C. Robinson (intro.), *Tyconius: Exposition of the Apocalypse* (Washington, DC: The Catholic University of America Press, 2017), p. 4.

both a literal and a spiritual sense. In his commentary on this book, Tyconius was in fact applying the rules for the interpreting of Scripture that he had laid out in his *Book of Rules* (c. 382) so that 'anyone who walks the vast forest of prophecy guided by these rules, as by pathways of light, will be kept from error'.[26]

Eschatologically, the present and the future could not be separated because Tyconius expected the end of the world at any moment. Rule Five in his *Book of Rules* was especially relevant to his eschatology. This Rule had to do with the 'mystical' meaning of biblical time. Thus, for example, one day was sometimes one hundred days. And the 1,260 days in which the two prophets or witnesses (now read as the church prophesying in both Testaments) bore witness (Revelation 11.3) was 126,000 days, or 350 years. Sometimes, one month meant one hundred months. Therefore, the 42 months during which the holy city was trampled (Revelation 11.2) was 4,200 months, or 350 years. A time period could be a year or a hundred years, in which case the 'time, and times, and half a time' (Revelation 12.14) could be either 3½ or 350 years. This 350 years, generated in various ways, was crucial to Tyconius' eschatology. It was the period of oppression and persecution between the crucifixion of Jesus and his second coming. Granted the crucifixion of Christ was in the year 33, this period was close to its end at the time Tyconius was writing his *Book of Rules*. So Tyconius really did believe that the end was at hand.[27]

---

[26] William S. Babcock (trans.), *Tyconius: The Book of Rules* (Atlanta, Georgia: Scholars Press, 1989), preface, p. 3.

[27] See *ibid.*, p. 99. For an argument that Tyconius didn't really mean what he apparently wrote, see Paula Frederiksen Landes, 'Tyconius and the

That said, by virtue of Rule Six, namely that the events of the final times recapitulated those that preceded them, the final trials of the immediate future were already a part of the Christian (read 'persecuted Donatist') present. The author of Revelation, he declared, 'never separates the present time from the last, when "spiritual wicked-ness" will be revealed. Because [that wicked spirit] neither now desists in suggesting evil works to people, nor then will he desist in doing the same things.'[28]

This blurring of the present and the future within the writings of Tyconius makes it difficult to discern his view of the Antichrist, in particular whether his emphasis is upon the Antichrist in the present rather than in the future. This question is also bedevilled, so to say, by the paucity of direct references to the Antichrist within his work. The modern opinion has it that, while Tyconius recognises a future Antichrist, his emphasis is upon the Antichrist in the present.[29] Yet the emphasis can as easily be read the opposite way. Thus, the *Book of Rules* contains only four direct references to the Antichrist. Of these, two refer to the Antichrist who was to come. A third, quoting 1 John 4.1–3, indicates that the spirit of the Antichrist that was to come was already in the world, while a fourth indicates that anyone who denied Christ was an Antichrist. The future Antichrist remains the predominant idea.

End of the World', *Revue d'études augustiniennes et patristiques* 28 (1982), 59–75.

[28] Gumerlock (trans.) and Robinson (intro.), *Tyconius*, 11.9, p. 114.
[29] See, for example, McGinn, *Antichrist*, p. 76; Brian E. Daley, *The Hope of the Early Church: A Handbook of Patristic Eschatology* (Grand Rapids, Michigan: Baker Academic, 1991), p. 248, n. 10.

As in the *Book of Rules*, so also in Tyconius' commentary on the book of Revelation, the emphasis was on the future Antichrist. The commentary contains three direct references to the Antichrist, all of which emphasise the Antichrist to come. Thus, in the first of these, the future Antichrist will be revealed in the whole world and will 'rule as the last king over all the earth', although he is already hidden within the church.[30] In the second, the persecution that was taking place of the Donatists in Africa was 'a figure of the future revelation of Antichrist throughout the world, who, now ... performs works of iniquity'.[31] The third suggests that the Roman emperor Otho (32–69), emperor for three months in 69, was a type of the Antichrist to come.[32]

Still, as the passages above suggest, the Antichrist was nevertheless already present and at work in the church. That this is so follows from Tyconius' theory of the church. For Tyconius, humanity consisted of two societies or cities, the people of God and the people of the Devil, the one coming from heaven, the other from the abyss.[33] However, some of those who belong to the people of the Devil were also to be found within the church. Thus, the church or the body of Christ was itself divided into two parts – a left and a right part. The left part was that of the Antichurch or the Antichrist, the right that of Christ. Thus, the battle between the church and the Devil occurred both inside and outside the church. Thus, *'Do not fear any of those things which you are about to suffer*

---

[30] Gumerlock (trans.) and Robinson (intro.), *Tyconius*, 3.10, p. 56.
[31] *Ibid.*, 6.7–8, p. 76.   [32] *Ibid.*, 17.10, p. 163.
[33] See *ibid.*, 17.18, p. 166.

[Revelation 2.10], surely from the whole body of the devil, which besieges the church in the whole world from inside and from outside.'[34] Thus did Tyconius set up the tension between the Antichrist outside the church and the Antichrists within it.

The false brethren of the Antichurch masquerade as true Christians. They are 'the Antichrist', 'the abomination of desolation', the 'mystery of iniquity', and 'the beast from the sea' already at work inside the church. As for the false bishops, they were the 'beast from the earth'. Although hidden, all these reveal themselves in their actions. False brethren 'confess him [Christ] with their mouth but by their actions say: "We have no king except Caesar".'[35] The true brethren receive a mark upon their hand and on their forehead, that is, 'in deed and in profession'.[36] The hypocritical false brethren actually receive 'the beast under the name of Christ'.[37]

Tyconius was no millenarian in the strict sense. He had no expectation that the saints would rule with Christ on earth after his return for a thousand years (Revelation 20.6). Rather, the 'millennium' was read spiritually as the period from the crucifixion of Christ until his second coming, during which the saints already reigned. It was also the period during which Satan was imprisoned (Revelation 20.2). At the end of the world, Satan would be released for three and a half years. At that time, the 'man of sin' who had been hidden within the church would be revealed. The false brethren previously hidden within the church would then persecute the church: '[T]hose

---

[34] *Ibid.*, 2.19, p. 45.   [35] *Ibid.*, 12.4, p. 123.
[36] *Ibid.*, 13.16, p. 138.   [37] *Ibid.*

in league with the devil, although saying that they are Christians, will fight against the church.'[38]

When Christ returned in judgement, there would be retribution: 'Vengeance will flow out even up to the rulers of the peoples. For in the last contest the vengeance of blood poured out will flow even to "the devil and his angels", as was predicted beforehand: "You have sinned with blood, and blood pursues you".'[39] Then the church would be purified, becoming in full the Jerusalem that it already was in part. The author of Revelation, declared Tyconius,

calls this [new] 'Jerusalem' the church, by recapitulating from the passion of Christ up to the day on which she rises and, having triumphed with Christ, she is crowned in glory. He mixes each time together, now the present, now the future, and declares more fully when she is taken with great glory by Christ and is separated from every incursion of evil people.[40]

The Antichrist, Immanent and Imminent

Unfortunately, the commentary of Tyconius on Revelation was not preserved. What we know of it has been reconstructed from its use in later works. Among these was the commentary on Revelation by Primasius, bishop of Hadrumetum in North Africa (fl. mid sixth century). He was sympathetic to Tyconius' interpretation, although he compared it to picking precious gemstones out of manure (*pretiosa in stercore gemma*).[41] Modern readers of Tyconius can only sympathise with this. Now Primasius endorsed

---

[38] *Ibid.*, 9.19, p. 100.   [39] *Ibid.*, 14.20, p. 147.
[40] *Ibid.*, 21.1, p. 181.   [41] See *ibid.*, p. 4.

Tyconius' view of Revelation as having relevance to the present. But, unlike Tyconius, who read it in terms of the struggle between enemies both within and outside the church, Primasius did so in terms of the battle between the church and the outside world. In so doing, Primasius was walking in Augustine's sandals. For Augustine too had read Tyconius' 'two cities' as referring only to the church and the world and not also to divisions within the church.

Augustine had also followed Tyconius in believing that the millennium had already begun. As we have seen earlier, according to Augustine, the binding of Satan had happened as the result of the victory of Christ in his life, death, and resurrection. Satan had, at that time, been thrown into the bottomless pit. The Devil, declared Augustine, is 'prohibited and restrained from seducing those nations which belong to Christ, but which he formerly seduced or held in subjection'.[42] Yet Satan dwelt still in the depths of the 'blind hearts' of those who hated Christians, and he still remained able to take even more possession of the ungodly for 'that man is more abundantly possessed by the devil who is not only alienated from God, but also gratuitously hates those who serve God'.[43] Thus the church, even now, was the Kingdom of God, and God's saints already reigned with him. The 'millennium' was not so much literally 'a thousand years' as figuratively all the years of the Christian era, whose number only God ultimately knew.

---

[42] Marcus Dods (trans.), *St. Augustin's City of God*, 20.7, in *NPNF, first series*, vol. II, p. 427. On Augustine's eschatology, see Daley, *The Hope of the Early Church*, pp. 131–50.

[43] Dods (trans.), *St. Augustin's City of God*, 20.7, in *NPNF, first series*, vol. II, p. 427.

Even though Augustine was non-committal about
when the end would come, he did remain committed
to a literal end of history and to the Antichrist who was
to come. The future Antichrist was already too much a
part of the Christian tradition for Augustine summar-
ily to dismiss him. To be sure, in the finer details of the
life and death of the Antichrist, he had little interest. But
that the Antichrist would come, he had no doubt: 'Elias
the Tishbite shall come; the Jews shall believe; Antichrist
shall persecute; Christ shall judge; the dead shall rise; the
good and the wicked shall be separated; the world shall
be burned and renewed. All these things, we believe,
shall come to pass.[44] Indeed, Christ would not come
again unless the Antichrist, 'His adversary, first come to
seduce those who are dead in soul'.[45]

The emphasis for Tyconius, we recall, remained on
the future rather than the present Antichrist. The opposite was the case with Augustine. Augustine was much
more interested in a 'spiritualised' Antichrist in the present than in a literal Antichrist to come. Thus, in a sermon
on the first letter of John, he focused on the presence of
many Antichrists, both inside and outside the church. All
heretics and schismatics, he declared, were Antichrists, as
were all those who left the church. 'Certainly,' he wrote,
'all who go out from the Church, and are cut off from the
unity of the Church, are antichrists; let no man doubt
it ... Therefore, whoso continue not with us, but go out
from us, it is manifest that that they are antichrists.[46]

---

[44] *Ibid.*, 20.30, *NPNF, first series*, vol. II, p. 451.

[45] *Ibid.*, 20.19, *NPNF, first series*, vol. II, p. 438.

[46] H. Browne (trans.), *St. Augustin: Ten Homilies on the First Epistle of John,*
Homily III, 7, in *NPNF, first series*, vol. VII, p. 478.

Demonising the other was, then as now, a useful political strategy against opponents.

The Antichrists were to be identified not by their words (for they *will* confess that Jesus is the Christ), but by their deeds. On this criterion, not only were there Antichrists outside the church, but also within it:

> For as many as the Church hath within it that are perjured, defrauders, addicted to black arts, consulters of fortune-tellers, adulterers, drunkards, usurers, boy-stealers, and all the other vices that we are not able to enumerate; these things are contrary to the doctrine of Christ, are contrary to the word of God. Now the Word of God is Christ: whatever is contrary to the Word of God is in Antichrist. For Antichrist means 'contrary to Christ'.[47]

Thus, the church was filled with Antichrists. These were like bad humours in the body of Christ, Augustine declared, that required vomiting up. Therefore 'each person ought to question his own conscience, whether he be an antichrist'.[48] In principle, therefore, any one of us could be an Antichrist. It behoved all of us to look within ourselves to ensure that we were not. This was Augustine's signature contribution to the story of the Antichrist. For Augustine, even though he was careful about predicting the end, the present was nonetheless eschatologically nuanced. The last hour *was* already present, not least because there were *already* many Antichrists. 'Could it [the present] have many antichrists', he asked, 'except it were "the last hour"?[49]

[47] *Ibid.*, 9, *NPNF, first series*, vol. VII, p. 479.
[48] *Ibid.*, 4, *NPNF, first series*, vol. VII, p. 476.
[49] *Ibid.*, 3, *NPNF, first series*, vol. VII, p. 476.

In the third book of his *On Christian Doctrine*, Augustine devoted considerable space to a discussion of Tyconius' *Book of Rules*. Augustine did not think that the Rules of Tyconius were sufficient to interpret the whole of Scripture, and, since they were written by a Donatist, he held that they should be read with caution. He did nonetheless admit that they were 'of very great assistance in understanding Scripture', in principle at least.[50] But it is perhaps not a matter for surprise that, in his discussion of Rule Five, Augustine ignored Tyconius' calculation of 350 years from the time of the death of Christ to the end of the world. For Augustine had completed the first three of the books of *On Christian Doctrine* in 397, a decade or so after, at least according to Tyconius, the world ought to have ended.

Failed predictions about the rise of the Antichrist or about the end of the world more generally were seldom sufficient to dent enthusiasm for or anxiety about the imminent end of the world. Imminent expectations of the future Antichrist and the return of Christ were always on the theological agenda. Troubled times always outweighed Augustine's calm and measured agnosticism. As Richard Landes puts it, 'Augustine's insistence, for example, that the Book of Revelations should not be read historically – taken up by every theologian from that day on in commentaries on the work – placed a near-impossible demand on believers who, wicks trimmed, looked anxiously for signs of the coming Parousia.'[51] Augustine's

---

[50] J. F. Shaw (trans.), *On Christian Doctrine in Four Books*, 3.30, in *NPNF*, first series, vol. II, p. 568.

[51] Richard Landes, 'Lest the Millennium Be Fulfilled', p. 158.

reluctance to predict the end of the world was not a deterrent. Augustine's own disciple Quodvulteus (d. c. 450), sometime bishop of Carthage, saw his own time as falling within the three and a half years of the Antichrist. Bernard McGinn points out that, in the middle of the fifth century, the number of the beast was interpreted by one commentator as referring to 'Gensericos', that is, Gaiseric, the Vandal king who sacked Rome in 455. He also reminds us that, as the year 500 approached, the date set by Hippolytus for the end of the world, the chronological work entitled the *Paschal List of Campania* noted that in 493 and 496 some 'arrogant fools' (*ignari praesumptores*) and 'crazies' (*deliri*) were announcing the coming of the Antichrist.[52]

Even when Hippolytus' prediction failed, expectations of the imminent end of the world continued. Pope Gregory the Great (c. 540–604) saw himself as ruling on the eschatological precipice, not least as a consequence of the social and economic chaos into which Italy had been plunged by the invasions of the Germanic Lombards. '[T]he barbarous and cruel nation of the Lombards', he wrote in his *Dialogues* (c. 590),

drawn as a sword out of a sheath, left their own country, and invaded ours: by reason whereof the people, which before for the huge multitude were like to thick corn-fields, remain now withered and overthrown: for cities be wasted, towns and villages spoiled, churches burnt, monasteries of men and women destroyed, farms left desolate, and the country remaineth solitary and void of men to till the ground, and destitute of all inhabitants: beasts possessing those places, where before great

---

[52] See McGinn, *Antichrist*, p. 77.

plenty of men did dwell. And how it goeth in other parts of the world I know not, but here in this place where we live, the world doth not foretell any end, but rather sheweth that which is present and already come.[53]

As he told the Kentish king Ethelbert in 601, wars, famines, plagues and earthquakes, tempests, changes in the air, and terror in the skies, all these indicated that, even though some of these things were yet to occur, the end of the world was close at hand.[54] That the end was close would also be signalled by the 'signs of power' being no longer present within the church: 'For prophecy is hidden, the grace of healings is taken away, the power of longer abstinence is weakened, the words of doctrine are silent, the prodigies of miracles are removed. And though the heavenly dispensation does not entirely withdraw them, yet it does not manifest them openly and in manifold ways as in former times.'[55]

Gregory was in no doubt that the future Antichrist would come. He took a leaf out of Hippolytus' book to the effect that the Antichrist would arise from the tribe of Dan. And, like Hippolytus, he invoked the description of Dan in Genesis 49.17 as a serpent lying on the ground.[56] If the Antichrist was not the Devil incarnate in

[53] Gregory the Great, *Dialogues*, 3.38, pp. 173–4. Available at www.tertullian.org/fathers/gregory_03_dialogues_book3.htm#C38
[54] See John R. C. Martyn (trans.), *The Letters of Gregory the Great*, 11.37 (Toronto: Pontifical Institute of Mediaeval Studies, 2004), vol. III, p. 784.
[55] James Bliss (trans.), *Morals on the Book of Job by St. Gregory the Great* (Oxford and London: John Henry Parker and J. Rivington, 1844), 34.3.7. Available at www.lectionarycentral.com/gregorymoraliaindex.html
[56] *Ibid.*, 31.24.43.

the strict sense, he was a man into whom the Devil had fully entered:

And he [the Devil] in his own person having in the last times entered into that vessel of perdition, shall be called 'Antichrist,' who will endeavour to spread his name far and wide, which same every individual now likens himself to, when, by the memorial of an earthly name, he strives to extend the gloriousness of his praise, and exults in transitory reputation.[57]

In Gregory's demonology, the afflictions caused by the Devil were his responsibility. Yet, paradoxically, they were also the consequence of God's overarching providence.[58] So too with the Antichrist. God allows, wrote Gregory, 'the ends of His Church to be agitated by the most cruel persecution through the coming of Antichrist, and yet forsakes her not, by permitting it'.[59] At the end of the world, the Antichrist would pass himself off as God, secretly assuming 'the brightness of the Deity'.[60] As the chief of all hypocrites, he would pretend to sanctity, the better to draw men into iniquity. But his reign would be brief: '[F]or a little time he is permitted to be exalted; that in proportion as he is let to glory for a while, he may be punished the more pitilessly for everlasting.'[61] That the Antichrist would be finally destroyed, Gregory was in no doubt. But he remained ambivalent as to whether the Antichrist would be killed by Christ or by Michael the archangel. It was an uncertainty that was to remain within the story of the Antichrist.

[57] Ibid., 14.21.25. See also 29.8.18.
[58] See Almond, The Devil, pp. 53–6.
[59] Bliss (trans.), Morals on the Book of Job by St. Gregory the Great, 29.6.10.
[60] Ibid., 4.9.14.   [61] Ibid., 12.43.48.

As for the Antichrist in the present, as in Tyconius, the body of the Antichrist was already active within the church, within the body of Christ. '[T]he author of iniquity', Gregory declared,

who has not yet come, is already visible in those who do his works. Hence John says; Now are there become many Antichrists [1 John 2, 18], because all wicked persons are even now his members, which being in truth born in wickedness, have prevented their head, by evil living. Hence Paul says, That he might be revealed in his time; for the mystery of iniquity doth already work [2 Thess. 2, 6. 7]. As if he were saying; Then Antichrist will be manifestly seen; for he now secretly works his hidden works in the hearts of the unrighteous.[62]

Thus, the hypocritical preachers of the Antichrist claim a show of sanctity, yet practise works of iniquity. The smell 'which they emit is pleasant, but the light they give is dark'.[63] And, like Augustine, Gregory recommended that each of us 'return to the hidden recess of his heart' to ensure that we were not among those in whom the Antichrist was already at work.[64] The Antichrist served not to emphasise the conflict between the church and the world so much as the battle between good and evil within the church.

For Gregory, the Antichrist was not merely a figure of the future, nor only of the present. He had been active in the members of his body since the time of the Fall:

O how many have beheld not the times of that temptation, and yet are involved in the storm of his temptation. Cain saw not the time of Antichrist, and yet was deservedly a limb of

---

[62] *Ibid.*, 29.7.15.   [63] *Ibid.*, 33.35.59.   [64] *Ibid.*, 29.7.14.

Antichrist. Judas knew not the fierceness of that persecution, and yet yielded to the might of his cruelty, by the persuasion of avarice. Simon was far removed from the times of Antichrist, and yet joined himself to his pride, by perversely seeking for the power of miracles [Acts 8.19–20]. Thus a wicked body is united to its head, thus limbs to limbs, when they both know not each other in acquaintance, and yet are joined together by wicked doings.[65]

Alongside the history of salvation, Gregory constructed a history of perdition.[66]

It is perhaps no surprise that Gregory saw Cain as a type of the Antichrist. He was, after all, the first murderer. It was easy, too, to identify the mark that God had put on Cain (Genesis 4.15) with the mark of the beast. Nor is it surprising that Judas, the betrayer of Jesus, should have been identified as an Antichrist. Gregory's 'Simon' who sought the power to do miracles was, of course Simon Magus. Thanks in large part to Gregory the Great, Simon Magus became, after Antiochus Epiphanes, the most important of the types of the Antichrist.

Simon, the Magical Antichrist

Already in the fourth century, in his *On the End of the World*, Pseudo-Hippolytus had pictured the Antichrist as a miracle worker on a par with Jesus. Little wonder that people were impressed by his powers and abilities. He would cleanse lepers, raise paralytics, expel demons, declare what was happening at a distance, raise the dead, and bring hosts of demons that would appear like angels.

[65] *Ibid.*, 29.7.15.   [66] See Hughes, *Constructing Antichrist*, p. 112.

He had powers and abilities way beyond those of mere mortals. You could be forgiven – actually when Christ came in judgement you wouldn't be – for believing this was Christ come again. And he could fly, too:

And in the presence of all he exhibits himself as taken up into heaven with trumpets and sounds, and the mighty shouting of those who hail him with indescribable hymns; the heir of darkness himself shining like light, and at one time soaring to the heavens, and at another descending to the earth with great glory, and again charging the demons, like angels, to execute his behests with much fear and trembling.[67]

The powers of the Antichrist in Pseudo-Hippolytus were, if not supernatural, at least those of a great magician. The capacity of the Antichrist to fly reminded Pseudo-Hippolytus of Simon Magus. He viewed Simon as a false Christ who was a type of those who would come in the Last Days proclaiming 'I am Christ.'

Simon Magus made his first appearance in the New Testament in *The Acts of the Apostles* 8.9–24, where, impressed by the wonders performed by Peter and John, he offered them money for their power. The apostles rejected his offer, urging him to pray for forgiveness. This was the starting point for the many narratives from the second and early third centuries onwards that created Simon Magus as a master of illusion, portrayed the battle between Peter and Simon as one between divine and demonic forces, and constructed Simon as the exemplary demonic magician. This is nowhere better exemplified

---

[67] Coxe (ed.), *The Extant Works and Fragments of Hippolytus, A Discourse … on the End of the World*, 29, in *ANF*, vol. V, p. 250.

than in the story of the death of Simon as told in the *Acts of the Apostles Peter and Paul* (fourth century). It was a story that, incorporated into the *Golden Legend* of Jacobus de Voragine in the middle of the thirteenth century, was transmitted in both art and literature for the following 300 years.[68]

According to the *Acts of the Apostles Peter and Paul*, Peter engaged in a magical contest with Simon Magus before the Emperor Nero in Rome. Nero had become persuaded that neither Peter nor Paul, nor Simon Magus, could be relied upon to tell the truth. Simon told Nero that, in order to demonstrate that Peter and Paul were liars, he would fly up to heaven on the following day. At Simon's request, Nero ordered a high tower to be built in the Campius Martius from which, Simon claimed, 'my angels may find me in the air; for they cannot come to me on earth among the sinners'.[69] Nero ordered Paul and Peter to be present, telling them that the truth would then be made clear.

On the following day, Simon, crowned with laurels, ascended the tower, spread his arms, and began to fly. When Nero saw Simon flying, he said to Peter, 'This Simon is true; but thou and Paul are deceivers.'[70] But Peter, looking steadfastly at the flying magician, said, 'I adjure you, ye angels of Satan, who are carrying him into the air, to deceive the hearts of the unbelievers, by

[68] On the history of the legends about Simon Magus, see Alberto Ferreiro, 'Simon Magus: The Patristic-Medieval Traditions and Historiography', *Apocrypha* 7 (1996), 147–65.
[69] M. B. Riddle (trans.), *Acts of the Apostles Peter and Paul*, in *ANF*, vol. VIII, p. 484.
[70] *Ibid.*

the God that created all things, and by Jesus Christ, whom on the third day He raised from the dead, no longer from this hour to keep him up, but to let him go.'[71] Immediately the demons let Simon go, and he fell to his death at a place called Sacra Via (see Plates 7 and 8). In spite of this, Nero ordered Peter and Paul to be arrested, Paul to be beheaded and Peter to be crucified – at the latter's request, upside down, 'for I am not worthy to be crucified like my Lord.'[72] Simon was the archetypal false prophet. From the time of Gregory the Great, the stories of Simon Magus and the Antichrist were intertwined.

On balance, Gregory summarises the Antichrist tradition as it was at the end of the sixth century, rather than adding much to it. But he did make one substantial innovation. This was to identify Leviathan and Behemoth as emblematic of the Antichrist (see Plate 9). In the book of Job, Leviathan and Behemoth were two primeval monsters, creatures of chaos and darkness, the one of the land, the other of the sea (Job 40.15–41.34). The wicked within the church, declared Gregory, were nought but the testicles of Behemoth:

For how many have not beheld Antichrist, and yet are his testicles: because they corrupt the hearts of the innocent by the example of their doings! For whoever is exalted with pride, whoever is tortured by the longings of covetousness, whoever is relaxed with the pleasures of lust, whoever is kindled by the burnings of unjust and immoderate anger, what else is he but a testicle of Antichrist? For while he willingly engages himself in his service, he furnishes by his example the progeny of error to others. The one works wickedly, the other cleaves to those

[71] *Ibid.*   [72] *Ibid.*

who work wickedly; and, so far from opposing, even favours them. What else then but a testicle of Antichrist is he, who, having cast aside the authority of the faith he has pledged to God, witnesses in favour of error?[73]

False teachers within the church were the teeth of Leviathan 'Because they mangle with their bite the life of the reprobate, and offer them, when withdrawn from the integrity of truth, in the sacrifice of falsehood.'[74] The flaming torches that come out of the mouth of Leviathan 'inflame the minds of their hearers to the love of misbelief, and from seeming to shine by wisdom, they doubtless thence burn with wickedness.'[75] In short, the church was the body of Christ, but the body of Antichrist existed within it. Gregory's concept of the Antichrist, in the tradition of both Tyconius and Augustine, made intelligible not only the threats to the church from without but the evils within.

The Last World Emperor

Adso's life of the Antichrist, we recall, contained a message of hope, at least for the queen to whom he had written. For Adso had told Queen Gerberga that the Antichrist would not come so long as the power of the Roman Empire survived. Since that power resided in the French monarchy embodied in Queen Gerberga's husband, Gerberga's anxieties, for the moment at least, could be eased. Her husband, the French king Louis IV d'Outremer, was not to be the last Roman emperor, and the Antichrist was not

[73] Bliss (trans.), *Morals on the Book of Job*, 32.16.28.
[74] *Ibid.*, 33.27.47.   [75] *Ibid.*, 33.34.58.

at hand. The Roman Empire remained a bulwark against the arrival of the Antichrist.

Queen Gerberga's anxieties might also have been lessened had she known that the Last World Emperor was imagined as a messianic hero. The Last Emperor, it was believed, would defeat the enemies of Rome, who, in a Christian empire, were God's enemies. He would create a millennial kingdom of peace and plenty, and convert the Jews. Adso had told the queen that the 'greatest and last of all kings', after having successfully governed his empire, would finally come to Jerusalem, and would lay aside his sceptre and crown on the Mount of Olives. 'This will be the end and the consummation', he went on to say, 'of the Roman and Christian Empire.'[76] As Richard Emmerson puts it, 'The legend of the Last World Emperor represents a merging of radical expectations of a millennial kingdom on earth with conservative eschatology that interprets the millennium as the age of the church brought to an end by Antichrist's certain reign.'[77]

The story of the Last Emperor was first played out in full in a text written in Syriac dating from the late seventh century known as the *Apocalypse* (or *Revelationes*) *of Pseudo-Methodius*. By the 720s, it had been translated into Greek and then into Latin. According to Paul Alexander, 'In the development of the Byzantine apocalyptic tradition, the translation of the Syriac text of Pseudo-Methodius into Greek marked the end of the era of Antiquity, and the beginning of that of the Middle Ages.'[78] It was written

[76] McGinn (trans.), 'Adso of Montier-en-Der', p. 93.
[77] Emmerson, *Antichrist in the Middle Ages*, p. 59.
[78] Paul J. Alexander (ed. Dorothy deF. Abrahamse), *The Byzantine Apocalyptic Tradition* (Berkeley: University of California Press, 1985), p. 14.

at a time when the new enemy of the Roman Empire had become the 'Ishmaelites', the author's term for the followers of the new Arabian religion of Islam.[79] By the time of the *Apocalypse of Pseudo-Methodius*, subsequent to the unification of Arabia by the prophet Muhammad (570–632), Muslim forces had conquered Syria, Palestine, and the Lebanon, along with Egypt, Mesopotamia, and Persia.

The *Apocalypse of Pseudo-Methodius* had two key features. The first of these was that the Roman Empire would play a decisive and positive role in the Christian account of the end of the world. The second was that the major player in the final act of the Roman Empire would be the Roman emperor. As a result of this apocalypse, the Last Emperor was to play a significant role in medieval and early modern theories of kingship. As Christopher Bonura writes,

The Last Emperor legend elevated monarchy to a sacral position integrally tied to the events of the End Times, and the Last Emperor became a model of the ideal Christian King. At the same time, since the Last Emperor would be monarch of the God-appointed universal Roman Empire, the legend became particularly important as numerous rulers vied for the status of legitimate inheritor of the title of Roman Emperor.[80]

---

[79] The question of the origin of the 'Last World Emperor' remains truly Byzantine (metaphorically and literally). See Christopher Bonura, 'When Did the Legend of the Last World Emperor Originate? A New Look at the Textual Relationship between *The Apocalypse of Pseudo-Methodius* and the *Tiburtine Sybyl*', *Viator* 47 (2016), 47–100. I have followed Bonura in giving the priority to the *Apocalypse of Pseudo-Methodius* over the *Tiburtine Sybyl*. I am indebted to Bonura and to Alexander, *The Byzantine Apocalyptic Tradition*, for this discussion.

[80] *Ibid.*, 49.

Until the time of the *Apocalypse of Pseudo-Methodius*, the role of the Roman Empire within Christian eschatology had been an ambivalent one. On the one hand, those Roman emperors such as Nero and Domitian who had persecuted Christians in the first century were imagined as types of the Antichrist. On the other hand, as we noted in Chapter 2 above, around the turn of the third century Tertullian was the first to identify 'the one who now restrains' (2 Thessalonians 2.7) with the Roman Empire. So he recommended that Christians should pray both for the emperors and for the stability of the empire in order to forestall the horrors of the end times. We know, Tertullian wrote, 'that a mighty shock impending over the whole earth – in fact, the very end of all things threatening dreadful woes – is only retarded by the continued existence of the Roman empire'.[81]

A role for the Roman Empire greater than a merely 'restraining' one became more feasible when the emperors Constantine and Licinius met in Milan in 313 and guaranteed religious toleration to Christians. The 'Father of Church History', Eusebius (c. 260–c. 340), saw it as the moment when Christ himself became present within the government of the empire.[82] That the empire was virtuous (Constantinian) rather than vicious (Neronic) was reinforced in 380 when Emperor Theodosius I made Christianity the empire's sole authorised religion. Even so, for the next 300 years the Roman emperor remained marginal *vis-à-vis* Christianity. It was only late in the

[81] Coxe (ed.), *Apology*, 32, in *ANF*, vol. III, pp. 42–3.
[82] See Ernest Cushing Richardson (trans.), *The Life of Constantine by Eusebius*, 1.1, in *NPNF, second series*, vol. I, p. 481.

seventh century, in the *Apocalypse of Pseudo-Methodius*, that the Roman Empire became fully and positively integrated into Christian eschatology. That it did so was the consequence of the significant role that the *Apocalypse of Pseudo-Methodius* gave the Roman emperor to play in the divine plan for the Last Days.

The eschatology of the *Apocalypse of Pseudo-Methodius* falls into two parts that span 6,000 years. An historical part begins with the departure of Adam and Eve from Paradise and climaxes in the rise of the Roman/ Byzantine Empire. It was this empire that held back the 'Son of Perdition' until it handed itself over to God:

> As long as this kingdom which possesses an abiding place of refuge is the center, the Son of Perdition will not be revealed, for that something which is in the center is the priesthood and the kingship and the Holy Cross. And this kingship of the Christians overpowers all kingdoms of the earth, and by it all leaders and all authorities will be paralyzed and come to nought and all its people will be left destitute, and by it they will be conquered and through it they will come to nought. And in the whole earth there will not be left one leader nor one authority when the Son of Perdition will be revealed, except the Kingdom of the Greeks which will hand over to the hand of God.[83]

A prophetical part then begins with the conflict between the Roman Empire and the Muslims that would last for ten year-weeks (seventy years) and would end with the destruction of the 'Son of Perdition'. It was in the seventh and last 'millennium' that the Muslims, 'the sons

[83] 'The Syriac *Apocalypse of Pseudo-Methodius*', 126 verso, in Alexander, *The Byzantine Apocalyptic Tradition*, p. 43.

of Ismael', would depart from the desert of Jeshrib and
assemble at Gaba'ot the Great. There the Greeks, 'the
fattened animals of the kingdom of the Greeks', would
suffer a great defeat – 'exterminated in Gaba'ot by Ismael,
the wild ass of the desert, who was sent in wrath of ire
against men and against animals and against cattle and
against trees and against plants. And it is a punishment in
which there is no love.'[84] This was not the consequence of
God's love for Muslims but the result of Christian wickedness, especially sexual libertinism – transvesticism,
homosexuality, lesbianism, and general 'a-whoring'.

The sons of Ismael would inflict great punishments
on the conquered in fulfilment of Paul's prediction in
2 Thessalonians 2.3: 'unless this chastisement comes
beforehand, and thereupon will be revealed the Man
of Sin, the Son of Perdition'. Pseudo-Methodius would
never himself be accused of holding back. 'These cruel
barbarians', he wrote,

are not human beings but are sons of desolation and upon desolation their faces are set upon the sword. They are despoilers
and for destruction they will be sent. And perdition they are
and for the perdition of everything they set out. And polluted
they are and in pollution they live … And they will be cruel
and murderers and bloodthirsty and destroyers and a testing
furnace for all Christians.[85]

Only a small remnant would remain faithful. The con-
querors would brag that there would be no deliverer for
the Christians.

They hadn't reckoned on the Last Emperor. For 'a
king of the Greeks will go forth against them in great

---

[84] *Ibid.*, 128 recto, p. 44.   [85] *Ibid.*, 130 verso, p. 46.

wrath' and defeat them in the desert of Jethrib.[86] Their servitude would be a hundred times more bitter than that of their former slaves, the Christians. Peace would then reign upon the earth, 'the like of which had never existed, because it is the last peace of the perfection of the world'.[87]

In his account of the Last Emperor, Pseudo-Methodius was drawing on three sources. The first of these was Pseudo-Ephraem's Syriac *Sermon on the End* (640/2 – 680/3). In this text, after the armies of Gog and Magog have been defeated by Michael the archangel (more of which anon), the Roman Empire would be restored, and peace would reign upon earth until the arrival of the Antichrist: 'And once more the empire of the Romans / Will spring up and flourish in its place. / It will possess the earth and its extremities, / And no one will exist who opposes it.'[88]

The second source upon which Pseudo-Methodius drew was the legend of Alexander the Great (356–323 BCE), particularly on the Syriac Christian *Alexander Legend* (late 620s CE). In this work, Alexander was portrayed as the founder of the Roman Empire. Alexander predicted that the end times would begin some 940 years from the time when he had imprisoned the 'Huns' in the north, that is, sometime in the first decades of the seventh century CE. Then the Huns, the Persians, and the Arabs would break free from their confines

---

[86] *Ibid.*, 133 recto, p. 48.   [87] *Ibid.*, 134 recto, p. 49.
[88] John Reeves (trans.), 'Sermon of Pseudo-Ephraem on the End of the World' (unpublished manuscript), p. 14. I am very grateful to John Reeves for allowing me to use this translation.

before being defeated by 'the might of the kingdom of the Greeks which is that of the Romans'.[89] The Romans would then subdue all the other kingdoms. The Roman Empire, we read, would then 'stand and rule to the end of time, and should deliver the earth to the Messiah who is to come'.[90]

The third influence upon Pseudo-Methodius was the depiction of the ideal Christian emperor in the so-called Syriac Julian Romance (sixth century). In the face of the persecutions inflicted upon the church by the Roman emperor known as Julian the Apostate (332–63), the Julian Romance anticipated an emperor, exemplified by Julian's successor, Jovian (332–64), who would 'come triumphantly to bring justice to a church persecuted by an anti-Christian emperor'.[91] Pseudo-Methodius envisioned the tyranny of the followers of Muhammad as parallel to that of Julian the Apostate. And just as the Julian Romance provided a justification for violence against the church to be met with violence by the church, so too did the *Apocalypse of Pseudo-Methodius* view violence as a legitimate response by Christians to those who threatened Christianity.

Under the influence of these sources, Pseudo-Methodius was able not only to predict that the Roman Empire would conquer the world before handing over its power to God, but also to create the individual through

[89] Ernest A. Wallis Budge (trans.), *A Christian Legend concerning Alexander*, in his *The History of Alexander the Great, Being the Syriac Version of the Pseudo-Callisthenes* (Cambridge University Press, 1889), p. 155.

[90] *Ibid.*, p. 158.

[91] Daniel L. Schwartz, 'Religious Violence and Eschatology in the Syriac Julian Romance', *Journal of Early Christian Studies* 19 (2011), 586.

whom this would all take place – the Last World Emperor, the king of the Greeks.[92]

Gog and Magog

The book of Revelation had predicted that, when the thousand years of Satan's imprisonment were completed, he would come out to deceive the nations at the four corners of the earth, Gog and Magog, in order to gather them for battle. They would then surround the camp of the saints and the holy city before 'fire came down from heaven and consumed them' (Revelation 20.9). The Devil would then be thrown into the 'lake of fire and sulphur' (Revelation 20.10) to be tormented for eternity. The author of Revelation had drawn his nations of Gog and Magog from the Old Testament book of Ezekiel (sixth century BCE), where, rather than Gog and Magog being nations or rulers, Gog was a prince of the land of Magog (Ezekiel 38.2). In the account in Ezekiel, Gog of Magog and his armies threatened Israel but were destroyed by God, after which a period of lasting peace ensued. By the middle of the second century BCE, 'Gog of the land of Magog' had transitioned to 'the land of Gog and Magog'.[93]

Among the early church fathers, 'Gog and Magog' were generally given an allegorical interpretation. Thus, for example, Augustine in his *City of God* rejected the notion that Gog and Magog were 'to be understood

---

[92] See Bonura, 'When Did the Legend of the Last World Emperor Originate?', 57.

[93] Collins (trans.), *Sibylline Oracles* 3.63–74, in Charlesworth (ed.), *The Old Testament Pseudepigrapha, Vol. I*, p. 369.

of some barbarous nations in some part of the world.'[94] Rather, and here he was following Jerome, he suggested that 'Gog' referred to those people in whom the Devil was at present shut (as if roofed in) and 'Magog' to the Devil who comes out from them (as if from under a roof).

Alongside this long-lasting allegorical tradition, however, there was a more literal one that identified Gog and Magog with specific peoples. Thus, for example, in the Syriac Christian *Alexander Legend*, the Huns enclosed behind the gate that Alexander had built were identified as peoples whose kings, along with others, were Gog and Magog (see Plate 10).[95] But it was in Pseudo-Ephraem's Syriac *Sermon on the End of the World* that Gog and Magog first became part of Christian eschatology. For those who poured through Alexander's gate when it collapsed were, among many others, 'Gog and Magog and Nāwāl and Agag, / Kings and mighty armies!'[96]

The identification of the eschatological hordes that broke through Alexander's gate with Gog and Magog travelled thence into the *Apocalypse of Pseudo-Methodius*. The first mention of them occurred in the historical section that dealt with Alexander the Great. There we read that Alexander saw in the East filthy and ugly nations. These 'sons of Japheth' (who was one of Noah's sons – Genesis 10.1) 'ate the vermin of the earth, mice and dogs

---

[94] Dods (trans.), *St. Augustin's City of God*, 20.11, in *NPNF, first series*, vol. II, p. 432.
[95] Budge (trans.), *A Christian Legend concerning Alexander*, p. 150. See Andrew Runni Anderson, *Alexander's Gate, Gog and Magog, and the Inclosed Nations* (Cambridge, Massachusetts: Medieval Academy of America, 1932).
[96] John Reeves (trans.), 'Sermon of Pseudo-Ephraem', p. 10.

and kittens, and they did not enshroud and bury their dead, and the embryos which the women aborted they ate as if it were some delicacy'.[97] When Alexander saw what they did, he expelled them and imprisoned them behind a gate of brass in the North. Pseudo-Methodius then foretold that, 'at the end of the ages, as was the saying of the prophet Ezekiel [Ezekiel 38.14–16 pretty loosely interpreted] which was prophesied concerning them, saying: In the end of times, at the end of the world, the followers of Agog and of Magog will come upon the land of Israel',[98] along with the followers of another twenty nations.

Gog and Magog re-entered the story in the eschatological section of the *Apocalypse of Pseudo-Methodius* after the Last World Emperor had defeated the Muslims and had inaugurated the 'millennial' period of peace. Then the gates of the North would be opened, and the nations imprisoned there would flood forth. Men would be frightened and would flee, hiding in mountains, caves, and tombs. The invaders from the North would eat the flesh of men and the creeping things of the earth, along with mice, snakes, and reptiles, the bodies of unclean animals and the abortions of sheep, not to mention the unmentionable – dead dogs and kittens. They would slaughter children and force mothers to eat the bodies of their sons. After one 'week', the nations would assemble in the plain of Joppe. God would 'send against them one of the captains of the hosts of the angels, and he destroys them in an hour'.[99]

---

[97] 'The Syriac Apocalypse of Pseudo-Methodius', 124 recto, in Alexander, *The Byzantine Apocalyptic Tradition*, p. 40.
[98] *Ibid.*, 124 verso, p. 41.   [99] *Ibid.*, 135 recto, p. 50.

Then the Last World Emperor would settle in Jerusalem for 'one week and a half-week, in numbers ten years and a half'.[100] At the end of that period, he would go to Golgotha, the *axis mundi*, the closest point between heaven and earth. There the Holy Cross would be set up in the place where Christ was crucified. The Last Roman Emperor would then place his diadem on top of the cross. He would stretch out his two hands to heaven and hand over the kingship to God the Father. Then the Son of Perdition would be revealed.[101]

Like Gregory the Great, Pseudo-Methodius followed the tradition begun by Hippolytus that the Antichrist would arise from the tribe of Dan. And, like Hippolytus, he looked to Genesis 49.17. He too invoked the description of Dan in Genesis as a snake that lies on the path that leads to the kingdom of heaven. The Antichrist's mother would be a married woman from the same tribe. For Jerome, we recall, the Antichrist was a Jew, albeit one from Babylon. But Pseudo-Methodius had a fresh take on the birthplace of the Antichrist. He expected the Antichrist to be born in Chorazin, to be raised in Beth-saida, and to rule in Capernaum. For a biblical text in support, he looked to Jesus' pronouncement of 'Woes' over the cities of Chorazin, Beth-saida, and Capernaum: 'Woe to thee Chorazin, and woe to thee Beth-saida, and thou, Capernaum, that hast

---

[100] *Ibid.*, 135 recto, p. 50.
[101] The *Apocalypse of Pseudo-Methodius* also has the Antichrist revealed during, rather than at the end of, the reign of the Last World Emperor. This may be the result of the weaving of two traditions. See Alexander, *The Byzantine Apocalyptic Tradition*, pp. 198–9.

exalted thyself unto heaven, thou wilt descend to Hell'
(Matthew 11.20–24).[102]

As we recall, Adso was to bring both of these traditions together. His Antichrist would be born in Babylon
but brought up and protected in the cities of Chorazin
and Beth-saida.[103] It was a confusion that was still present
in the late fourteenth century within popular literature.
Thus, for example, in *The Travels of Sir John Mandeville*
we read:

In Chorazin shall Antichrist be born, as some men say. And
other men say he shall be born in Babylon; for the prophet
saith: *De Babilonia coluber exest, qui totum mundum devorabit*;
that is to say 'Out of Babylon shall come a worm that shall
devour all the world.' This Antichrist shall be nourished in
Bethsaida, and he shall reign in Capernaum: and therefore
saith holy writ; *Vae tibi, Chorazin! Vae tibi, Bethsaida! Vae tibi,
Capernaum!* that is to say, 'Woe be to thee, Chorazin! Woe to
thee, Bethsaida! Woe to thee, Capernaum.'[104]

Pseudo-Methodius' Antichrist was, above all, a miracle worker. He cleansed the lepers, made the blind to see,
the paralytics to walk, exorcised the possessed, darkened
the sun, and changed the moon to blood. The saints, duly
impressed, would be led astray 'because he was made a
habitation of all the demons and all their activity will be

[102] 'The Syriac *Apocalypse of Pseudo-Methodius*', 135 recto, in Alexander,
The Byzantine Apocalyptic Tradition, p. 50. Shortly before this, Pseudo-
Methodius also has the Antichrist conceived in Chorazin and born in
Saidan.
[103] McGinn (trans.), 'Adso of Montier-en-Der', p. 91.
[104] John Mandeville, *The Travels of Sir John Mandeville* (London:
Macmillan, 1900), ch. 13, p. 74.

completed in him'.[105] He would enter Jerusalem and sit in the temple of God 'and will pretend to be like God, for he is a man of sin clothed in a body from the seed of man'.[106] At the coming of Christ from heaven, he would be delivered to the fires of hell and outer darkness. There he would weep and gnash his teeth along with all those who had believed in him.

The destruction of the barbarous nations before the arrival of the Antichrist was also popularised by its inclusion in the *Tiburtine Oracle*, one of the Sibylline Oracles, from the early eleventh century. The Latin versions of this text gave an account of the Last World Emperor and the fate of Gog and Magog (although they were not specifically named). There we find a king of the Romans and the Greeks by the name of Constans. He was 'tall of stature, of handsome appearance with shining face, and well put together in all parts of his body'.[107] This would be a time of plenty. Fruit, oil, bread, and wine would be cheap. Constans would be the ideal Christian emperor. He would devastate the pagan lands and destroy idolatrous temples. He would call all the pagans to baptism and set up crosses in their former temples. Whoever did not convert would be punished by the sword. He would live for the maximum possible time, 120 years. Then the Jews too would convert to Christianity.

---

[105] 'The Syriac *Apocalypse of Pseudo-Methodius*', 136 recto, in Alexander, *The Byzantine Apocalyptic Tradition*, p. 51.

[106] *Ibid.*

[107] Bernard Mc Ginn (trans.), 'The Latin Tiburtine Sibyl', in Bernard McGinn (ed.), *Visions of the End: Apocalyptic Traditions in the Middle Ages* (New York: Columbia University Press, 1998), p. 49.

Towards the end of his reign, the twenty-two nations that Alexander had imprisoned in the North would arise. The Last World Emperor would then call his army together and utterly destroy them. He would then travel to Jerusalem, remove the crown from his head, and put aside his imperial robes. Then he would 'hand over the empire of the Christians to God the Father and to Jesus Christ his Son'.[108]

As in the *Apocalypse of Pseudo-Methodius*, so also in the *Tiburtine Oracle* the Antichrist, the Prince of Iniquity and the Son of Perdition, would then be revealed. He would come from the tribe of Dan, sit in the temple in Jerusalem, and do great wonders and signs through magic. The Syriac version of the *Apocalypse of Pseudo-Methodius* did not include Elijah and Enoch in its eschatology, although they were included in its Greek and Latin versions. So too, in the *Tiburtine Oracle*, during the reign of the Antichrist Elijah and Enoch would return to announce the coming of Christ. They would be killed by the Antichrist but resurrected by the Lord after three days. Then there would be a great persecution of the Christians 'such as has not been before nor shall be thereafter'.[109] For the sake of the elect, those days would be shortened. The Antichrist would be slain, not by Christ as in the *Apocalypse of Pseudo-Methodius* and as in the Greek version of the *Tiburtine Oracle*, but 'by the power of God through Michael the Archangel on the Mount of Olives' (see Plate 11).[110]

The inclusion of Gog and Magog in the story of the Last World Emperor was driven by the Alexander Legend, specifically by his imprisonment of the barbarous

[108] *Ibid.*, p. 50.   [109] *Ibid.*   [110] *Ibid.*

nations behind the gate, their eventual incursion beyond it in the Last Days, and their identification with Gog and Magog. But there was another reading of 'Gog and Magog' that was to become part of Christian eschatology and that predated their identification with Alexander's barbarians, and gave them a more specific role in the story of the Antichrist. We find it as early as 397 in a work by the African bishop Quintus Julius Hilarianus entitled *The Progress of Time*. Following the chronology of Hippolytus, Hilarianus calculated that the end of history could be expected in the year 500, 6,000 years to the same day and month in which the world was both created and redeemed, namely, 24 March.

At the end of the sixth millennium since the creation, wrote Hilarianus, the Antichrist would arise. They would be deadly times, like those 'when Antiochus tried to make one people commit apostasy under his reign'.[111] He would do what Antiochus did not have time to, namely destroy the faithful. He would eventually be slain by Christ. For the next thousand years, the resurrected saints would live on the earth until Satan was released from his prison. He would seduce the nations of Gog and Magog and bring them together ready to do battle at the Camp of the Saints. Rather than the defeat of the forces of Gog and Magog preceding the arrival of the Antichrist, they have now become his armies. Then 'Fire will descend from heaven and all men will be consumed.'[112] Then would follow a further resurrection, when all would be judged by God.

[111] Bernard McGinn (trans.), 'Quintus Julius Hilarianus, *The Progress of Time*', in McGinn (ed.), *Visions of the End*, p. 53.
[112] *Ibid.*

In the Meantime!

Adso of Montier-en-Der, we recall, had comforted Queen Gerberga by informing her that the Antichrist would not come until the Roman Empire, represented by her husband, had fallen. And that, he had assured her, was not going to happen any time soon. In support, he quoted Paul's second letter to the Thessalonians. 'This is why', he wrote, 'the Apostle Paul says that the Antichrist will not come into the world "Unless the defection shall have come first" [2 Thessalonians 2.3], that is, unless first all the kingdoms that were formerly subject shall have defected from the Roman Empire.'[113] In reading Paul in this way, Adso was relying directly upon a commentary on the second letter to the Thessalonians written a century earlier by Haimo, a monk of St Germain at Auxerre (fl. c. 840–70). In this commentary, more generally, Haimo had interpreted Paul as teaching literally how the end of the world would come.

Although Adso had read Haimo, the latter differed significantly in his understanding of the second letter to the Thessalonians. Whereas Adso believed that Rome was yet to fall, Haimo believed that it had already done so, not least because his was a period during which the unity of the Carolingian Empire (800–88) begun by the Frankish king Charlemagne was at a particularly low point, only to be reunited briefly by (the wonderfully named) Charles the Fat before collapsing again. Thus, Haimo summarised his interpretation of 2 Thessalonians 2.4 in the following way: 'With these words, the Apostle

---

[113] McGinn (trans.), 'Adso of Montier-en-Der', p. 93.

demonstrates to the Thessalonians that the Lord will not come in judgment before the collapse of Roman rule, *which we already see completed*, and the appearance in the world of Antichrist, who will kill the witnesses of Christ.'[114] In the main, Haimo was following Jerome, and particularly his *Letter 121*, but the notion that Rome had already fallen was against the tradition up until that time and genuinely innovative.

So, if Haimo placed his own time between that of the end of the Roman Empire and the arrival of the Antichrist, when, then, would the Antichrist arrive? On this, Haimo remained vague, putting it down to divine providence: 'at a time set by God', he declared.[115] Nevertheless, Haimo could already discern the 'mystery of iniquity' (2 Thessalonians 2.7) working in history. It began, he believed, with Nero:

This is called a 'mystery' because what the devil works openly through Antichrist when he kills the holy martyrs Elijah and Enoch and all the rest, this he already does secretly through his own members, Nero and his princes, killing through those princes the apostolic martyrs. Thus the mystery of iniquity was begun by Nero, who, with his father the devil secretly urging him on, killed the holy martyrs in his zeal for idols. It continued up to Diocletian and Julian the Apostate, who slew many saints. So just as Christ, who is the head of all the elect, was prefigured secretly and in mystery long before his

---

[114] Kevin L. Hughes (ed. and trans.), *Haimo of Auxerre: Exposition of the Second Letter to the Thessalonians*, 2.4, in Steven R. Cartwright and Kevin L. Hughes, *Second Thessalonians: Two Early Medieval Apocalyptic Commentaries* (Kalamazoo, Michigan: Medieval Institute Publications, 2001), p. 26 (my italics). On Haimo, see especially Hughes, *Constructing Antichrist*, pp. 144–67.

[115] Hughes (ed. and trans.), *Haimo of Auxerre*, 2.8, p. 28.

coming in the death of Abel, in the sacrifice of Isaac, and in King David, who slew Goliath ... so too the devil who will be in Antichrist is prefigured secretly and in mystery in his members – obviously, in evil kings.[116]

As for the Antichrist himself, Haimo's teaching was pretty traditional. He was called 'the man of sin', declared Haimo, because he was 'the source of all sins', 'the son of damnation' [perdition] because he was 'the son of the devil, not by nature, but through imitation'.[117] Thus, the Antichrist would be morally responsible for all of his misdeeds. Although the devil would possess him completely, 'he will not give up his senses, so that he might say foolishly that he does not know God, nor will he be seized by the devil like madmen. For if he were, he would have no sin in whatever he does, just as those who suffer madness do not, for they do not know what they do.'[118] In short, for Haimo, he was fully human, and fully responsible, and Haimo was the first unequivocally to say so.[119]

As the Antichrist, he would exalt himself over the pagan gods, 'Hercules, for example, and Apollo and Jove, who falsely are called "gods"'.[120] He would also lord himself over Christians. But worse, for Haimo, he would set himself up over everything that is worshipped, that is, the Holy Trinity, 'which alone should be worshiped [sic] and adored by all creatures'.[121] As to his taking 'his seat in the temple of God, declaring himself to be God' (2 Thessalonians 2.4), Haimo understood this in two

---

[116] *Ibid.*, 2.7, p. 27.   [117] *Ibid.*, 2.3, p. 25.   [118] *Ibid.*, 2.9, p. 29.
[119] See Hughes, *Constructing Antichrist*, p. 161.
[120] Hughes (ed. and trans.), *Haimo of Auxerre*, 2.4, p. 25.
[121] *Ibid.*

ways. On the one hand, the Antichrist would be born in Babylon from the tribe of Dan, come to Jerusalem and circumcise himself, declare to the Jews that he was their Messiah, be recognised as such by the Jews, rebuild the temple destroyed by the Romans, and declare himself Christ. Or, on the other hand, he would take a place in the church as if he were a god. Haimo had no preference for the Antichrist as the eschatological tyrant outside the church or the Great Deceiver within it.

Haimo also took a leaf out of Jerome's letter in his contrasting of Christ and the Antichrist: 'just as every fullness of divinity reposed in Christ, so the fullness of vice and every iniquity will dwell in that person called Antichrist, because he is the opposite of Christ'.[122] That said, the Antichrist did not have the same supernatural powers as Christ. The second letter to the Thessalonians 2.9 had declared that the lawless one's actions would be 'signs and lying prodigies' [wonders]. But the signs and wonders that the Antichrist would do were only *apparently* miraculous. He was actually only a great magician, like Simon Magus, who would 'delude men through magical art and delusion'.[123] Haimo was undoubtedly familiar with the story of Simon laid out in the *Acts of the Holy Apostles Peter and Paul*. The Antichrist, he declared, 'deceived the one who, thinking he was killing Simon, beheaded a ram in his place'.[124] Nevertheless, the magical tricks of the Antichrist would be sufficient to persuade the Jews and pagans. Because they had already rejected

---

[122] *Ibid.*, 2.4, p. 26.   [123] *Ibid.*, 2.8, p. 29.

[124] *Ibid.*, 2.8, p. 29. For the relevant passage, see Riddle (trans.), *Acts of the Apostles Peter and Paul*, in *ANF*, vol. VIII, p. 482.

Christ, God permitted the Antichrist to lead them astray and to be ultimately damned for both.

Eventually, as we have now learnt to expect, the Antichrist would be destroyed. Like Gregory the Great, Haimo was uncertain whether he would be killed by the Lord Jesus or the archangel Michael. In either case, it would be 'by the power of the Lord Jesus'.[125] And, following Jerome, he had the Antichrist meeting his death on the Mount of Olives. The death of the Antichrist, however, in spite of its being brought about by Christ, was not in itself the coming of Christ in judgement. Haimo, too, adopted the tradition that there would be a gap between the death of the Antichrist and the Day of Judgement. 'It should be noted', he wrote, 'that the Lord will not come immediately to judge when Antichrist has been killed, but, as we learn from the Book of Daniel, after his death the elect will be given forty-five days for penance.'[126] Even so, Haimo's timetable remained pretty rubbery, for 'it is completely unknown', he immediately added, 'how long the span of time may be before the Lord comes'.[127]

Haimo may have been uncertain when the Day of Judgement would be. Adso was putting it off into the (almost) never-never. Adso's contemporary, Thietland of Einsiedeln (fl. 943–65), expected it, if not immediately, at least eighty years or so in the future. Thietland's views on the Antichrist occurred within his commentary on the second letter to the Thessalonians and included asides on the meaning of the book of Revelation. Nothing original

---

[125] Hughes (ed. and trans.), *Haimo of Auxerre*, 2.8, p. 28.
[126] *Ibid.*, 2.9, p. 29.   [127] *Ibid.*

about the Antichrist here – rather a mix of Haimo and Augustine.

But, most crucially, he did toughen up Augustine's 'soft' symbolic eschatology into a 'hard' literal one. He was motivated to do so by the fact that at least some of his contemporaries expected the end of the world at any moment. So it is not perhaps surprising that, using the authority of Augustine, if not his intention, Thietland pushed the literal coming of the Antichrist and the return of Christ into the not too distant future. In short, Thietland expected the rise of the Antichrist and the release of Satan in 1033, a thousand years after the death of Christ. Thus, speaking of the author of the book of Revelation, he declared, 'He calls this the last part of the world, and claims it is from the suffering of our Lord and our redemption to the coming of the Antichrist. He therefore fixed the number of a thousand years for the completion of this entire time.'[128]

Well, as we know, Thietland got it wrong, as did all of his contemporaries who expected the coming of the Antichrist, the return of Christ, and the final judgement one thousand or so years after Christ. Adso had won this particular eschatological round. And Augustine's reluctance to take Christian eschatological chronology too literally was vindicated, at least until the next recalculation.

---

[128] Steven R. Cartwright (ed. and trans.), *Thietland of Einsiedeln on 2 Thessalonians*, 2.8a, in Cartwright and Hughes, *Second Thessalonians*, p. 56.

4

Antichrists, Present and Future

~

They are seven kings, of whom five have fallen, one is living, and
the other has not yet come; and when he comes, he must remain
only a little while.

Revelation 17.9–10

Muhammad the Antichrist

In the winter of the year 1190, we read in *The Annals*
of Roger de Hoveden (fl. 1174–1201), King Richard the
Lionheart of England was *en route* to the Holy Land to
do battle against the Muslims, then under the leadership of Saladin. While in Italy, he heard of a religious
man in Calabria (Fiore), by the name of Joachim, a monk
of the Cistercian order. It was said that Joachim had a
spirit of prophecy and foretold things to come. He was
a man learned in the Holy Scriptures who 'interpreted
the visions of Saint John the Evangelist, which Saint John
had revealed in the Book of Revelation'.[1]

In conversation with King Richard, Joachim gave him
an interpretation of the seven kings of Revelation 17.9–10:

Of these, five have perished; namely Herod, Nero, Constantius,
Mahomet, and Melsermut; one is, namely Saladin, who is now
oppressing the Church of God; and, together with it, the

---

[1] Henry T. Riley (ed.), *The Annals of Roger de Hoveden: Comprising the
History of England, and of other Countries of Europe from A.D. 732 to
A.D. 1201* (London: H. G. Bohn, 1853), vol. II, p. 177.

Sepulchre of our Lord, and the Holy City of Jerusalem and the land on which stood the feet of our Lord are kept in his possession. But he shall shortly lose the same.[2]

Richard then went on to ask Joachim when this would happen. Seven years after the capture of Jerusalem, declared Joachim. Joachim comforted Richard's worry that he had come too soon with the words, 'Your arrival is very necessary, inasmuch as the Lord will give you victory over His enemies, and will exalt your name beyond all the princes of the earth.'[3] The seventh king who had not yet come was, according to Joachim, the Antichrist, of whom more anon. The fourth was Mahomet or Muhammad, the founder of Islam.

In the West, the view that Muhammad was among the types of the Antichrist was not original to Joachim. It began in Muslim Spain in the middle of the ninth century, when a few Christians began to react against the moderation with which their fellow Christians treated Islam and the ease with which they had adopted Islamic culture.[4] They were to become known as the Córdoban maryrs.

The Córdoban martyrs' movement began when these 'resistance' Christians deliberately set out to provoke their Muslim fellow-citizens. A Christian priest by the name of Perfectus described Muhammad as one of the false Christs and prophets predicted in the gospel of

---

[2] *Ibid.*, vol. II, p. 178.   [3] *Ibid.*

[4] See Edward P. Talbert (trans.), *Paul Alvarus, Description of Christian Youth*, in Olivia Remie Constable (ed.), *Medieval Iberia: Readings from Christian, Muslim, and Jewish Sources* (Philadelphia: University of Pennsylvania Press, 2012), pp. 61–2.

Matthew (24.24). Little surprise that his Muslim listeners were outraged at this description of their prophet: 'seduced by demonic delusions, devoted to sacrilegious sorcery, he corrupted with his deadly poison the hearts of many idiots … Lacking any spiritual wisdom, he made them subjects of Prince Satan, with whom he will suffer the most abominable punishments in hell.'[5]

The earliest Latin 'lives of Muhammad' in Muslim Spain, adapting Byzantine models, arose in this context. While these 'lives of Muhammad' incorporated authentic biographical details, they nonetheless constructed Muhammad as a parody of Christ. Thus, in a ninth-century letter that John of Seville sent to Paul Alvarus (c. 800–61), we read,

Mammet [Muhammad], the heretic of the Arabs, the seal of pseudoprophets, the precursor of the Antichrist, was born in the time of the Emperor Heraclius, in the seventh year [of his reign], the six hundred and fifty-sixth [year] of the current era [618 AD] … The followers of that aforesaid wicked prophet were told that he glittered with so many miracles that, snatching away the wife of another man because of the burning of his lust, he actually coupled with her carnally … When death came upon him, he promised that he would be resurrected on the third day, but through the negligence of those who were watching over him, he was found and devoured by dogs. He reigned as prince for ten years, and at the end of them was buried in hell.[6]

---

[5] Quoted in John V. Tolan, *Saracens: Islam in the Medieval European Imagination* (New York: Columbia University Press, 2002), p. 87.

[6] Janna Wasilewski, 'The "Life of Muhammad" in Eulogius of Córdoba: Some Evidence for the Transmission of Greek Polemic to the Latin West', *Early Medieval Europe* 16 (2008), 335, n. 8.

A more expansive life of the prophet Muhammad was included in the *Liber apologeticus martyrum* (*Apologetic Book of Martyrs*), a work written by Eulogius of Córdoba to eulogise those Christians who, like Perfectus (and eventually Eulogius himself), were martyred between the years 851 and 859. Their crime was to have publicly criticised the prophet and described him as a 'precursor of Antichrist' (*praevium Antichristi*). Eulogius had happened upon this life of Muhammad during a visit to a monastery of Leyre, just south-east of Pamplona. He saw it as his chance to drive a wedge between Christians and Islam.

Eulogius' Muhammad was a demonically inspired false prophet – a 'pestilential and demoniacal little man, who, seized by an unclean spirit, exercising the mystery of his iniquity as a true precursor of Antichrist, instituted as it pleased him a law of I know not what novelty, at the inspiration of demons for the destruction of multitudes'.[7] He was 'an avaricious usurer' and 'a shrewd son of darkness' who presented himself as a prophet and ordered his followers to kill their adversaries with the sword. He stole the wife of a neighbour and 'subjected her to his lust'. He composed certain sayings about the hoopoe bird and the frog 'so that the stench of one might belch forth from his mouth and the babbling of the other might never cease from his lips'. He predicted that he would be revived on the third day after his death by the angel Gabriel, who would appear to him in the form of a vulture. His body,

---

[7] Kenneth B. Wolf, *Eulogius of Córdoba and His Understanding of Islam*, p. 5. Available at www.academia.edu/20312136/Eulogius_of_C%C3%B3rdoba_and_His_Understanding_of_Islam

left unguarded, was eaten by dogs. It was appropriate, the
story concluded, 'that a prophet of this kind fill the stomach of dogs, a prophet who committed not only his own
soul, but those of many others to hell'.[8] This was a lustful
and violent Antichrist.

Eulogius' apocalyptic view of Muhammad found
sympathetic support in *Indiculos luminosus*, the work
of his friend and biographer Paul Alvarus. The rule of
Islam was, in his view, nothing but a preparation for the
final and imminent appearance of the Antichrist. Islam
was the fourth beast of the book of Daniel that would
'devour the whole earth' (Daniel 7.23). Muhammad, for
his part, was a precursor of the Antichrist, 'the eleventh king' who would subdue the three kingdoms of the
Greeks, the Romans, and the Goths. As for Daniel's 'a
time, two times, and half a time' (Daniel 7.25), Alvarus
interpreted this as meaning that the period of Muslim
rule would be three and a half periods of 70 years, or 245
years. Granted he took the beginning of the Muslim era
to be around 618, he clearly expected the end of the world
in the not too distant future. And he took the then ruler
of Córdoba, the appropriately named Mahomet I, to be
himself the 'precursor in our time of the man of damnation'.[9] As John Tolan neatly puts it, Alvarus and Eulogius
'oppose the Muslim triumphalist view of history with an
apocalyptic vision promising Christian vengeance'.[10]

This identification of Muhammad with the Antichrist,
or at least his precursor, was to spread into northern

---

[8] Kenneth B. Wolf (trans.), *History of Muhammad*, in Constable (ed.),
     Medieval Iberia, pp. 58–60.
[9] *PL* 121.535.   [10] Tolan, *Saracens*, p. 91.

Europe. Peter the Venerable, the abbott of Cluny (c. 1092–1156), had commissioned the translation of the Qur'ān into Latin to demonstrate 'how foul and frivolous a heresy it is'.[11] In his *Summary of the Entire Heresy of the Saracens*, he positioned Muhammad halfway between the heretic Arius and the Antichrist:

The highest aspiration of this heresy [Islam] is to have Christ the Lord believed to be neither God, nor the Son of God, but, although a great man and beloved by God, nonetheless a mere man, and certainly a wise man and a very great prophet. What once, indeed, were conceived by the devil's device, first disseminated by Arius and then advanced by that Satan, namely Mohammad, will be fulfilled completely according to diabolical design through the Antichrist. In fact, since the blessed Hilary said that the origin of the Antichrist was in Arius, then what he began, by denying that Christ is the true Son of God and by calling him a creature, the Antichrist will at last consummate by asserting that in no way was he God or the Son of God, but also that he was not a good man; this most impious Mohammad seems properly to be provided for and prepared by the devil as the mean between both of them, as one who became in a certain sense both an extension of Arius and the greatest support for the Antichrist who will say worse things before the minds of the unbelievers.[12]

Muhammad as a type of Antichrist was to have a long history as it became a key element in the ongoing

---

[11] Irven M. Resnick (trans.), *Peter the Venerable: Writings against the Saracens* (Washington, DC: The Catholic University of America Press, 2016), p. 50. On Peter and Islam more generally, see James Aloysius Kritzeck, *Peter the Venerable and Islam* (Princeton University Press, 2016).

[12] *Ibid.*, p. 47.

geopolitical struggles between the West and the Muslim empires. As we will see in more detail later, Protestantism would fruitfully combine it with the imaginative vision of the Pope as the Antichrist. Humphrey Prideaux's assertion in 1697 of dual Antichrists in the East and the West was to set the pattern for British interpretations of Islam for the following 200 years: '*Mahomet* began this Imposture about the same time that the *Bishop* of *Rome* ... assumed the title of *Universal Pastor* ... so that *Antichrist* seems at this time to have set both his Feet upon *Christendom* together, the one in the *East*, and the other in the West.'[13]

Al-Dajjal, the Deceiver

Considering the Christian view that the prophet Muhammad was a type of the Antichrist, if not the Antichrist himself, it is perhaps ironic that, by the ninth century, Islam and Judaism too had their own apocalyptic Antichrist figures – in Islam al-Dajjal (the Deceiver), in Judaism Armilus. The Christian Antichrist was absorbed into early Islam from the Syriac Antichrist accounts, particularly those of the Pseudo-Ephraem and Pseudo-Methodius traditions, as he was thence into early medieval Jewish traditions. This was no doubt the consequence of textual commerce whereby, as John C. Reeves aptly notes, 'the literary products of one culture are appropriated, tweaked, adapted, adjusted, and rebutted by others who are themselves the producers and/or consumers

---

[13] Humphrey Prideaux, *The True Nature of Imposture Fully Displayed in the Life of Mahomet* (London, 1697), p. 16.

of competing apocalypses'.[14] As a result, the Antichrist figures in Christianity, Judaism, and Islam find their place within similar apocalyptic scenarios of the end of history.[15]

Only at an interpretative stretch can the Dajjal be said to appear in the Qur'ān.[16] He does, however, play an important role in Islamic eschatology in the Hadith literature – the later collections of the sayings and acts of Muhammad. As with the Christian Antichrist, the Muslim Antichrist was a complicated and ambiguous character. But we can construct a more or less coherent account of the Muslim Antichrist, as it was construed in the ninth century, from the Hadith accounts, in particular the *Sahih Bukhari* and the *Sahih Muslim*.[17]

According to one hadith, Muhammad told his companions of a Christian, Tamim Dari, who had converted to Islam. With a number of others, Tamim Dari had taken shelter from a storm at sea on an island. There they encountered a beast with hair so thick and long that its front could not be distinguished from its back. The beast told them of a person who wished to meet them in a nearby monastery. There they found a well-built man

---

[14] John Reeves, *Trajectories in Near Eastern Apocalypses: A Postrabbinic Jewish Apocalyptic Reader* (Atlanta: Society of Biblical Literature, 2005), p. 17.

[15] For a table plotting the apocalyptic similarities, see *ibid.*, p. 18.

[16] See Sura 108, 'Abundance', where we read of 'the one cut off'.

[17] The *Sahih* of al-Bukhari and the *Sahih* of Muslim are the two most authoritative Hadith collections. On the Hadith, see Muhammad Zubayr Siddiqi, *Hadith Literature: Its Origin, Development and Special Features* (Cambridge: The Islamic Texts Society, 1993). The topic remains under-researched in Western Islamic studies. The most useful recent account of the Dajjal may be found in Zeki Saritoprak, *Islam's Jesus* (Gainesville: University Press of Florida, 2014).

with his hands tied to his neck and iron shackles on his legs. He told them that he was the Dajjal, and that he would soon be permitted to leave the monastery and be let loose to travel the land. He informed them that he was prohibited from going into Mecca or Medina. He would not attempt to do so as there would be angels with swords in their hands to prevent him doing so. Muhammad thought that this man was probably the Dajjal.

While Muhammad initially thought that the Dajjal was imprisoned on an island in the Mediterranean or Arabian Seas, he went on to point out that the Dajjal was in the East and that it was from there that he would eventually appear. Although there is no declaration in the Hadith literature that the Dajjal would be Jewish, it was said that he would be followed by 70,000 Jews of Isfahan in Iran wearing Persian shawls.[18] Later traditions would elaborate on these followers of the Dajjal. They would be bastards, drunkards, and singers. They would commit all the acts forbidden by Islam, including adultery and sodomy in public.

Like the Christian Antichrist, you would know the Dajjal when you saw him. He was large and stout, of a red complexion. He was also blind in one eye that appeared like a swollen grape (although there was uncertainty whether it was his left or right eye) and 'big' curly hair. Thus, for example, Muhammad said that, in a dream, 'I turned my face to see another man with a huge body, red complexion and curly hair and blind in one eye. This eye looked like a protruding grape. They said (to me), He is

---

[18] See Abdul Hamid Siddiqui, *Sahih Muslim: Being Traditions of the Sayings and Doings of the Prophet Muhammad* (Lahore: Sh. Muhammad Ashraf, 1976–81), vol. IV, p. 1524.

Ad-Dajjal.'[19] He would be unable to have children. In a clear take-up from the Christian Antichrist, his most distinctive feature was the word 'Kafir' ('disbeliever') written on his forehead.

Like the Christian Antichrist, he would also deceive men through his miraculous powers, often inverting the order of nature. Thus, Muhammad told his followers,

the Dajjal would appear and there would be along with him water and fire and what the people would see as water that would be fire and that would burn and what would appear as fire that would be water and any one of you who would see that should plunge in that which he sees as fire for it would be sweet, pure water.[20]

In a variation on this, we read that the Dajjal would create a Paradise that would be really hellish and a fire that would be really paradisal.

On another occasion, the prophet reported that the Dajjal would kill a man and then raise him from the dead:

Ad-Dajjal will say (to his audience), 'Look, if I kill this man and then give him life, will you have any doubt about my claim?' They will reply, 'No.' Then Ad-Dajjal will kill that man and then will make him alive. The man will say, 'By Allah, now I recognize you more than ever!' Ad-Dajjal will then try to kill him (again) but he will not be given the power to do so.[21]

Another hadith has a much more elaborate version of this story. According to this, a believer would confront the Dajjal with the words, 'O people, he is the Dajjal about whom Allah's Messenger [Muhammad] (may peace

---

[19] *Sahih Bukhari*, 9.88.242. Available at www.sahih-bukhari.com
[20] Siddiqui, *Sahih Muslim*, vol. IV, p. 1516.
[21] *Sahih Bukhari*, 9.88.246.

be upon him) has informed (us).' The Dajjal would then order his followers to beat him up. Then the Dajjal would ask him if he believed in him. And the believer would say, 'You are a false Masih [Messiah].' The Dajjal would then order him to be torn in pieces with a saw 'from the parting of his hair up to his legs'. After that, the Dajjal would walk between the two pieces. The Dajjal would then order him to stand up. He would then ask him, 'Don't you believe in me?' And the believer would say, 'It has only added to my insight concerning you (that you are really the Dajjal).' The Dajjal would then try to kill him again but was unable to do so. So the Dajjal caught hold of him by his hands and feet and threw him into the air. And 'the people would think as if he had been thrown in the Hell-Fire whereas he would be thrown in Paradise'. He would be among the most eminent of 'persons in regard to martyrdom', the Prophet declared.[22]

Whereas the Dajjal was undoubtedly a man, he was unable to be killed by any other mere mortal. On one occasion in Medina, there was a discussion between Muhammad and his followers whether a local Jewish youth by the name of Ibn Sayyad was the Dajjal. When one of Muhammad's followers suggested that he should kill the youth, the Prophet replied, 'If he is the same (Dajjal) who would appear near the Last Hour, you would then not be able to overpower him, and if he is not that there is no good for you to kill him.'[23]

---

[22] Siddiqui, *Sahih Muslim*, vol. IV, p. 1519.

[23] *Ibid.*, 4.1513. In *Sahih Muslim*, the Ibn Sayyad stories may be found at 4.1510–15. See also David H. Halperin, 'The Ibn Sayyad Traditions and the Legend of Al-Dajjāl', *Journal of the American Oriental Society* 96 (1976), 213–25.

The Hadith sources suggest that Muhammad thought that the Dajjal, and therefore the end of the world, was imminent. The Dajjal appeared particularly in the hadith of the Prayer of Refuge:

O Allah! I seek refuge with You from the affliction of the Fire, the punishment of the Fire, the affliction of the grave, the punishment of the grave, and the evil of the affliction of poverty. O Allah! I seek refuge with You from the evil of the affliction of Al-Masih Ad-Dajjal. O Allah! Cleanse my heart with the water of snow and hail, and cleanse my heart from all sins as a white garment is cleansed from filth, and let there be a far away distance between me and my sins as You made the East and West far away from each other.[24]

The Dajjal also appeared among the signs of the end times. In one hadith, for example, Muhammad told his companions that the end would not come until the ten signs had been completed. Among these, the Dajjal featured along with a cloud of smoke that blanketed the earth, the beast, the rising of the sun from the west, the descent of Jesus son of Mary, the release of Gog and Magog from behind the wall, and landslides in the East, in the West, and in Arabia, and a fire from Yemen.[25] Elsewhere, the Dajjal was listed as one of the six signs of the end, along with the smoke, the beast from the earth, the rising of the sun from the West, general turmoil, and the deaths of many.[26]

---

[24] *Sahih Bukhari*, 8.75.388.
[25] See for example Siddiqui, *Sahih Muslim*, vol. IV, p. 1503–4. See also *Sahih Bukhari*, 9.88.237, where eleven signs of the Last Hour are mentioned, the second of which is the appearance of 'about thirty dajjals'.
[26] Siddiqui, *Sahih Muslim*, vol. IV, p. 1525.

According to the longest of the accounts of the career of the Dajjal in the *Sahih Muslim*, he would appear somewhere between Syria and Iraq and spread trouble in all directions. He would stay on the earth for forty days, 'one day like a year, and one day like a month and one day like a week and the rest of the days would be like your days', in short, around one year and ten weeks. He would move quickly 'like cloud driven by the wind'. For those who accepted him, there would be bountiful food. For those who rejected him, there would be drought and poverty. He would walk through the wasteland and say 'Bring forth your treasures,' and they would appear before him like a swarm of bees. He would then call a young man, strike him with a sword and cut him in pieces. This was the time of the death of the Dajjal. God would send Jesus Christ, son of Mary. Christ would descend with his hands resting on the shoulders of two angels at the white minaret on the eastern side of Damascus. Every non-believer would perish at his breath. He would then search for the Dajjal. He would capture him at the gate of the city of Ludd (Lydda) in Palestine and kill him.[27]

Eccentric appearance, fabulous powers, and wickedness in abundance aside, the basic doctrine of the apocalyptic Dajjal had become part of the creed of Islam by the ninth century. As the Sunni Muslim scholar Ahmad ibn Hanbal (d. 855) summed it up: 'And belief that the False Messiah will rise up, with the word "unbeliever" written

---

[27] *Ibid.*, vol. IV, pp. 1516–17. In some later traditions, Jesus is assisted by the Mahdi – an apocalyptic redeemer who rules the world. Elsewhere, it is the Mahdi himself who kills the Dajjal. Neither *Sahih Muslim* nor *Sahih Bukhari* refers to the Mahdi.

between his eyes, and [belief] in the hadiths that have
come about this. And faith that this shall really be so, and
that Jesus will descend from Heaven and slay him at the
Lydda gate.'[28]

Armilus, the Jewish Antichrist

Like Christianity and Islam, medieval Judaism too had
its Antichrist figure – Armilus, absorbed into Judaism
from Christianity.[29] He was a 'creature of Satan and of
stone', as one twelfth-century text obscurely put it. The
meaning is made clearer (sort of!) in a midrash (commentary) from the same time: 'And after this, Satan
will descend and go to Rome to the stone statue and
have connection with it in the manner of the sexual
act, and the stone will become pregnant and give birth
to Armilus.'[30] Another text informs us that the stone
was in the shape of a beautiful girl who was created in
the first six days of creation. In this case, she was made
pregnant not by Satan but by 'worthless people from
the nations of the world'.[31]

[28] John Alden Williams (ed.), *Themes of Islamic Civilization* (Berkeley:
University of California Press, 1971), p. 30.
[29] The sources on Armilus may most easily be accessed in Raphael
Patai, *The Messiah Texts: Jewish Legends of Three Thousand Years*
(Detroit: Wayne University Press, 1988), pp. 156–64. I have used
those texts which cover the period from the seventh to the twelfth
centuries. I have left out of the discussion two outlying texts: an
undated Yemeni manuscript about an eschatological false prophet not
named as 'Armilus'; and another undated text from the 'Doenmeh
notebook' from a different Armilus tradition. For a brief discussion,
see also McGinn, *Antichrist*, pp. 109–11, 314–15. The main texts are
also available in John Reeves, *Trajectories in Near Eastern Apocalypses*.
[30] Patai, *The Messiah Texts*, p. 157. [31] *Ibid.*

Armilus was monstrous in appearance, perhaps more so than the Christian or Muslim Antichrists. He was certainly a giant: 12 cubits high and 2 wide, according to one source, 100 cubits and 11 spans high, and 10 spans wide, with a mouth 1 span across according to another. In several sources, he was reported as having two skulls. One tradition reported that his hair was dyed, one that it was red, another that his face was hairy and his forehead leprous. Several reports had him as bald. His eyes were variously malformed – small, deep, red, and crooked, one eye small and the other big. He was also said by several to be deaf in one ear. If anyone said anything good to him, he would bend to him his 'stopped-up ear', his 'open ear' to anything evil.[32] His body too was monstrous. According to the earliest source, the *Sefer Zerubbabel* (seventh–ninth century), his hands hung down to his feet, which, according to another, were green. One midrash had his right arm only as long as a hand and his left 2½ cubits long.

The career of Armilus developed over time. At its earliest, in the *Sefer Zerubbabel*, it was said that he would rise up and rule in Imus [Emmaus?] and that (perhaps not surprisingly) all those who saw him would be frightened. Then Menahem ben Amiel (the Messiah) would come to him from the Valley of Shittim. He would blow into the face of Armilus and kill him. By the mid tenth century, he was playing a part in Judaism's two-Messiah tradition. According to this, there will come a warrior Messiah who will die in battle (Messiah ben Joseph or Ephraim) and an eschatological spiritual messiah (Messiah ben David) who

32 *Ibid.*, p. 160.

will gather the Jews in Israel and usher in the Messianic age.

Thus, in the *Ma'ase Daniel* (mid tenth century), the whole earth submits to Armilus, and he kills those who refused to do so. The army of Gog and Magog, all of whom had four eyes – two in front and two in back – join with him. Then the Messiah ben Joseph appears, and all Israel gathers around him. They all go to Armilus, who declares that *he*, Armilus, is the Messiah. When they see he is unable to prove through miracles that he is what he claims to be, the people of Israel reject him and go to the desert of Ephraim. Furious at this rejection, Armilus commands that they all be killed. He murders the Messiah ben Joseph, and the children of Israel flee. After forty days of mourning, they rise up and kill Armilus. Then God appears from heaven and, in place of the destroyed Jerusalem, brings down a heavenly Jerusalem for them. Messiah ben David then arrives and slays the army of Gog and Magog.[33]

There is another final variation on these themes of Armilus and the Messiahs. According to this, Armilus kills the warrior Messiah and is then himself killed by the spiritual Messiah. Thus, for example, in the eleventh-century *Midrash vaYosha'*, Armilus wages war against Israel for three months before going to Jerusalem and killing Messiah ben Joseph. Armilus is then killed by Messiah ben David before God gathers together the dispersed people of Israel.[34] Similarly, in the twelfth-century *Nistarot R. Shim'on ben Yohai*, after Messiah ben Ephraim has been defeated in battle by Armilus and dies in exile

---

[33] *Ibid.*, pp. 162–4.   [34] *Ibid.*, pp. 159–60.

in a desert of marshes, Messiah ben David 'will sprout up there … And he will blow upon that wicked Armillus and slay him'.[35] God then destroys Jerusalem and evicts the foreigner, the uncircumcised, and the impure. He gathers together the people of Israel to dwell in a new Jerusalem, in which are 'seventy-two pearls which will shine from one end of the world to another'.[36]

The Antichrist of Roger de Hoveden

In the year 1190, we recall, King Richard I of England was informed by Joachim of Fiore that, of the seven kings of Revelation 17.9–10, six had already come and one was yet to come. That the Antichrist was yet to come would have been no surprise to the king. That the one yet to come would be a persecutor of the church, like his six predecessors, would also have occasioned little surprise among Joachim's listeners. But then Joachim did surprise them. 'Now as to this Antichrist,' Joachim said, 'He is already born in the City of Rome, and will be elevated to the Apostolic See.'[37] The first six kings whom Joachim identified were all persecutors from outside the church. But the seventh would not only be inside, but would be the pope of Rome. In the history of the Antichrist, this was a momentous occasion. From this time on, the Adsonian eschatological tyrant outside the church would be juxtaposed with a *papal* deceiver within it. And, for the next 800 years, from the year 1200 to the present day, Adso's biography of the tyrannical

[35] *Ibid.* p. 160.   [36] *Ibid.*, p. 161.
[37] Riley (ed.), *The Annals of Roger de Hoveden*, vol. II, p. 178.

Antichrist would be set over against Joachim's story of a papal Antichrist.

The Annals of Roger de Hoveden 'record' King Richard's response, one that reflected the tradition of Adso. 'I thought', said the king,

> that Antichrist was to be born in Antioch, or at Babylon, of the descendants of Dan, and was to reign in the temple of the Lord at Jerusalem ... and was to reign therein three years and a half, and was to dispute against Elias and Enoch, and was to slay them, and was afterwards to die, and after his death the Lord was to give sixty days for repentance, during which those persons might repent who had wandered away from the paths of truthfulness, and had been seduced by the preaching of Antichrist and his false prophets.[38]

Roger de Hoveden was, perhaps, not as surprised as King Richard, for he went on to say that the dispute about whether the Antichrist would be the pope of Rome within the church, as Joachim was suggesting, or a king of Jerusalem outside it, as the Adsonian tradition had it, was still undecided. Roger then gave his elaborate and extensive account of the Antichrist. In a declaration of the authority of his version, Roger wrote that he was relying on 'ecclesiastical men of great learning in the Holy Scriptures'.[39] In particular, he mentioned Walter de Coutances (archbishop of Rouen and Apamia), Gerard (archbishop of Auxienne), John (bishop of Evreaux), and Bernard (bishop of Bayeux). Moreover, and very significantly, he was getting information directly from them, for they were also, like Roger, on crusade with King Richard and no doubt present at the conversation with

---

[38] *Ibid.*, vol. II, p. 179.   [39] *Ibid.*, vol. II, p. 180.

Joachim. At the least, they told him where to look for an authoritative account.[40] So Roger's was very much the episcopal 'authorised version' at the beginning of the thirteenth century and, we might conclude, the version that would have been known at that time, among both the elite and the populace, across Europe.

In fact, Roger's *Annals* contained two accounts of the life of the Antichrist. These provide for us a perfect snapshot of the Antichrist in the year 1200. The first of these was pretty much a verbatim account of the biography of the Antichrist as Adso had created it. There are only two minor differences. The first of these concerns the place where the Antichrist will be killed – on the Mount of Olives according to Adso, on a mountain in Babylon according to Roger. The second of these relates to the time for repentance after the death of the Antichrist – forty days according to Adso, one day according to Roger – although both Adso and Roger agree that no one knows how long after this period it will be before God comes in judgement.[41]

I cannot identify the source of the second, briefer account of the life of the Antichrist given by Roger de Hoveden in his *Annals*. Suffice it to say that it does follow, with some variations, the basic outlines of the Adsonian tradition. That said, it has several notable features that put it at odds with it. The first of these is the identification of the Antichrist with the Devil: 'Antichrist, that is, the Devil, shall reign, and shall work miracles and

[40] See Richard H. Heiser, 'The Court of the Lionheart on Crusade, 1190–2', *Journal of Medieval History* 43 (2017), 505–22.
[41] Riley (ed.), *The Annals of Roger de Hoveden*, vol. II, pp. 185–6.

1 The two witnesses, Enoch and Elijah, killed by the Antichrist.

2 St Michael killing the dragon.

3 The beast from the sea and the beast from the earth.

4 The martyrdom of Isaiah.

5 The Antichrist at the gates of Jerusalem.

6 Antiochus Epiphanes IV and his army before Jerusalem.

7 The fall of Simon Magus.

8 St Peter and Simon Magus.

9 The Antichrist riding Leviathan.

10 Alexander building a wall to enclose the people of Gog and Magog.

11 St Michael vanquishes the Antichrist.

12 The birth of the Antichrist according to Hildegard of Bingen

13 The death of the Antichrist mirroring that of Simon Magus.

Vnd er würt aller vntugent vnd boßheit vol · Wenn der tüfel tůt
alles ſin vermügen dar zů · Vnd das wcp ſt das bůch /das da heiſt
Compendium Theologie·in dem ſibenden Capitel·

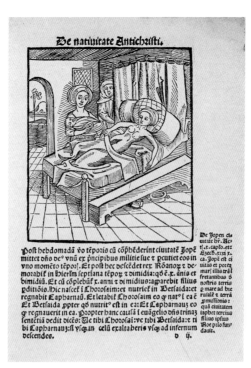

14 The birth of the Antichrist by Caesarean section – a
demonic version.

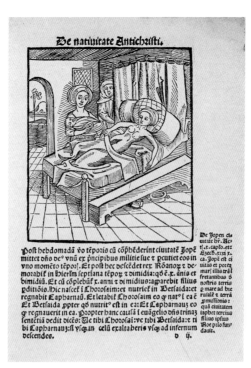

De natiuitate Antichriſti.

Poſt hebdomadā vo tēporis cū cōphēderint ciuitatē Jopē
mittet oñs ve° vnū er pncipibus milirie ſue τ pcuriet eos in
vno momēto tēpor.Et poſt hec veſcēdet rex Roanox τ ve-
morabit in bierſim ſeptiana tēpor τ vimidia:qō ē.x. ānis et
bimidiū.Et cū cōplebūt x.anni τ vi midius:apparebit filius
pditiōis.Jbic naſcet i Choroſaim:et nutriet in Berſaida:et
regnabit Capharnaū.Et letabit Choroſaim eo q nat°i eā
Et Berſaida ppter qō nutrit° eſt in ea:Et Capharnaū co
q regnauerit in ea.propter hanc cauſā i euāgelio oñs trinas
ſentētiā dedit vices: Te tibi Choroſai:ve tibi Berſaida:τ ti
bi Capharnaū3:ſi vſq·in celū exaltaberis vſq ad infernum
veſcendes.   v ij.

De Jopen ci
uitate ht̃.Ac-
Ezecb̃.xxi x.
ca.Jopē eſt ci
uitas et portū
mar̃ illiu trā
fretantibus o
noſtrū terris
p mare ad vie
ruſalē τ terrā
pmiſſionis :
quā ciuitatem
iopbet tercius
filius ipſius
Noe pilo fun°
dauit.

15 The birth of the Antichrist by Caesarean
section – an obstetric version

16 The seven-headed beast coming from the sea.

17 A papal Antichrist? Miniature of Pope John XXII.

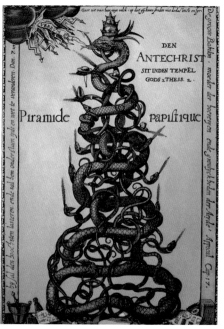

18 The Roman church hierarchy as the serpent of hell crowned with a papal tiara.

19 'The Sermon and Deeds of the Antichrist' by Luca Signorelli.

20 The Devil whispering into the ear of the Antichrist.

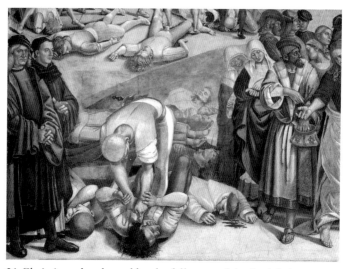

21 Christians slaughtered by the followers of the Antichrist.

22 The Antichrist appears to raise a man from the dead.

23 The slaughter of the two witnesses, Enoch and Elijah.

24 The death of the Antichrist.

25 Followers of the Antichrist destroyed by heavenly rays.

26 Pope Leo X as the Antichrist.

27 The pope as the Whore of Babylon seated on the beast with seven heads.

28 Napoleon, 'The Beast as Described in the Revelations'.

29 A scene from *Rosemary's Baby*: 'He has his Father's eyes.'

30 A scene from *The Final Conflict: The Seven Daggers of Megiddo.*

great signs in the people.[42] Second, where Gregory the Great, Haimo of Auxerre, and Adso were all uncertain whether the Antichrist would be killed by Jesus Christ or the archangel Michael, Roger's second account has Michael killing the Antichrist. Almighty God, we read, 'shall send Michael, the Archangel, having a sharp two-edged sword in his hands, that is to say, the sword of the Holy Spirit, and shall slay him, and shall cleave him into two parts from head to foot, that so the world may not be destroyed, but may be renewed for the better.[43] These differences aside, Roger was clearly more concerned with promoting the big picture of the Adsonian tradition than with sweating the minor differences in detail.

Apocalypse Maybe?

While the history of the future Antichrist had, more or less, received its definitive form by the year 1200, the imminence of his arrival had become much less certain in the early part of the second millennium. This is not to suggest that the importance of the Antichrist had diminished. But, as Bernard McGinn has noted, there did remain an

important difference between a general consciousness of liv-ing in the last age of history and a conviction that the last age itself is about to begin, between a belief in the reality of the Antichrist and the certainty of his proximity (or at least of the date of coming), between viewing the events of one's own time in the light of the End of history and seeing them as the last events themselves.[44]

[42] *Ibid.*, vol. II, p. 186.   [43] *Ibid.*, vol. II, p. 187.
[44] McGinn (ed.), *Visions of the End*, p. 4.

In either case, an apocalyptic worldview in which the Antichrist had a central role remained prevalent, sufficiently so for it to be as much rhetorical as literal to accuse others of being the Antichrist. However blurred, the tensions between the literal and the spiritual Antichrist, the Antichrist to come and the Antichrist already present, the real and the rhetorical Antichrist, were in play.

Thus, the literal Antichrist was yet to come, but spiritual Antichrists were already present. The discourse of the Antichrist became an effective means of 'demonising' opponents within the church as well as enemies outside it. Pope Gregory VII (c. 1015–85), for example, was never one to pull his rhetorical punches in pursuit of papal supremacy over opponents, secular or religious. For him, the arrival of the Antichrist was imminent. In a letter written to all Christians in 1084, he declared that it was no wonder that he had stirred up so much opposition to his reforms: 'For the nearer the day of Antichrist approaches, the harder he [Satan] fights to crush out the Christian faith.'[45] The Antichrist might not yet have arrived. But Gregory saw him 'busy everywhere by means of his members'.[46] Elsewhere, he wrote of 'precursors', 'heralds', and 'limbs' of the Antichrist.[47] Gregory declared Wibert (or Guibert) of Ravenna (c. 1029–1100), elected pope in 1080 in opposition to Gregory, to be 'a perjurer against the Holy Roman Church, notorious throughout the whole Roman world for the basest of

---

[45] Ephraim Emerton (trans.), *The Correspondence of Pope Gregory VII* (New York: Columbia University Press, 1932), p. 195.
[46] *Ibid.*, p. 100.   [47] *Ibid.*, pp. 9, 11, 188.

crimes ... Antichrist and heretic.[48] The compliment was returned in spades. Gregory's opponent, Cardinal Beno, declared, whether ingenuously or not is hard to determine, that Gregory was 'either a member of Antichrist, or Antichrist himself'.[49]

This blurring of the Antichrist to come with the Antichrist or Antichrists already present was not uncommon. Thus, for example, the Augustinian priest Gerhoh of Reichersburg (1093–1169) wrote his apocalyptic works *The Investigation of Antichrist* and *The Fourth Watch of the Night* during the 1160s, in the midst of the conflict over papal or imperial supremacy between Pope Alexander III and the Emperor Frederick Barbarossa. In *The Fourth Watch of the Night*, Gerhoh read the gospel story of the four watches of the night when the apostles battled stormy waters on the Sea of Galilee (Matthew 14.22–33) as an allegory of the history of the church during four trials brought about by the Antichrist. The first watch was the age of the 'bloody Antichrist' of the persecution of Christians by the Romans that ended with Constantine. The second was that of the 'fraudulent Antichrist' of the age of heresy that ended with Pope Gregory the Great. The third watch, that of the 'impure Antichrist', culminated in Gregory VII's attempt to reform the church of its clerical corruption. The fourth watch of the 'avaricious Antichrist' then began: 'In this fourth watch widespread avarice swollen with desire for gain rules the whole Body of Christ from head to foot.'[50] In short, the Antichrist had

---

[48] *Ibid.*, p. 162.   [49] McGinn, *Antichrist*, p. 121.
[50] McGinn (ed.), *Visions of the End*, p. 104.

always been present as the sum of all those who, since the beginnings of Christianity, have opposed the true church.

Certainly, for Gerhoh, the end times were not far away. Gerhoh read Augustine more literally than figuratively. Satan, he believed, had been released a thousand years after the death of Christ, since when began both the split in the papacy and the conflict between pope and emperor initiated by the conflict between Pope Gregory VII and Emperor Henry IV. 'From that time', he wrote in his *The Investigation of the Antichrist*,

the priesthood was made like a smoking cloth through the evil of simony and the wickedness of incontinence so that in many it was evident as a fear not of evil works but of good ones … Under a disguise of piety they hid their purpose, so that what they did in an evil and bestial manner might seem to be done at God's inspiration.[51]

For Gerhoh, the collective Antichrist of the past and present did not negate the final Antichrist. The final Antichrist would arise out of the corrupt 'avaricious Antichrist' within the church. This meant that Gerhoh had to go soft on some of the details of the Adsonian Antichrist. Nevertheless, the general features of the career of the Antichrist remained consistent. He would rage 'against the Holy Church in the cruellest fashion'.[52] He would show himself as God, 'indeed is even lifted up above everything that is termed God, or worshipped as God'.[53] Still, even during the time of the final Antichrist, a Reformation within the church would occur, and the

[51] *Ibid.*, p. 100.   [52] *Ibid.*, p. 106.   [53] *Ibid.*, pp. 106–7.

church 'will be thus purified from the pollutions of filth and simony and will be adorned with gold crowns'.[54] Before the final coming of Christ, he wrote, 'the Church, which is the true and living house of the living God, is to be reformed to its ancient practice of apostolic perfection in those who are called and ought to be spiritual men'.[55] The 'Last Roman Emperor' was no longer the key figure in the preparations for the return of Christ. Taking the papal against the imperialist side in the battle between pope and emperor, Gerhoh promoted the pope to top position in the earthly hierarchy. It was the purified church, opposed to wealthy corruption and devoted to poverty, with the pope at its head, that was to play the key role in preparing for the return of Christ and the defeat of the Antichrist. Only when the church was reformed would the Antichrist be humbled – 'when the Lord Jesus slays him with the breath of his mouth and destroys him with the brightness of his coming'.[56]

This interweaving of ecclesiastical reform and eschatological expectation in the twelfth century was exemplified in Bernard of Clairvaux (1090–1153), the leading spokesperson for the Cistercian monastic order. Bernard was not convinced that the Antichrist was imminent. Thus, for example, in a letter to Geoffrey of Chartres, he reported on a conversation about the Antichrist that he had had with his friend Norbert of Xanten (c. 1080–1134), the founder of the Premonstratensian monastic order. Norbert 'spoke of the coming of Antichrist', Bernard

---

[54] *Ibid.*, p. 107.   [55] Quoted in McGinn, *Antichrist*, p. 124.
[56] McGinn (ed.), *Visions of the End*, p. 106.

wrote, 'and, on my asking him when he thought this would be, he declared himself quite certain that it would be during this present generation. But when I heard the reasons he had for his certainty, I did not feel compelled to agree with him.'[57]

That said, Bernard was not averse to using the rhetorical device of 'the Antichrist' in criticism of others, especially in the rivalry between Popes Innocent II and Anacletus II, each of whom had been consecrated as pope on the same day, 23 February 1130. Bernard threw himself into the brawl in support of Innocent and against Anacletus. Thus, in an attempt to persuade Hildebert, archbishop of Tours, to support Innocent, he wrote,

Innocent has been set up for the fall and rise of many. Those who are of God have freely chosen him, but he who stands over against him [Anacletus] is either Antichrist or his follower. The abomination of desolation is standing in the Holy Place, to gain possession of which he has set fire to the sanctuary of God.[58]

Elsewhere, in a letter to Geoffrey of Loreto, he described Anacletus as 'That beast, spoken of in the book of the Apocalypse, to whom power has been given to blaspheme and make war on the saints.'[59] Of Anacletus' supporter, Gerard of Angoulême, he declared, 'by dividing those

---

[57] Bruno Scott James (trans.), *The Letters of St. Bernard of Clairvaux* (Chicago: Henry Regnery Company, 1953), Letter 59, p. 86. For an excellent overview of Bernard's thought on the Antichrist, see Bernard McGinn, 'Saint Bernard and Eschatology', in M. Basil Pennington (ed.), *Bernard of Clairvaux: Studies Presented to Dom Jean Leclercq* (Washington, DC: Consortium Press, 1973), pp. 161–85.

[58] James (trans.), *The Letters of St. Bernard*, Letter 127, p. 188.

[59] *Ibid.*, Letter 128, p. 190.

whom Christ saved by uniting, he makes himself not a Christian but Antichrist, guilty of the cross and death of Christ'.[60] This was now eschatology in the service of global politics.

Like Gerhoh, Bernard's expectations of the imminence, or otherwise, of the Antichrist were set within a history of the church. According to this, the church would pass through four stages over its life that mirrored the four temptations faced by monks during their daily lives. These monastic temptations were derived by Bernard from those outlined in Psalm 91.5–6: 'You will not fear the terror of the night, or the arrow that flies by day, or the pestilence that stalks in darkness, or the destruction that wastes at noonday.'[61]

Bernard's four ages of church history, derived from Psalm 91, were most clearly laid out in the thirty-third of his sermons on the 'Canticle of Canticles' (more commonly known as 'The Song of Songs') around the year 1139. Thus, the primitive church was assailed by 'the terror of the night' (*timor nocturnus*), for it was then that 'everyone who slew the saints thought he was offering a service to God'.[62] In the second age, when the church had triumphed, 'the terror of the night' was replaced by

---

[60] *Ibid.*, Letter 129, p. 194.

[61] McGinn, 'Saint Bernard and Eschatology', p. 173, and Robert Rusconi, 'Antichrist and Antichrists', in Bernard McGinn (ed.), *The Encyclopedia of Apocalypticism: Vol. II* (New York: Continuum, 1998), p. 298, both list this as Psalm 90. In the Vulgate version, derived from the Greek Septuagint that Bernard would have used, this psalm is also numbered as 90. Modern English translations, which I follow, number it as 91.

[62] A Priest of Mount Melleray (trans.), *St. Bernard's Sermons on the Canticle of Canticles* (Dublin: Browne and Nolan, Limited, 1920), p. 405.

the 'arrow that flieth in the day' (*sagitta volans in die*). This was the age of heresies, in which vain men hungering after earthly glory 'began to afflict their holy mother by teaching diverse and perverse doctrines'.[63] It was remedied by the wisdom of the doctors, as was the first age, by the patience of the martyrs. The second age was followed by Bernard's own, 'the business that walks around in the dark' (*negotium perambulans in tenebris*), exemplified in the disease of hypocrisy and ambition within the church:

Today the foul disease has spread itself throughout the whole body of Christ's mystical Bride, the more incurable in proportion as it is widely extended, and the more deadly the deeper it penetrates. Were one to rise up against holy mother Church, teaching open heresy, he would be cut off like an infected member, and cast forth to rot. Were a persecuting enemy to appear against her, she might perhaps hide herself from his violence. But now whom shall she cast forth, and from whom shall she hide herself? All are her friends and nevertheless all are her enemies. All are her children and, at the same time, all are her adversaries. All are her domestics, yet none give her peace. All are her neighbours, whilst all seek the things that are her own. They are Christ's ministers, but they serve Antichrist.[64]

The final and worst age was still to come, that of the midday demon (*daemonium meridianum*). He would appear in order to seduce the remnant who remained faithful, persevering in their simplicity of life: 'This is Antichrist who simulates the day, yea, and the Meridian, "and is lifted up above all that is called God, or that is worshipped".[65] The

---

[63] *Ibid.*, p. 406. [64] *Ibid.*, pp. 406–7. [65] *Ibid.*, p. 408.

Antichrist would be destroyed by Christ 'with the Spirit of his Mouth and with the brightness of his coming'.[66]

Towards the end of his life, Bernard seems to have had more of an expectation that the fourth age was at hand or, even, that it had already arrived. Perhaps, like many of us as we get older, he had no doubt that things were worse than when he was younger. Holiness was rare, iniquity abounded, and 'our age is lacking in men', he declared in the preface to his life of Saint Malachy of Armagh in 1149, some four years before his death.[67] I suppose, he went on,

he has come or is at hand of whom it is written, Want shall go before his face. If I mistake not, Antichrist is he whom famine and sterility of all good both precedes and accompanies. Whether therefore it is the herald of one now present or the harbinger of one who shall come immediately, the want is evident.[68]

Sexy Beast

The Benedictine nun Hildegard of Bingen (1098–1179) brought a new emphasis to the story of the Antichrist. For her, the church was deeply corrupted by sexuality. Thus, in her major work, *Scivias* (c. 1151), Hildegard described her vision of the Antichrist, born from the vagina of the church:

[66] *Ibid.*
[67] H. J. Lawlor (trans.), *St. Bernard of Clairvaux's Life of St. Malachy of Armagh* (London: Macmillan, 1920), preface.
[68] *Ibid.*

And I saw again the figure of a woman whom I had previously seen in front of the altar that stands before the eyes of God; she stood in the same place, but now I saw her from the waist down. And from her waist to the place that denotes the female, she had various scaly blemishes; and in that latter place was a black and monstrous head. It had fiery eyes, and ears like an ass's, and nostrils and mouth like a lion's; it opened wide its jowls and terribly clashed its horrible iron-coloured teeth ... And behold! That monstrous head moved from its place with such a great shock that the figure of the woman was shaken through all her limbs [see Plate 12].[69]

In the same vision, she saw the death of the Antichrist, incorporating into her vision the Pseudo-Hippolytan tradition of Antichrist as a kind of Simon Magus figure, attempting to ascend into heaven: 'And a great mass of excrement adhered to the head; and it raised itself up upon a mountain and tried to ascend the height of Heaven. And behold, there came suddenly a thunderbolt, which struck that head with such great force that it fell from the mountain and yielded its spirit up in death' (see Plate 13).[70]

Her commentary on this vision remained within the tradition of Adso. But her sexualising of the Antichrist gave it a new flavour. Thus, the mother of the Antichrist became the Anti-Mary, the promiscuous whore. Having separated herself from friends and family, 'she will secretly engage in vile fornication with men, though only a few, defiling herself with great appetite for wicked

---

[69] Mother Columba Hart and Jane Bishop (trans.), *Hildegard of Bingen, Scivias* (New York: Paulist Press, 1990), 3.11, p. 493.
[70] *Ibid.*

doings ... And in the burning heat of this fornication, she will conceive the son of perdition without knowing which man's semen engendered him.'[71] As the Devil was closely involved in the fall of Eve, so he would be in the creation of the Antichrist. Taking delight in her promiscuity, the Devil would breathe on the embryo and possess it with all his power in her womb, with the result that 'that destroyer will issue from the womb of that mother full of the Devil's spirit'.[72]

The Antichrist would be skilled in magic and would appear to perform miracles, bringing fire and lightning from heaven, raising thunder and hailstorms, uprooting mountains, and drying up water. He would appear to make the healthy sick and the sick healthy, cast out demons, and even raise the dead. Thus, God told Hildegard, 'many will be deceived, for they will blind their own inner Vision with which they should have regarded me'.[73]

At the core of the teaching of the Antichrist was his attack on virginity. Thus, in Hildegard's *Book of Divine Works* (1163–73), the Antichrist would tell his followers that the principle of chastity was against the natural law according to which human bodies should be both hot and cold, and that it was unnatural to suppress bodily heat. He would teach that 'there is no sin when flesh warms itself on flesh ... The accursed son of corruption will lead human beings astray by teaching them to live according to the burning impulses of the flesh and to accede to every desire of the flesh.'[74]

---

[71] *Ibid.*, 3.11.25, p. 502. [72] *Ibid.* [73] *Ibid.*, 3.11.27, p. 503.
[74] Matthew Fox (ed.), *Hildegard of Bingen's Book of Divine Works with Letters and Songs* (Santa Fe, New Mexico: Bear and Company, 1987), 3.10.30, pp. 254–5.

Having deceived his followers with a faked death and resurrection, the Antichrist would place an inscription upon the forehead of his followers. This was more than simply the 'name or number of the beast' (Revelation 13.17). The Devil has had this inscription since the beginning. It was, in fact, the inscription by which Satan had been cast out of heaven by God for seeking to become God. It had never been previously shown to a human being. But it would be given to the Antichrist to mark on his followers as the sign of their new evil natures:

> He will have inscriptions marked on the foreheads of his followers. In this way he will inscribe all evil upon them, just as the old serpent did for human beings by deceiving them and arousing their passion [inflaming their lust] in order to keep them in its power. By means of this inscription and in opposition to baptism and Christ's name, the Antichrist will so capture human beings through magical spells that they will no longer wish to be free of him.[75]

When the Antichrist, having murdered Enoch and Elijah, had fulfilled the Devil's will on earth, he would, in his pride and presumption, seek to know the secrets of heaven. Thus, in the tradition of Simon Magus, he would assemble all his followers and inform them that he wanted to go to heaven. But God's power would manifest itself and destroy him, 'striking him with such jealousy that he will fall violently from the height of his presumption, in all the pride with which he stood against God. And, so ending, he will vomit forth his life in the death of eternal perdition.'[76] The people, seeing the Antichrist

---

[75] *Ibid.*, 3.10.32, p. 257.
[76] Hart and Bishop (trans.), *Hildegard of Bingen, Scivias*, 3.11.38, p. 507.

fallen and his body rotting and stinking, would repent of their errors and turn back to the truth.

As to the time of the Antichrist, Hildegard remained uncertain. She was clear in her belief that she was living in the end times: 'the insane murderer, the son of perdition, will come soon', she declared.[77] But not too soon! 'But you, O humans, have a time to traverse from now on, until the coming of that murderer who will try to pervert the Catholic faith.'[78] Indeed, her vision for the future included that of the five ages of the end times, only the last of which was the age of the Antichrist: 'Then I looked to the North, and behold! Five beasts stood there. One was like a dog, fiery but not burning; another was like a yellow lion; another was like a pale horse; another like a black pig; and the last like a gray wolf.'[79] The clergy of her own time, the age of the dog, were forerunners of the Antichrist, but the age of the Antichrist, that of the grey wolf, was clearly some little time off.

In holding that the Antichrist, however monstrous, was born in the normal fashion, Hildegard of Bingen was in line with the overall tradition concerning his birth. The son of Satan was born of a woman, as was the son of God. But in the second half of the fifteenth century, images of the birth of the Antichrist by Caesarean section began to proliferate in woodcuts to a German life of the Antichrist, *Endkrist*, and even made their way to Spain. There was no textual tradition to this effect. But the illustrators were probably intending that, since the Antichrist was contrary to Christ in all things, he could

[77] *Ibid.*, 3.11.25, p. 501.   [78] *Ibid.*, 3.11.23, p. 500.
[79] *Ibid.*, 3.11, p. 493.

not be born in exactly the same way as Christ. That his life began with the death of his mother added to his ignominy. Those illustrations that accompanied Antichrist texts represented demons present at his birth. Thus, for example, a German woodcut from 1475 pictured a demon at the foot of the bed looking happily on as the Antichrist is born from a large wound in his mother's stomach. Another demon at the head of the bed prepares to take his mother's soul, pictured in the form of another infant, although the presence of an angel in the window might suggest her salvation rather than her damnation (see Plate 14). 'He was full of everything wicked and evil', we read.[80]

Alongside the satanic illustrations of the birth of the Antichrist went obstetrical versions. In these, the demons were absent and only human figures appeared. Thus, for example, in a 1498 illustration from an edition of a work by Pseudo-Methodius and headed 'On the Birth of Antichrist' (*De nativitate Antichristi*), the Antichrist was already delivered, wrapped in swaddling clothes, and held by a midwife. The Antichrist's mother gazed unhappily at the gash in her stomach (see Plate 15). Unlike the vernacular satanic illustrations in the block books, these obstetric versions appeared in printed books intended for a more educated audience. In either case, it is clear that the illustrators saw a symmetry between the 'unnaturalness' of the Caesarian birth and the evil of the Antichrist.

[80] This same print occurs in a Spanish version of *Endkrist* entitled *El libro del Anticristo*. See Renate Blumenfeld-Kosinski, *Not of Woman Born: Representations of Caesarean Birth in Medieval and Renaissance Culture* (Ithaca: Cornell University Press, 1990), plate 24. I am indebted to Blumenfeld-Kosinski for this discussion.

Magnus Antichristus

Joachim of Fiore, we recall, surprised King Richard and his entourage on their way to the Holy Land in 1190 by declaring that, far from the Adsonian tradition of the Antichrist as a Jew from the East, the Antichrist would be born at the very centre of the West, in Rome. He would be both a king and a priest – the last of seven regal persecutors of the church, and a false pope.

It was an account of the Antichrist that Joachim had given six years before, in May of 1184 in the city of Veroli, in an appearance before Pope Lucius III (c. 1100–85). On this occasion, Joachim told the pope that there would be seven persecutions before Christ would return in judgement. The last of these would be that of the Antichrist. As Robert E. Lerner has noted, 'Any tattered or grizzled prophet called in for the occasion might have told Pope Lucius more or less the same.'[81] Joachim, however, placed his account of the Antichrist within an innovative and original history of the church.

According to this, the seven persecutions of the Jews in the Old Testament (ranging from that of the Egyptians to that of Antiochus) paralleled the seven stages in church history from the beginning of the New Testament onwards: 'Just as in the Old Testament, when the seven tribulations were finished, the Savior who was to redeem

---

[81] Robert E. Lerner, 'Antichrists and Antichrist in Joachim of Fiore', *Speculum* 60 (1985), 555. I am especially indebted to Lerner for this discussion. See also Marjorie Reeves, *The Influence of Prophecy in the Later Middle Ages* (Oxford: Clarendon Press, 1969). For an excellent overview of Joachim, see Brett E. Whalen, *Dominion of God: Christendom and Apocalypse in the Middle Ages* (Cambridge, Massachusetts: Harvard University Press, 2009), ch. 4.

the human race came into the world, so when just as many persecutions against the Church have been completed, the punishing Judge of this world will make his appearance.'[82] The first four persecutions of the church had already occurred – those of the Jews, the Pagans, the Arians and the Saracens, with three yet to come. Of these, the last would be that of the Antichrist, 'since it is necessary that Antichrist appear before the great day of the Lord'.[83]

Joachim's most developed account of the Antichrist as the seventh king is elaborated in his *Book of Figures* (*Liber figurarum*). Within that work, we find an exposition of the meaning of the seven-headed dragon of Revelation 12, now aligned with the seven persecuting kings of Revelation 17 (see Plate 16). There we read that there will be victory for the Christians over the sixth head of the dragon over which the sixth king (Saladin) reigns. However, after a few years, the wound inflicted on the sixth head of the dragon will heal, and 'the king who is over it (whether it be Saladin if he is still alive or another in his place) will gather together a much larger army than before and he will wage general war against God's elect'.[84]

At the same time, the seventh head of the dragon – the great Antichrist, *magnus antichristus* – would also arise, together with a multitude of false prophets. He would 'pretend to be king, priest and prophet'.[85] While the sixth king would wage war from the East, the seventh would come from the West to assist him. The Antichrist would perform great signs before the Eastern king, 'just as Simon Magus had done in the sight of Nero'.[86] Joachim

---

[82] McGinn (ed.), *Visions of the End*, p. 131.   [83] *Ibid.*, p. 133.
[84] *Ibid.*, p. 137.   [85] *Ibid.*, p. 138.   [86] *Ibid.*, p. 137.

came close to identifying the Antichrist with the pope. 'Just as the Beast from the Sea [Revelation 13]', he wrote,

is held to be a great king from his sect who is like Nero and almost emperor of the whole world, so the Beast ascending from the earth [Revelation 11] is held to be a great prelate [*magnum prelatum*] who will be like Simon Magus and like a universal pope [*universalis pontifex*] in the entire world. He is that Antichrist of whom Paul said he would be lifted up and opposed to everything that is said to be god, or that is worshipped, and that he would sit in God's temple showing himself as God [2 Thessalonians 2.4].[87]

These two kings would both be defeated by Christ: 'These two will make a conspiracy to wipe the name of Christ from the earth. But Christ will conquer them, he who is Kings of Kings and Lord of Lords.'[88]

According to the mainstream apocalyptic tradition up to that time, the final judgement would occur immediately after the defeat of the Antichrist or, perhaps, after a short period of rest for the saints. But Joachim has yet another significant innovation. It concerns a new reading of the book of Revelation, to the effect that chapters 17–22 were about the future. Augustine, we recall, believed that the binding of Satan for (a figurative period of) a 'thousand years' (Revelation 20.2–3) occurred at the time of Christ's passion, that this period coincided with the 'thousand-year' reign of the saints with Christ (Revelation 20.4–6), and that, at the end of this period, Satan would be released (Revelation 20.7). Satan would

---

[87] Quoted in McGinn, *Antichrist*, pp. 141–2.
[88] McGinn, *Visions of the End*, p. 138.

then enter into the Antichrist who would persecute Christians before being finally defeated.

Joachim would project all these events into the future. He aligned the binding of Satan not with the death and resurrection of Christ, but with the defeat of the Antichrist already born. Unlike Augustine, for whom the 'thousand-year' reign of the saints was a spiritual one already happening, Joachim declared it an earthly one that would begin with the Antichrist's defeat and coincided with the binding of Satan. Peace and justice would then reign on earth for the 'millennium', although 'God alone knows the number of the years, months, and days of that time'.[89]

For Joachim, the time was near when the Antichrist, assisted by the Devil and his demons, would begin his onslaught. It would coincide with the end of the second and the beginning of the third 'age' (*status*). The first of these, according to Joachim, was the time of the Old Testament Law and the Father. During that period, people were not yet able to attain 'the freedom of the Spirit'.[90] The second age was that of the Gospel and the Son. This remained into Joachim's own time. It was a period of freedom greater than that under the Law but not as complete as that of the third age.

The third age, that of the Holy Spirit, would come

toward the End of the world. The third age would no longer be under the veil of the letter, but in the full freedom of the Spirit when, after the destruction and cancellation of the false gospel of the Son of Perdition and his prophets, those who teach

---

[89] *Ibid.*, p. 140.   [90] *Ibid.*, p. 133.

many about justice will be like the splendor of the firmament and like the stars forever.[91]

Christian society would be spiritualised, under the guidance of 'spiritual men' (*viri spirituales*). Not so much the 'rule of the saints', this was to be the 'rule of the monks'.

'The rule of the spiritual men' was to begin in the year 1260. There was any number of ways in which Joachim might have generated this date. But he seems to have derived it from his parallel histories of the Old Testament and New Testament. Thus, in a passage in the *Book of Figures*, Joachim declared,

From the days of Zerubabel 1,260 years are counted under which the Old Testament takes its beginning and end ... Therefore, according to the New Testament, it is clear that it will be concluded under the same number, that is, one thousand and two hundred and sixty years, after which, when it pleases him (but soon), the Judge will come to judgement.[92]

That all said, Joachim's futuristic reading of the later chapters of the book of Revelation, against the Augustinian grain, led him to a severe interpretative problem. He had dealt with the defeat of Antichrist prior to the beginning of the millennial period. But how now to deal with the loosing of Satan who 'will come out to deceive the nations at the four corners of the earth, Gog and Magog, in order to prepare them for battle' (Revelation 20.8)? Simple! He added another final Antichrist: 'Among all the Antichrists who will appear in the world two are worse than the others: the one who

---

[91] *Ibid.*, p. 134. No need to put too fine a point on it, but it should be noted that there was an overlapping of these ages.
[92] Quoted in Rusconi, 'Antichrist and Antichrists', pp. 303–4.

is denoted by the seventh head [of the dragon] and the one denoted by the tail … God's saints have specifically spoken of one Antichrist and nonetheless there will be two, one of whom will be the Greatest Antichrist.[93]

This final Antichrist would be Gog, the commander of the satanic army. God would judge him and his army with fire and brimstone poured down from heaven. He and the Devil 'will be cast into the lake of fire where the Beast [the first Antichrist] and the False Prophet already are'.[94] '[A]nd with that stroke', as Robert E. Lerner writes, 'the abbot effected the first major departure in medieval Antichrist thinking since the days of the Fathers.'[95] To add to that, and perhaps even more significantly, Joachim had significantly revised traditional Christology. For Joachim had added a further appearance of Christ on earth. Christ had returned a second time to destroy the great Antichrist before the millennium, but now he would also return for a third time at the end of the millennium, this time to defeat Gog, the final Antichrist.

---

[93] McGinn (ed.), *Visions of the End*, pp. 140–1.   [94] *Ibid.*, p. 140.
[95] Lerner, 'Antichrists and Antichrist in Joachim of Fiore', p. 560.

5

Of Prophets, Priests, and Kings

~

And I saw a beast rising out of the sea, having ten horns and seven
heads; and on its horns were ten diadems, and on its heads were
blasphemous names.

Revelation 13.1

Antichrists, Regal and Papal

On 20 November 1210, William Aurifex, along with
nine others, was burned for heresy. These were not
common folk but rather, as Caesarius of Heisterbach
(c. 1180–c. 1240) put it, 'learned men', in whom the Devil
had instilled perverse understanding.[1] William, although
a cleric and trained in philosophy, was their 'prophet'. He
was known as 'Aurifex', hence his being remembered as
William *the goldsmith*, although he may well have been a
philosophical alchemist.

William and his colleagues were followers of Almaric
of Bena (d. 1204–7). Almaric had lectured in logic and
theology at the University of Paris. Pushing well beyond
the limits of orthodoxy, he taught that God was in all
things, that hell was ignorance, that heaven was only
in the here and now, and that the truly 'spiritual' man
cannot sin. Eventually, he was denounced for heresy

---

[1] *Caesarii Heisterbacensis dialogus miraculorum*, 5.22, in Walter L.
Wakefield and Austin P. Evans, *Heresies of the High Middle Ages:
Selected Sources Translated and Annotated* (New York and London:
Columbia University Press, 1969), p. 259.

by Pope Innocent III and forced to reject his teachings publicly. Humiliated by his public recantation, he took to his bed and died soon afterwards. In 1215, the Fourth Lateran Council condemned his teachings. 'We also reprobate and condemn', it declared, 'the perverse teaching of the impious Amaury [Almaricus, Amalricus] de Bene, whose mind the father of lies has so darkened that his teaching is to be regarded as not so much heretical as insane.'[2]

William's teaching was a particularly 'upbeat' rendition of Almaric's. He proclaimed that the bread on the altar in which the body of Christ was present was the same as any other bread. He denied the resurrection of the body and said that there was no heaven or hell. He who possessed knowledge of God, he believed, had heaven within, just as he who was in mortal sin had hell within him, 'like a decayed tooth in the mouth'.[3] He and his followers mocked those who kissed the bones of martyrs and blasphemed the Holy Spirit. His was apparently a theology of sexual libertinism:

If anyone was 'in the Spirit', they said, even if he were to commit fornication or to be fouled by any other filthiness, there would be no sin in him, because that Spirit, who is God, being entirely distinct from the body, cannot sin. Man, who is nothing, cannot sin so long as that Spirit, who is God, is within him, for He 'worketh all in all'.[4]

---

[2] *Medieval Sourcebook: Twelfth Ecumenical Council: Lateran IV 1215.* Available at https://sourcebooks.fordham.edu/basis/lateran4.asp. See also Norman Cohn, *The Pursuit of the Millennium* (London: Paladin, 1970), pp. 152–6.
[3] Wakefield and Evans, *Heresies of the High Middle Ages*, p. 259.
[4] *Ibid.*

We do not know if William was directly influenced by Joachim of Fiore, but he was clearly, like his inspiration Almaric, working in a Joachite mode. For he told Master Ralph of Namur (who was to inform against him to the bishop of Paris) that the Father had worked under the Law, and the Son under the eucharist, baptism, and the other sacraments. Now, under the Holy Spirit, the sacraments were no more, since God would speak through those in whom he was incarnate, namely seven men, of whom he, William modestly declared, was himself one.

Like Joachim, his prophesying was apocalyptic. He predicted that, within five years, there would be four plagues. In the first of these, the people would be destroyed by famine; in the second, the nobles would kill each other by the sword; in the third, the earth would open up and swallow the townspeople; and in the fourth, fire would come down upon the prelates of the church, who were the members of the Antichrist. But he went one large step further in his apocalypticism than Joachim. Joachim, we recall, had expected the Antichrist to be a false pope. William said that the *true* pope was the Antichrist. '[T]he pope was Antichrist', he declared, 'Rome was Babylon; the pope himself reigns upon Mount Olivet, that is, in the grossness of power.'[5] And again unlike Joachim, who saw the Antichrist as both a priest and a king, William revisited the tradition of the Last World Emperor. After the defeat of the Antichrist, the whole earth would be made subject to the king of France and to his son, the future Louis VIII, who was still dauphin at the time. He would live 'in the age of the Holy

[5] *Ibid.*, p. 260.

Spirit and will not die'.[6] Rather mysteriously, the future king would be given twelve loaves 'which are the knowledge and power of the Scriptures'.[7]

Some forty years after the death of William Aurifex, in the spring of 1247 Emperor Frederick II (1194–1250) was marching his army through Tuscany. According to the *Chronicle* of the Franciscan monk Salimbene (1221–88), an aged and saintly abbot, fearing that the emperor would destroy his abbey, which lay in Frederick's path from Lucca to Pisa, fled to the Franciscan convent of Pisa. He believed that in Frederick II 'all the mysteries of iniquity should be fulfilled'.[8] In short, he believed that the emperor was the Antichrist. Now, the abbot was a follower of Joachim of Fiore. And he had taken with him to Pisa all the books of Joachim Fiore that he possessed – a 'luggage full of eschatological catalysts', as Robert E. Lerner neatly puts it – from which, no doubt, the abbot had deduced that Frederick II was the regal Antichrist from the West whom Joachim had expected.[9]

The impact of the abbot's Joachism was immediate. Brother Rudolf of Saxony, we read, 'a great logician, theologian, and disputer, left the study of theology by reason of those books of Joachim's ... and became a most

---

[6] *Ibid.*   [7] *Ibid.*

[8] G. G. Coulton, *From St. Francis to Dante: Translations from the Chronicle of the Franciscan Salimbene, 1221–1288* (Philadelphia: University of Pennsylvania Press, 1972), p. 79.

[9] Robert E. Lerner, 'Frederick II, Alive, Aloft and Allayed, in Franciscan–Joachite Eschatology', in Werner Verbeke et al. (eds.), *The Use and Abuse of Eschatology in the Middle Ages* (Leuven University Press, 1988), p. 364. I am indebted to Lerner for this discussion.

eager Joachite'.[10] Salimbene too joined the Joachite fraternity. Other Franciscans followed in the footsteps of the abbot from Lucca. The apocalypticism of Joachim was rapidly to become a key part of Franciscan theology. As Lerner remarks, 'Although the exact ways in which Joachism spread within the Franciscan Order apart from the torch-passing incident at Pisa are unknown, there is no doubt that within a half a year to a year after the spring of 1247 Guelf Joachism was endemic among the [Franciscan] Friars Minor.'[11]

The Franciscans were no doubt encouraged to endorse Joachism by the identification of themselves as those 'spiritual men' (*viri spirituales*) who, according to Joachim, would be the leaders in the age of the Holy Spirit. In addition, one of the books that may have been brought by the abbot that the Franciscans were to absorb was the so-called *Commentary on Jeremiah*. This work was attributed to Joachim, but it was actually written by followers of Joachim in the early 1240s. In this work, 'Joachim' foretold the coming of two great mendicant religious orders, an *ordo minorum* and an *ordo predicancium*. The Franciscans saw themselves as the *ordo minorum* expected by Joachim, and his apocalyptic status among the Franciscans grew accordingly.

On the other side, Frederick II was a more than likely candidate to be the Antichrist. Although Salimbene declared him gallant and, on occasion, kind, courteous, and delightful, with a sense of humour, 'Of faith in God

---

[10] Coulton, *From St. Francis to Dante*, p. 79.
[11] Lerner, 'Frederick II, Alive, Aloft and Allayed', p. 364.

he had none; he was crafty, wily, avaricious, lustful, malicious, wrathful.'[12] Of his cruelty, there was little doubt. Salimbene told of an occasion when the emperor gave two men an excellent dinner, one of whom he immediately sent off to sleep, the other to hunt. That same evening, wishing to know which had digested the better, 'he caused them to be disembowelled in his presence'.[13] Nice company for a glass of wine or two, perhaps, but don't accept an invitation to dinner.

The apocalypticism of Joachim may well have had an influence on earlier criticisms of Frederick II that emanated from the papal court. Thus, for example, Pope Gregory IX's (c. 1170–1241) manifesto of 1239, *Ascendit de Mari Bestia*, clearly cast Frederick II in the role of the Antichrist. 'The beast filled with the names of Blasphemy has risen up from the sea', it declared:

Cease to be surprised that he who now arises to destroy the name of the Lord from the earth directs an injurious sword against us. Rather, so that you may be able to resist his lies with open truth and to confute his fallacies with pure argument, carefully consider the beginning, middle, and end of this beast Fredrick.[14]

In a papal letter of 1240, *Convenerunt in unum*, he wrote in similarly apocalyptic terms: 'What other Antichrist should we await, when, as is evident in his works, he is already come in the person of Frederick? He is the

---

[12] Coulton, *From St. Francis to Dante*, p. 241.   [13] *Ibid.*, p. 243.
[14] McGinn (ed.), *Visions of the End*, pp. 173–4. This text, as well as a number of others from the court of Popes Gregory IX and Innocent IV, may have been composed by Cardinal Rainer of Viterbo and his circle.

author of every crime, stained by every cruelty, and he has invaded the patrimony of Christ seeking to destroy it with Saracen aid.'[15]

Not surprisingly, the emperor was already returning apocalyptic fire. Thus, in July 1239, in a letter entitled *In Exordio Nascentis Mundi*, he declared:

He, who is pope in name alone, has said that we are the beast rising from the sea full of the names of blasphemy and spotted like a leopard. We maintain that he is the monster of whom we read: 'Another horse arose from the sea, a red one, and he who sat thereon took away peace from the earth so that the living slaughtered one another' [Revelation 6.4.] … He has scandalised the whole world. Construing his words in the true sense, he is that great dragon who leads the world astray [Revelation 12], Antichrist, whose forerunners he says *we* are … *He* is the angel coming from the abyss bearing vials full of bitterness to harm the sea and the earth [Revelation 16.1–3].[16]

The conflict between emperor and pope continued when Cardinal Sinibaldo Fieschi was elected as Pope Innocent IV (c. 1195–1254) in 1243. In his letter *Iuxta vaticinianum Isaiae*, he pictured the emperor as the Antichrist: 'Since Frederick has in his forehead the horn of power and a mouth bringing forth monstrous things, he thinks himself able to transform the times and the laws and to lay truth in the dust, and hence he blasphemed against the Most High and uttered outrages against Moses and God.'[17] In 1245, at the Council of Lyons, Innocent IV deposed the emperor. Again, Frederick returned fire, this time showing how the numerical value of the name

---

[15] *Ibid.*, p. 169.   [16] *Ibid.*, pp. 174–5 (my italics).
[17] *Ibid.*, pp. 169–70.

'Innocencius papa' signified the number of the beast –
666: 'When the number is fully added up, the name of
the mark of the beast, that is, of the Antichrist who is
Pope Innocent, equals 666 ... There is no doubt that he
is the true Antichrist.'[18]

The belief that Frederick II was the Antichrist, and
the resulting expectation that he and his army would be
defeated when Christ returned in 1260, were to come to
nought. He died of dysentery in December 1250. The
reluctance to believe in his death, both among those who
thought good of him as well as those who thought ill, was
widespread. Salimbene declared that he 'could never have
believed that he was indeed dead, had I not heard it from
the mouth of Pope Innocent IV'.[19] 'For I was a Joachite',
he continued, 'believing and expecting and hoping that
Frederick would do yet more evil.'[20]

Death by dysentery was an inglorious end for one
expected to engage in history's greatest ever eschatological battle with Christ and his army of angels. It was
not, however, the end of the story of Frederick II as the
Antichrist. As the worst persecutor of Christianity since
the Emperor Nero, or so it was believed, it is not surprising that he was configured, like the Antichrist Nero, as
someone who was still alive or who would, at the eschatologically right time, be restored to life. It came to be
believed, for example, that he was hiding in a mountain.
The English chronicler Thomas of Eccleston reported on
news brought to the Franciscans in London by a Brother
Mansuetus. According to Mansuetus, a certain Sicilian

[18] *Ibid.*, p. 176.   [19] Coulton, *From St. Francis to Dante*, p. 245.
[20] *Ibid.*

brother had a vision, at the same time as Frederick II's death, of 5,000 knights plunging into the sea, which hissed as though their armour was molten. One of the knights was 'the Emperor Frederick entering into Mount Etna', the mouth of Hell.[21] Among his supporters, he was destined to live on as the Last Roman Emperor dwelling 'in his mountain fastness, who will one day return, establish the reign of Justice, castigate the Church, and lead the people of Christ into Jerusalem'.[22]

Alternatively, there was the expectation that he would 'return' in one of his children. Circulating from the mid 1250s, with the expectation of the return of Christ imminent in 1260, a work entitled the *Book of the Prophets' Afflictions* predicted a third Frederick, who would be a terroriser of the church. Salimbene was familiar with this work. He once read it to a friend of his, Azzo, marquis of Este, as they sat together with another friar under a fig tree.[23]

With the passing of the year 1260, and with the failure of Joachim's prediction that Christ would return in that year, the enthusiasm of the Franciscan Joachites waned. As Robert E. Lerner notes, 'the mysteries were supposed to have been "revealed" in 1260, but they patently were still shrouded in enigmas'.[24] Salimbene also lost his faith in Joachism: 'After the death of the ex-Emperor

---

[21] Father Cuthbert, *The Friars and How They Came to England: Being a Translation of Thomas of Eccleston's De Adventu F.F. Minorum in Angliam* (London: Sands & Co., 1903), p. 228.
[22] Ernst Kantorowicz, *Frederick the Second 1194–1250* (New York: Frederick Ungar Publishing Co., 1957), p. 506.
[23] Coulton, *From St. Francis to Dante*, p. 113.
[24] Lerner, 'Frederick II, Alive, Aloft and Allayed', p. 379.

Frederick, and the passing of the year 1260, then I let that whole doctrine go; and I am purposed to believe no more than I can see.'[25]

The Antichrist Mysticus

Even if Frederick failed to rise again, Joachism did not. But when it did revive among the Franciscans towards the end of the thirteenth century, their attention was to focus more on an Antichristian pseudo-pope than an Antichristian emperor. The debate about the Antichrist now became imbedded in the conflict within the Franciscans about the nature of poverty within the Franciscan tradition. This was a battle between those who, following the lead of Saint Francis of Assisi (1181/2–1226), endorsed a life of absolute poverty *versus* those who adopted a more lenient view that allowed the use of, if not the ownership of, property and possessions. From the 1280s onwards, the supporters of absolute poverty (the 'Spirituals') began to align themselves with Joachite thought and to weave Saint Francis and the 'spiritual Franciscans' into a Joachite reading of the end times. Their key spokesman was Peter Olivi (c. 1248–98), a Scholastic theologian who was to reject the dominant Scholastic philosophy of the time as a 'carnal', Islamicised Aristotelianism, and instead embrace Joachism as a 'spiritual' apocalypticism.

As we recall, Joachim had prophesied dual Antichrists – the Great Antichrist who would later be followed by Gog, the commander of the satanic army. In an original

[25] Coulton, *From St. Francis to Dante*, p. 158.

variation on Joachim, and on the Antichrist tradition more generally, Peter Olivi had the Great Antichrist *preceded* by another Antichrist, namely, the Antichrist mysticus – the mystical, hidden, or secret Antichrist. At the most general level, Olivi's doctrine of dual Antichrists – the great and the secret – was a consequence of his key principle for the interpretation of Scripture. This was to the effect that behind the literal meaning of any passage, there lay a secret or mystical meaning. Thus, in speaking of the book of Revelation, he declared, 'Know that anywhere in this book where it treats of the Great Antichrist in prophetic fashion, it also implies the time of the Mystical Antichrist preceding him.'[26]

Crucial to Olivi's interpretation of the Antichrist was where he located *himself* on the pages of history, and particularly that time when he wrote his commentary on the book of Revelation in the last few years of his life right at the end of the thirteenth century. Like Joachim, Olivi saw the history of the world up to the time of Christ in seven periods, and from the time of Christ to the end of history in a further seven periods. The first period of the second set of seven was the founding of the primitive church under the apostles. It began with Christ's resurrection and the sending of the Holy Spirit. The second was that of the persecutions of the church and its martyrs, beginning with Nero (or even with the stoning of Stephen). The third was the period of the doctrinal establishment of the faith in opposition to the heresies that sprang up.

[26] McGinn (ed.), *Visions of the End*, p. 210. This principle was itself part of a more general one to the effect that prophetic Scripture may have multiple references.

It began with the reign of Constantine and the Council of Nicea. The fourth, beginning with 'Saint Anthony the anchorite', was the period when Christians retreated from the world in favour of solitude and extreme asceticism.

The fifth period began with Charlemagne, and included the owning of possessions by both monks and clergy. The sixth was that of the reformation of the monastic traditions, the expulsion of the sect of the Antichrist, the final conversion of the Jews, and the rebuilding on earth of the church on the model of its earliest form. This sixth period began, in part, in the time of Saint Francis, but it would begin more fully 'with the destruction of the great whore Babylon', when the angel of Christ would gather the army of Christ. Finally, the seventh period would be the paradisal time of the church on earth, beginning with the death of the Antichrist and ending in the final and general judgement of the elect and the damned.[27]

As with Joachim, so also with Olivi. He combined his pattern of double sevens with a division of world history into the ages of the Father, the Son, and the Holy Spirit. The age of the Father ran until the time of Christ, the age of the Son extended from the Christ to the time of Saint Francis (periods one to five), while the age of the Spirit would begin in the sixth period and reach fulfilment in the seventh. Olivi located himself in the overlap between the end of the fifth period and the beginning of the sixth, and therefore believed that he was already in the third age (which began with Saint Francis or Joachim

[27] Warren Lewis (trans. and ed.), *Peter of John Olivi: Commentary on the Apocalypse* (New York: Franciscan Institute Publications, 2017), 'Prologue', pp. 5–8.

of Fiore). Although the third age had already begun, he nevertheless saw himself in a predominantly carnal rather than spiritual world, at the end of a period increasingly exemplified by the acceptance of a carnal philosophy (Aristotelianism) and the rejection of true spirituality (Franciscan poverty).

On the other hand, he also believed that, with the rise of Franciscanism and its ideal of poverty at the beginning of the thirteenth century, his was also a time of the recovery and of the renewal of Christian ideals. Thus, in a century in which the fifth and sixth periods overlapped, the struggle between Joachim's 'spiritual men' of the sixth and the 'carnal men' of the fifth was to be expected. Thus, too, while the Great Antichrist would only come at the final end of the fifth period, the Mystical Antichrist was already present in this overlap between the fifth and sixth periods.

Who then were the two Antichrists?[28] It is clear that, on the one hand, the Mystical Antichrist is a collective figure already working secretly since the Fall of man: 'In one way, the whole beastly mass of evil people ascends from the sea, that is, from the surpassing depth of malice or from the profound and bitter abyss of the original and, then, the actual corruption of human nature.'[29]

This collective Mystical Antichrist would soon be exemplified in an individual. Olivi seems uncertain

---

[28] On modern debates of this question and the difficulties in determining what Olivi intended, see David Burr, *Olivi's Peaceable Kingdom: A Reading of the Apocalypse Commentary* (Philadelphia: University of Pennsylvania Press, 1993), ch. 6. I am especially indebted to Burr for this discussion.

[29] Lewis (trans. and ed.), *Peter of John Olivi*, 13.20, p. 413.

whether the Mystical Antichrist would be a king or a pseudo-pope, or perhaps a combination of both. On balance, he seems to favour the Mystical Antichrist as a pseudo-pope, not least because he viewed his own time as that of a battle within the church between Franciscans and the papacy over radical poverty. '[A]t that time', he wrote, 'almost everyone will fall away from obedience to the true pope and follow the pseudo-pope, who will indeed be "pseudo" because he errs in a heretical way against the truth of evangelical poverty and perfection, and perhaps also because he will not be canonically elected but schismatically introduced.'[30]

In any case, the rise of the Mystical Antichrist will bring about a persecution of the elect. This will end only when a pagan (probably Muslim) army destroys Babylon (Rome) and the carnal church. There will then be a resurgence of the true church. Another persecution will soon begin, brought about by the Great Antichrist and symbolised both by the beast from the sea – a revived pagan power under a (probably) Muslim ruler – and the beast from the earth – a pseudo-pope probably drawn from the Franciscans themselves.

In contrast to the Mystical Antichrist who is both collective and individual, Olivi saw the Great Antichrist as an individual. Again, whether the Great Antichrist was a king or a pseudo-pope – a tyrant or a heretic, or both – is unclear. Olivi seems not to care: 'I myself do not worry much about whether he who will properly be Antichrist, be adored as God, and call himself King of the Jews, will be a king, pseudo-pope, or both. It is sufficient for me to

[30] Quoted in Burr, *Olivi's Peaceable Kingdom*, p. 145.

know that he will be deceitful and contrary to Christ.'[31] In either case, the state of the world would be so awful that Christ would then intervene to end it.

Olivi's timetable for the apocalypse is both confusing and imprecise. As David Burr wryly puts it, 'Olivi seems to be suggesting that the Holy Spirit speaks in very round figures, accurate to the nearest three centuries or so.'[32] Generally, for prophetic predictors, this is a pretty good if ultimately unhelpful strategy. And Olivi's predictions were complicated by including *both* the Mystical *and* the Great Antichrist. Still, that said, as we have seen above, the time of the *collective* Mystical Antichrist was already present. Olivi does seem to be expecting the *individual* Mystical Antichrist in the immediate future, probably around 1300 or 1301.

Thus, for example, on one calculation, in his commenting on the number of the beast in Revelation 13.18, the number 666 represented the number of years from the end of the fourth period to the Mystical Antichrist. Granted that he saw the rise of Islam as taking place at the end of the fourth period, around the year 635, this would place the Mystical Antichrist around 1301. Olivi also spoke of seven centuries between the rise of Islam and the coming of the Great Antichrist. This would place his arrival around the year 1335. In yet another calculation, Olivi dated the loosing of Satan 1,000 years after the beginning of Christendom with Constantine (say, the year 300) to around the year 1300. Olivi could line this up (more or less) with the 1,260 days (years) of Revelation 12.6 and the 1,290 days (years) of Daniel 12.11 after the

---

[31] Quoted in *ibid.*, p. 142.   [32] *Ibid.*, p. 175.

death of Christ. Thus, all of this led to the time of the Antichrists as being around the end of the thirteenth and the beginning of the fourteenth centuries.

Be all that as it may, by the middle of the fourteenth century, the third age of the Holy Spirit would have begun, with the expectation that it (and history) would end somewhere around the year 2000. As David Burr put it in 1993, 'We are coming into the home stretch and can look forward to little except our encounter with Gog.'[33] That's well past. So, as *I* write – not even that to look forward to!

Be that as it may, both Joachim of Fiore and Peter Olivi had been reluctant to point the apocalyptic finger at any *particular* pope as the Antichrist – or, at least, were not willing to name him. Not so with Olivi's Franciscan teaching colleague in Florence, Ubertino of Casale (1259– after 1325). He continued Olivi's combination of commitment to the ideal of radical poverty, his apocalypticism, and his critique of the church. Suspended from teaching as a result of his attacks on the 'carnal' church, he retired to Monte Alverna (where Saint Francis had received the stigmata) and wrote his *The Tree of the Crucified Life of Jesus* in 1305.

Like Olivi, he saw himself in a period of decadence mitigated only by the Franciscan and Dominican monastic orders. 'At the close of the fifth *status* (*period*) of the Church's pilgrimage', he declared, 'the self-indulgent were teeming like oxen, the avaricious crawling like reptiles, the arrogant as fierce as beasts, bringing an all-out defiling influence upon her life and causing

---

[33] *Ibid.*, p. 176.

her to be gnawed by a deceptive, ungodly, and heretical horde.'[34] Thus, Ubertino's own period, the sixth, saw the renewal of the true life of the gospel and the attack on the followers of the Antichrist by poor men who possessed nothing.

Ubertino identified Pope Boniface VIII (c. 1230–1303) with the beast from the sea of Revelation 13.1 and his successor, Pope Benedict XI (1240–1304), with the beast from the earth of Revelation 13.11. Thus, in Ubertino there were not only two Antichrists, the Mystical and the Great Antichrists, but also two Mystical Antichrists – Boniface VIII and Benedict XI, the latter of whose name numbered 666. The Great and the Mystical Antichrists had two evil possibilities within them: 'a fearful open evil, destructive beyond belief in all things, and an awesome hypocrisy and deceit'.[35] In the Great Antichrist, these roles were consecutive, the latter to be succeeded by the former. But 'in the two figures who are the Mystical Antichrist they are fulfilled in reverse, because the first was the open destroyer, the second the shrewd and cowardly deceiver'.[36]

The stakes in the battle between the Franciscan Spirituals and the papacy were upped by Pope John XXII (1234–1334) when he declared that the views on poverty both of the Spirituals who demanded absolute poverty and their opponents, the Conventuals, who endorsed a more relaxed version were incorrect, and that continuing to hold them was a heresy. They then became a target of

---

[34] Regis J. Armstrong et al., *Volume III of Francis of Assisi: Early Documents* (New York: New City Press, 2001), p. 146.
[35] McGinn (ed.), *Visions of the End*, p. 214.   [36] *Ibid.*

the Inquisition and were included as a heresy in Bernard Gui's *Inquisitor's Manual* (1324). Gui noted that they varied in their expectations of when the Great Antichrist would come, ranging from 1325 to 1350. But he got solid 'intelligence' from those he interrogated on their understanding of the dual Antichrists:

[T]hey teach that the Antichrist is dual; that is, there is one who is spiritual or mystical, and another, the real, greater Antichrist. The first prepares the way for the second. They say, too, that the first Antichrist is that pope under whom will occur and, in their opinion, is now occurring the persecution and condemnation of their sect.[37]

Popes Boniface VIII and Benedict XI had now been replaced by Pope John XXII as the Mystical Antichrist (see Plate 17).

It seemed to matter little to the Franciscans when the expected dates for the arrival of the Antichrist came and went. Galling as it must have been to see the expected time of the Antichrist pass with no sign of him, apocalypticism had become a core part of their self-identity. Salimbene, we recall, lost his faith in Joachism when the expected arrival of the Antichrist in 1260 failed to happen. But his loss of faith was rare. Generally, the Franciscans' understanding of their key role in Christian apocalyptic and their capacity to identify the key figures transcended their disappointment at the failure of the Antichrist to arrive. As Leigh Penman remarks, 'the mental world which engendered the prophecy is ... normally far broader and more resilient than the prophecy

---

[37] Wakefield and Evans, *Heresies of the High Middle Ages*, p. 425.

itself'.[38] Ironically, the worldview is sustained, even reinforced, by its failures in prophetic prediction – a kind of
eschatological 'doubling down'.

Mystical Prophets and an Angelic Pope

The Franciscan alchemist John of Rupescissa (c. 1310–
c. 1368)[39] remained committed to his Franciscan apocalypticism in spite of, or perhaps because of, his personal
travails. During a hearing before the papal curia in 1354,
when asked why he presumed to know the future when
so many learned doctors of the church did not, he replied
that his years of persecution and imprisonment readied
him to receive divine gifts: 'For nearly twelve years now
I have been cooked in prison cells, and the fiery boilings
do not cease, but continually burn hotter against me …
And therefore it pleases God to reveal to me – "fantastic"
and insane – the secret'.[40]

The secret that had been revealed to him was the
nature of the apocalypse that was to come and the millennium that was to follow it. A prolific writer, his final
thoughts on these matters were contained within his *Vade
mecum in tribulatione* (*Walk with Me in the Tribulation*) in

---

[38] Leigh T. I. Penman, 'A Seventeenth-Century Prophet Confronts
His Failures: Paul Felgenhauer's *Speculum Poenitentiae, Buß-Spiegel*
(1625)', in Clare Copeland and Jan Machielsen (eds.), *Angels of Light?
Sanctity and the Discernment of Spirits in the Early Modern Period*
(Leiden: Brill, 2013), p. 190.
[39] Also known as '*Jean de Roquetaillade*'.
[40] Quoted in Leah DeVun, *Prophecy, Alchemy, and the End of Time: John
of Rupescissa in the Late Middle Ages* (New York: Columbia University
Press, 2014), p. 2.

late 1356. This was a work that laid out the expected series of events between 1356 and 1370. It was translated into seven vernacular languages. In addition, various versions of the text were translated into English, French, Italian, German, Castilian, Catalan, and Czech. A Muslim version was intended to comfort Muslim minorities under Christian rule by assuring them that apocalyptic relief from their travails was imminent. It was, in short, 'a pivotal text of the European apocalyptic tradition'.[41]

Vade mecum in tribulatione, composed of twenty 'intentions', was intended to enable its possessor 'to take precautions against the imminent dangers and lead himself and others in what is to be done'.[42] Rupescissa began his account of the end time in the first intention by announcing that, before the year 1370, it was God's intention to unite the whole world in one Catholic faith under the Roman pope, not only to convert the Jews, Saracens, Turks, and Tartars, but also to wipe from the earth all schismatics, heretics, and bad Christians. To this end, it would be necessary for all the clergy, starting at the top with the cardinals, to be brought back to the way of life of the apostles. This Reformation of the church would only occur after such severe persecutions up to around 1365 that the church would almost perish. This persecution would be the inevitable result of the wickedness of most of the clergy, 'hardened in detestable arrogance toward Christ, in riches and greed, in the cult of the gluttonous stomach and of Venus'.[43]

---

[41] Matthias Kaup, *John of Rupescissa's Vade Mecum in Tribulatione* (London: Routledge, 2017), preface.
[42] *Ibid.*, Prefatory Letter, 8.   [43] *Ibid.*, Intention 3.23.

In the years between 1360 and 1365, nature would be turned upside down: 'First the worms in the earth will put on such great courage and boldness that they will most cruelly devour nearly all the lions, bears, leopards and wolves. Both the larks and the blackbirds, very small birds, will rip apart the rapacious falcons and hawks.'[44] The human hierarchy too would be levelled. There would be 'an affliction among the nobles beyond what it is possible to believe'.[45] The monastic orders, including the Franciscans, would be severely afflicted, although the Franciscan order would be restored after the tribulation and would spread throughout all the world. Disasters 'beyond all human imagination will increase, storms from the heavens, that have never been seen elsewhere, monstrous floods of water, unheard of in many parts of the world – apart from the general deluge – famines severe beyond all measure, epidemics, lethal diseases and inflammations of the gullet and other ulcerous maladies'.[46] The greater part of the population would be killed and 'the hardened reprobate' exterminated.

During this period, the first of the Antichrists would arise in the East. His disciples would preach in public in Jerusalem, with signs and portents to seduce all those who saw or heard them. The Jews would follow their false Messiah – the Eastern Antichrist – and attack Christendom, joined by the Saracens, Turks, and Tartars. In many places, the churches would be destroyed, and scarcely one in ten believers would stay faithful to the church. Before 1365, the army of the Eastern Antichrist would be on the march, laying waste for forty-two

---

[44] *Ibid.*, Intention 5.29.   [45] *Ibid.*   [46] *Ibid.*, Intention 5.31.

months (three and a half years) all Hungary and Poland, along with parts of Germany and Italy.

Around the same time, there would arise a Western Antichrist, 'a modern Nero, a false Roman emperor and death-bringing heretic, who will soon appear to afflict severely the general Church'[47] for some forty-two months. He would be the 'beast rising up out of the sea' of Revelation 13. This Antichrist would blind his followers mentally so that they would believe without any hesitation that he was the true Messiah. Since the time of the Fall, the Devil had kept certain words hidden in his mind that he would now reveal to the Western Antichrist. The Western Antichrist would then write them on parchments and place them on the forehead or hand of his followers. This was the mark of the beast of Revelation 13.16–17. Whoever bore those words on his body would not doubt 'the Antichrist and his law, and will firmly believe that he is the Messiah, and will not doubt that Jesus Christ was a seducer'.[48] Eventually all those who embraced the inscription would be damned, and those who resisted would be saved.

However, around the middle of 1362, God would send two prophets, 'two very poor, girdled, humble' Franciscan monks. They were the 'two witnesses' of Revelation 11 and would prophesy for the next three and a half years. The younger of the two was the 'mystical Elijah', the other the 'mystical Enoch', predating by a thousand years the return of the original Elijah and Enoch. Christ would cause the mystical Elijah to be elected as the pope who would restore the church:

[47] *Ibid.*, Intention 8.46.   [48] *Ibid.*, Intention 17.95.

He will certainly as Christ drive all the corrupt, lascivious and avaricious priests with this scourge – literally made of ropes from the little poor ones, the humble girdled ones – out of the Temple so that they do not serve him in sacrifice, and he will dismiss the simoniacs [those who sold spiritual goods for profit] from their clerical office, and he will hand over those who offend nature to the secular arm, to be sacrificed in fire, so that nature will be purified. He will chastise adultery. He will confine the arrogance of the clergy in excrement. He will restore to the bishoprics the ancient liberty to elect their prelates. He will drive the voracious wolves away from the flock. He will place the saintly men on a candlestick and hide the unworthy ones under a bushel.[49]

Rupescissa's Restorer Pope was one version of the 'Angelic Pope' who, it was believed, was yet to come in the Last Days. This Angelic Pope was the counterpoint to the idea of the pope as Antichrist. As Bernard McGinn points out, 'the place of the papacy in apocalyptic hopes must be always viewed from a dialectical point of view, an antithesis between hope for a coming papal messiah and dread of a pope who would be man's final enemy'.[50] It was a sign of deep disappointment in the worldliness of many of the incumbents of the See of Rome, allied with an optimistic assertion of the key role that a truly spiritual papacy had to play in any Christian apocalyptic programme.

It was Joachim of Fiore who first put forward the notion of an ideal pope yet to come. Joachim's ideal pope would play a key role in the third age of the Holy Spirit.

---

[49] *Ibid.*, Intention 12.63.
[50] Bernard McGinn, 'Angel Pope and Papal Antichrist', *Church History* 47 (1978), 155.

In 1267, sixty-five years after the death of Joachim, the English Franciscan Roger Bacon (c. 1219/20–c. 1292) prophesied the coming of an eschatological pope, as a result of whose goodness, truth, and justice, 'the Greeks will return to the obedience of the Roman Church, the greater part of the Tartars will be converted to the faith, and the Saracens will be destroyed. There will be one flock and one shepherd.'[51]

It was, however, in the 1290s that the Angelic Pope and the papal Antichrist were combined into the one vision of the end times. Thus, for example, in *The Angelic Oracle of Cyril*, we read of a future conflict between the true pope (orthopontifex) and the evil and wicked false pope (pseudopontifex), perhaps reflecting the replacement of the saintly and pro-Franciscan Pope Celestine (1215–96) after his abdication by the worldly politician and anti-Franciscan Boniface VIII in 1294. Similarly, Ubertino of Casale looked to the coming of an Angelic Pope after the defeat of both the Mystical and the Great Antichrists. He was the angel who would descend from heaven in Revelation 18.1 – 'Perhaps that Angel will be the same Supreme Pontiff spoken of above or another successor of his perfection'.[52] It is perhaps no surprise, as we will see, that the Protestant reformers will emphasise the papal Antichrist, while Catholics will continue to look to a future Angelic Pope.

It only remained for the idea of the Angelic Pope to be united with that of the Last World Emperor for both church and state to have crucial roles in the end of history. The first detailed account of this combination

[51] McGinn (ed.), *Visions of the End*, p. 190.   [52] *Ibid.*, p. 215.

was in John of Rupescissa. His Angelic Pope would also restore the world to last until its final end. To assist him, he would raise up the French king to be the Last World Emperor, an ideal Christian king of 'such a great holiness that no emperor or king since the beginning of the world ever will have equalled him in holiness except the King of Kings and Lord Jesus Christ'.[53]

Rupescissa was predicting that conflicts between Franciscans and the papacy on the one hand and church and state on the other would be eschatologically resolved. The Franciscan Angelic Pope and the Last World Emperor would unite to restore the world and destroy 'all the law and tyrannical power of Mohammed'.[54] Both the emperor and the pope would 'personally visit Greece and Asia, extinguish the schism, liberate the Greeks from the Turks, subjugate the Tartars to the faith, restore the kingdoms of Asia'.[55] The Angelic Pope and the Last World Emperor would reign for nine and a half and ten and a half years respectively.

According to Rupescissa, Christ would descend and defeat the Antichrists at the beginning of the millennium in 1365. With their demise, Satan too would be imprisoned for a thousand years. At the same time, those who died as martyrs under the Antichrists would rise again, and the conversion of the Jews and all other unbelievers would begin. In the moment before the total conversion of the world, the final remaining hard-core followers of the Antichrists ('Gog and Magog') would be chased away until the end of the millennium.

[53] Kaup, *John of Rupescissa's Vade Mecum in Tribulatione*, Intention 12.65.
[54] *Ibid.*, Intention 12.66.   [55] *Ibid.*

Around the year 2000, 700 years into the millennium, there would again be a time of increasing laxity. But it would be another 300 years before, around the year 2365, Gog and Magog would return. With them, or shortly afterwards, the Final Antichrist would arrive. To resist him, the original Elijah and Enoch would come from the earthly Paradise. At some unspecified time after that, the signs of the final end of the world would appear, and the world would end – albeit on a date known only to God.

The Radical Antichrist

By the year 1400, there were two competing accounts of the Antichrist – the Adsonian tradition and the Joachite tradition. As we have noted, the former viewed the Antichrist as an outsider to the church, the latter its very pinnacle. It reflected the polarity between the Antichrist as external tyrant and the Antichrist as internal heretic and hypocrite. So it is interesting to see these two traditions in competition with each other at exactly that time in the writings of Walter Brut (?–1402). He described himself as a sinner, a layman, a farmer, and a Christian of Welsh origins. But we can also add to that Herefordshire gentleman, soldier, preacher, Welsh freedom fighter, Latinist, and, finally, a Lollard – a follower of the English religious radical John Wycliffe (c. 1329–84).[56] It was for his Lollard theological opinions that he was called before John Trefnant, bishop of Hereford, on

[56] On the life of Walter Brut, see Maureen Jurkowski, 'Who was Walter Brut?', *The English Historical Review* 127 (2012), 285–302. See also Curtis V. Bostick, *The Antichrist and the Lollards: Apocalypticism in Late Medieval and Reformation England* (Leiden: Brill, 1998).

15 October 1391 to answer numerous charges of heresy.[57] Among other things, he was accused of holding that 'the Pope is Antichrist, and a seducer of the people and utterly against the law and life of Christ'.[58] Brut was sent away to make written responses to the charges, which he duly did in January 1392.

Brut rejected the Adsonian tradition outright. 'But forasmuch', he wrote, 'as many tales and fables are told of Antichrist and his coming and many things, which do rather seduce than instruct the hearers … we will show that the same fable sprang from the error of people imagining, and from no truth of the Scriptures prophesying.'[59] Thus, according to Brut, the Antichrist would not be born in Babylon of the tribe of Dan, nor would he come as an adversary or a king. The Jews would not be seduced by him. He would not kill Enoch and Elijah, nor would he be slain by lightning. Moreover, the predicted '1,290 days' of Daniel did not refer to the three and a half years during which the Antichrist would reign, but rather to the number of years from the time of the desolation of Jerusalem 'unto the revealing of Antichrist'.[60]

Having disposed of the Adsonian Antichrist, Brut was able to find the true Antichrist in the bishops of Rome, who, in failing to follow Christ's law of love, showed their true nature: 'Therefore, seeing they say that they are

---

[57] For the trial and documents, see William W. Capes (ed.), *The Register of John Trefnant, Bishop of Hereford (A.D. 1389–1404)* (Hereford: Wilson and Phillips, 1914). For an English translation, see S. R. Catley and J. Pratt (eds.), *The Acts and Monuments of John Foxe, Vol. III* (New York: AMS Press, 1965), pp. 131–88.

[58] Catley and Pratt, *The Acts and Monuments of John Foxe, Vol. III*, p. 132.

[59] *Ibid.*, p. 144.   [60] *Ibid.*, p. 146.

Christ's, and the chief friends of Christ; if they make and justify many laws contrary to the gospel of Jesus Christ, then it is plain that they themselves on earth are the principal Antichrists, because there is no worse plague and pestilence than a familiar enemy.'[61] Using the same biblical evidence as his Adsonian opponents, Brut marshalled an array of references to prove that the Roman bishop was 'the chief Antichrist upon the earth, and must be slain with the sword of God's word, and cast, with the dragon, the cruel beast, and the false prophet that hath seduced the earth, into the lake of fire and brimstone to be tormented world without end'.[62]

Brut's accusation was not so much of any individual pope, but of the papacy in general. The epitome of all human evil, the Antichrist, was now embodied not in any individual pope, but in all of them. The popes were *all* the enemies of Christ. More broadly, it was the papacy as an institution that was the Antichrist. As accusations go at that time, this was as big as you get. The institution to which Christ had entrusted the keys to the Kingdom of Heaven was now the Antichrist. The result was that 'the whole round world is infected and seduced ... ignorant that within a little while shall come the day of her destruction and ruin'.[63] Unfortunately for Brut, his own destruction and ruin came sooner. On 3 October 1393, Walter Brut disavowed the thirty-seven heretical conclusions of which he had been convicted and meekly submitted himself to the bishop of Hereford. Nothing more is heard of Brut until the reports of his death in 1402. Having saved himself from death for heresy, he was

[61] *Ibid.*, p. 147.   [62] *Ibid.*, p. 138.   [63] *Ibid.*

executed for treason for participating in the Welsh uprisings against Henry IV.

In viewing the institution of the papacy as the Antichrist, Brut was following in the footsteps of John Wycliffe. That 'the Antichrist' could refer to a 'collective' as much as to an individual had been a part of the story of the Antichrist since Tyconius. But the genuinely innovative move made by Wycliffe was in his restricting of the 'collective' Antichrist to the papacy and the hierarchy of the church more generally. Although Wycliffe rejected the view of the Adsonian Antichrist that he would be a Jew from the tribe of Dan, he nevertheless accepted that there would be an *individual* Antichrist who would excel in wickedness. Eventually, he was to narrow candidacy for this position to one who, whether pope or emperor or something else, would most vehemently act against the 'law of Christ' (*lex Christi*).

That said, Wycliffe's emphasis was not on the apocalyptic imminence of the Antichrist; nor was he particularly interested in predicting the time of the end. 'It is certain', he declared, 'that the time of the last judgement approaches as has been shown from the many signs and proofs that we have gathered from scripture. But just how near and precisely when it will occur no one except the foolish anxiously concern themselves ... for we will never attain that answer.'[64] Consequently, Wycliffe was able to focus on those parts of the contemporary church that he was able to identify as the Antichrist.

For Wycliffe, the Antichrist was everywhere in the church. And he had been thus since the time of the

---

[64] Quoted in Bostick, *The Antichrist and the Lollards*, p. 71.

so-called *Donation of Constantine* in 315. This document, in reality an eighth-century forgery, purported to record the Emperor Constantine's bestowal of authority over Rome and the Western part of the Roman Empire to the pope and his successors.[65] For Wycliffe, from that moment when the popes and the clergy had obtained worldly possessions and temporal power and rejected the poverty and humility of Christ, they had become Caesar's clergy and not Christ's. And therefore, not to be 'of Christ' was to be 'of the Antichrist':

For the Pope may obviously be the Antichrist, and yet not just that sole single individual, who beyond any one else promulgates laws antithetical to the law of Christ; but rather the multitude of popes holding that position since the Donation of Constantine, along with the cardinals and bishops of the church, plus their accomplices [are Antichrist].[66]

Indeed, he went on to conclude, 'the person of the Antichrist is a monstrous composite'.[67]

Until his death in 1384, Wycliffe's heresies were 'merely academic'. He was, after all, only an Oxford scholar. But his 'heretical' teachings gained significant traction after his death beyond the walls of Oxford University, sufficiently so for the Council of Constance on 4 May 1415 to condemn some forty-five of his assertions. Number 20 among these read: 'The pope is antichrist

---

[65] It was demonstrated to be a medieval forgery by Valenzo Valla in the early fifteenth century.

[66] Quoted in Bostick, *The Antichrist and the Lollards*, p. 72.

[67] Johann Loserth (ed.), *Iohannis Wyclif: Operis Evangelici Liber Tertius et Quartus sive De Antichristo Liber Primus et Secundus* (London: Wyclif Society, 1896), p. 107, lines 25–30 (my translation).

made manifest. Not only this particular person but also the multitude of popes, from the time of the endowment of the church, of cardinals, of bishops, and of their other accomplices, make up the composite, monstrous person of antichrist' (see Plate 18).[68] The Council of Constance also ordered that all Wycliffe's works should be publicly burned, and declared that he 'was a notorious and obstinate heretic who died in heresy', and that 'his body and bones are to be exhumed, if they can be identified among the corpses of the faithful, and to be scattered far from a burial place of the church'.[69]

The Council of Constance had been called for three reasons: first, to bring an end to the schism within the church as a result of its then having three different popes; second, to reform the corrupt morals of the church; and third, to eradicate heresies spread by John Wycliffe in England, and Jan Hus (c. 1370–1415) and Jerome of Prague (1379–1416) in Bohemia. Hus, Jerome, and intellectual life in Prague generally were significantly influenced by Wycliffe's writings. These had reached Bohemia soon after Wycliffe's death in 1384. Although never a Wycliffite, Jan Hus nonetheless 'imbibed deeply from the well of Wyclif's writings'.[70]

[68] 'Council of Constance 1414–18', *Papal Encyclicals Online*. Available at www.papalencyclicals.net/councils/ecum16.htm. Wyclif was not considered a devotee of university education. Number 29 of his condemned teachings reads: 'Universities, places of study, colleges, degrees and academic exercises in these institutions were introduced by a vain pagan spirit and benefit the church as little as does the devil.'

[69] *Ibid.*

[70] Thomas A. Fudge, *Jerome of Prague and the Foundations of the Hussite Movement* (Oxford University Press, 2016), pp. 40–1.

Like Wycliffe, Hus believed that the beginning of the decline of the church from its original purity was the *Donation of Constantine*. But he drew back from Wycliffe's claim that the papacy *itself* as an institution was the Antichrist. Rather, in his most important work, the *Treatise on the Church* (1411), not only popes and those within the church, but *all* those who lived *contrary to Christ* were Antichrists. Thus, authority was only to be accorded to those who acted in accordance with the precepts of Christ. 'By their fruits ye shall know them' (Matthew 7.16), he declared.[71] Moreover, he wrote, those who had become popes were not always paragons of virtue. Not only unlettered laymen and heretics had become popes, but even a woman.[72]

As for an Antichrist occupying the papal throne, he declared,

it is evident that a pope living contrary to Christ, like any other perverted person, is called by common consent antichrist. In accordance with John 2.22, many are become antichrists. And the faithful will not dare to deny persistently that it is possible for the man of sin to sit in the holy place. Of him the Saviour prophesied when he said: 'When ye see the abomination of desolation, which is spoken of by Daniel, standing in the holy place.'[73]

Hus' suggestion that a pope could be the Antichrist was one of the thirty teachings for which he was condemned

---

[71] David S. Schaff (trans.), *The Church by John Huss* (New York: Charles Scribner's Sons, 1915), pp. 47, 133.

[72] See *ibid.*, p. 127. Hus is referring to the legend of Pope Joan. See Alain Boureau, *The Myth of Pope Joan* (University of Chicago Press, 2000).

[73] Schaff (trans.), *The Church by John Huss*, pp. 128–9.

at the Council of Constance. His writings were burned, as was he on 6 July 1415. The Antichrist was now in transition from apocalyptics to politics. The so-called Hussite revolution was the active religious, political, and social resistance to the determination of the papacy to eradicate the heresies of Wycliff and Hus in Bohemia.[74]

If Hus was always a little guarded in identifying the Antichrist, his disciples were not. For his more radical followers not only the odd pope, and not only the papacy as a whole, 'but the whole fabric of late medieval Christendom reeked of the stink of Antichrist'.[75] This was the context within which Nicholas of Dresden (fl. early 1400s) wrote his *Tables of the Old and New Color* in Prague around 1411. It consisted of nine 'tables', or nine 'groups of citations of authorities', intended to contrast the primitive with the modern church, or, as the subtitle puts it, 'The way of life of Christ contrasted with the way of life of the Antichrist'.[76] Intended for a popular readership, it was probably accompanied by banners or pictures to be carried in processions or hung on church walls.

From these tables we can construct Nicholas' views of the pope, beginning with the contrast between the

[74] See Howard Kaminsky, *A History of the Hussite Revolution* (Berkeley and Los Angeles: University of California Press, 1967). See also Philip N. Haberkern, *Patron Saint and Prophet: Jan Hus in the Bohemian and German Reformations* (Oxford University Press, 2016).

[75] McGinn, *Antichrist*, p. 185.

[76] Howard Kaminsky et al. (eds.), 'Master Nicholas of Dresden, The Old Color and the New: Selected Works Contrasting the Primitive Church and The Roman Church', *Transactions of the American Philosophical Society* 55 (1965), 38. The tables may have been originally accompanied by pictures. See also Kaminsky, *A History of the Hussite Revolution*, pp. 40–9.

pope riding on a horse and Christ carrying the cross, and that between the pope receiving the *Donation of Constantine* and Christ having nowhere to lay his head.[77] The pope and his administrators in the Roman curia were seen as the wielders of power, property, and wealth, driven by greed and lust: 'Money is what the Curia likes best, / It empties many a purse and chest. / If you are stingy with your marks, / Stay away from popes and patriarchs. / But give them marks, and once their chests are filled / You will be absolved from the bondage of all your guilt.'[78] The final table was devoted to eighteen citations showing that what was said of the Antichrist by biblical and ancient authorities was applicable to the pope, and that the kingdom of the Antichrist was the Roman church.[79]

This was not so much a rallying cry for the reformation of the church as a clarion call to eschatological revolution. 'Oh Lord', Nicholas exclaimed elsewhere, 'will I live to see that blessed hour when the Whore of Revelations will be stripped bare and their flesh consumed by the fire of tribulation?'[80] It was a call that was heard by Jakoubek of Stříbro (c. 1370–1429), the founder of the Hussite movement. For him, the battle between Bohemia and Rome was that between a renewed church in Bohemia and the papal Antichrist now ruling Rome who had infiltrated the church at the time of the *Donation of Constantine*. 'Antichrist is a false Christ or Christian', he wrote, 'contrary to the truth and life and teaching of Christ in a fraudulent way, superabounding in the highest

[77] Kaminsky, *A History of the Hussite Revolution*, p. 39.   [78] *Ibid.*, p. 61.
[79] *Ibid.*, pp. 62–5.   [80] Quoted in *ibid.*, p. 48.

level of malice, covered with evil totally or in large part, possessing the highest level in the Church and claiming the highest authority over every person, clerical and lay, from fullness of power.'[81] That the papal Antichrist needed to be overthrown was at the centre of Hussite revolutionary theology. Thus, the manifesto from a Hussite congregation at Bzi Hora on 17 September 1419:

We declare in this letter, publicly and to all, that our meeting on the mountains and in the fields is for no other purpose than for freely hearing the faithful and salutary message based on the Law of God ... We also ask God, now that we have recognized the cunning and damaging seduction of our souls by false and hypocritical prophets, guided by Antichrist against the Law of God, that we may be aware of them and diligently be on our guard against them ... For we now clearly see the great abomination standing in the holy place, as prophesied by the prophet Daniel: the ridicule, blasphemy, suppression and repudiation of all of God's Truth, and the enormous glorification of all Antichristian hypocritical evil, under the name of holiness and benevolence.[82]

Nevertheless, by the 1430s, the radical edge was disappearing from the Hussite movement. With an accommodation reached between the more moderate Hussites and Rome, the 'papal Antichrist' quietly receded into the rhetorical background. He was to return a century later as reformation and revolution again threatened the Roman church. In the meantime, expectations of the imminent arrival of the Antichrist were now to be heard, not so much in the European north as in the south – in

---

[81] Quoted in McGinn, *Antichrist*, p. 331, n. 44.
[82] Quoted in Kaminsky, *A History of the Hussite Revolution*, p. 300.

the midst of the Italian Renaissance. As Marjorie Reeves remarks, 'Foreboding and great hope lived side by side in the same people … The concept of a humanist age of Gold had to be brought into relation with the ingrained expectation of Antichrist.'[83]

[83] Marjorie Reeves, *The Influence of Prophecy in the Later Middle Ages*, p. 431.

6

The Antichrist Divided

~

And I saw a woman sitting on a scarlet beast ... holding in her hand
a golden cup full of abominations and the impurities of her fornication; and on her forehead was written a name, a mystery: 'Babylon
the great, mother of whores and of earth's abominations'.

Revelation 17.3–5

The Return of Adso's Antichrist

Alongside the Joachite tradition of the papal Antichrist,
that of the Adsonian Antichrist continued. It was to
receive its most significant pictorial representation at the
end of the fifteenth century in Luca Signorelli's (c. 1450–
1523) 'The Sermon and Deeds of the Antichrist', arguably the most important portrayal of the Antichrist in
the history of Western art (see Plate 19). The Antichrist
fresco was part of Signorelli's depiction of the Apocalypse
in the chapel of the Madonna di San Brizio in Orvieto
cathedral. Surrounded by a large crowd, the Antichrist
preaches on a pedestal in front of which lie silver and
gold that he would give to corrupt the faithful. He could
easily be mistaken for Christ, since he closely resembles
Renaissance portraits of Christ, except for the fact that
he is receiving his instructions from the Devil (see Plate
20). This is an Antichrist who beguiles his listeners into
believing that he is the true Christ.

To the left, a Jewish follower of the Antichrist corrupts
the virtue of a woman by giving her money, while another

cuts the throat of a Christian who rejects the Antichrist's claims (see Plate 21). In the centre, a group of his converts watch as the Antichrist appears to raise a man from the dead (see Plate 22). To the right of the Antichrist, grey-clad Franciscans, black-clad Benedictines, and a Dominican in white consult their Antichrist texts, while one gestures towards the Antichrist overseeing a fake resurrection. The overall scene is Jerusalem, for in the background there is a newly erected Renaissance style Jewish temple, in front of which the two witnesses, Enoch and Elijah, are being executed (see Plate 23). At the top of the picture, Michael the archangel casts down the Antichrist, who has attempted to ascend to heaven in the manner of Simon Magus, to the ground from the sky (see Plate 24), while numbers of his followers are destroyed by rays from above (see Plate 25). This was Adso's life of the Antichrist in pictorial form.

It has been suggested that, in his 'The Sermon and Deeds of the Antichrist', Signorelli was referencing the Dominican friar Girolamo Savonarola (1452–98). Well, probably not.[1] But the suggestion does point to the role that Savonarola played in Italian politics as the most significant apocalyptic preacher at that time. Savonarola's apocalypticism was part of a more general eschatological effervescence that had been bubbling in Europe from around 1480.[2] For his part, Savonarola had become the effective ruler of the city of Florence from 1494 until 1498, the year before Signorelli began his work in

---

[1] See Jonathan B. Riess, *The Renaissance Antichrist* (Princeton University Press, 1995), pp. 136–8.
[2] See Denis Crouzet, 'Millennial Eschatologies in Italy, Germany, and France: 1500–1533', *Journal of Millennial Studies* 1 (1999), 1.

Orvieto. During those years, the populace of Florence had accepted Savonarola's view that the French invader, King Charles VIII, was the Last World Emperor, come to punish a corrupt church, and that Florence, so long as it repented, would be the new Jerusalem.[3]

For Savonarola himself, the end was at hand, and now was the time for Florentines to repent. I have declared to you, he said in a sermon in January 1495, 'that God's dagger will strike, and soon ... Believe me it will be soon ... So, I say this: now is the time for penance. Do not make a jest of this *cito* [*soon*], for I tell you: if you do not do what I have told you, woe to Florence, woe to the people, woe to the great and small!'[4] A year later, in his *Compendium of Revelations*, he elaborated on his vision of the end of the world and of the future for Florence:

I beheld a tempest darkening in the air with rushing clouds, winds, lightnings, thunderbolts, hail – all mixed together with fire and sword. An innumerable multitude of men was destroyed so that those who survived on earth were few ... From that time ... the city [of Florence] would be more glorious, more powerful and more wealthy than it had previously been.[5]

His views on the Antichrist are somewhat opaque, part Adsonian, part Joachite. In Joachite style, he looked

[3] For a good summary of Savonarola, see 'Introduction', in Anne Borelli and Maria Pastore Passo (trans.), *Selected Writings of Girolamo Savonarola: Religion and Politics, 1490–1498* (New Haven: Yale University Press, 2006), pp. xv–xxxvi. See also Donald Weinstein, *Savonarola and Venice: Prophecy and Patriotism in the Renaissance* (Princeton University Press, 1970).
[4] Borelli and Passo (trans.), *Selected Writings of Girolamo Savonarola*, pp. 74–5.
[5] McGinn (ed.), *Visions of the End*, pp. 281–2.

forward to a golden age with Florence at the centre. This was part of the attraction of Savonarola for his Renaissance Humanist contemporaries. He also looked towards an 'Angelic Pope' farther down the eschatological line. Moreover, that Rome, the pope, and its clergy were all corrupt was at the core of his message of reformation. Yet he seems never to have called the pope 'the Antichrist' as Joachites tended to do. Indeed, in his *A Dialogue concerning Prophetic Truth* (1496–7), he rejected the Joachite notion of a hidden Antichrist, papal or otherwise. 'Who could believe', he asked, 'that the Antichrist … has already come and is hidden from all Christians? For his coming will not be concealed, nor is it reasonable that the universal Church of the faithful, which thinks that he is yet to come, is being deceived.'[6] Nor did he accept the notion that the Antichrist had already come in the persons of Muhammad or Nero.

Thus, Savonarola's Antichrist was very much in the future. He was in no doubt that the Antichrist would arise in Jerusalem and only at the time when there were Christians in those parts – 'such Christians as are able either to stand against the Antichrist or to endure steadfastly those most abominable afflictions.'[7] The Antichrist would eventually be destroyed in the fifth age of the world, after which, in Joachite style, the world would be renovated.

In the 'bonfire of the vanities' in February 1497, Savonarola had ordered that all objects that were likely

---

[6] Borelli and Passo (trans.) *Selected Writings of Girolamo Savonarola*, p. 106.
[7] *Ibid.*, p. 107.

occasions of sin were to be burnt. That covered a pretty fair range. So mirrors, cosmetics, clothing, playing cards, musical instruments, books of divination, magic, and astrology, song manuscripts, paintings, and sculptures were all consigned to the flames in the Piazza della Signoria. Eventually, charged with heresy and sedition by Pope Alexander VI (Rodrigo Borgia, 1431–1503), he and two of his followers joined 'the vanities' and were themselves burned to death in the same square in May 1498, condemned by both the church and the Florentine state.

Ironically, Savonarola himself came to be thought of as a demonic Antichrist figure. His powers, once thought of as angelic, were now perceived as demonic. Thus, for example, Giovanni Francesco Poggio Bracciolini (1447–1522), a canon of Florence cathedral, described him as 'another Antichrist', insanely given over to the power of Satan.[8] The Augustinian monk Friar Leonardo da Fivizzano (c. 1450–1526) believed that the Antichrist was alive in Savonarola not least because his promotion of civil discord among the Florentines revealed his secret hatred of the city.[9] The Humanist philosopher and priest Marsilio Ficino (1433–99) began by thinking that Savonarola was God's chosen. But he came to see him as a prince of hypocrites led by a spirit diabolic. Of this, he declared, there were many proofs: 'a certain utterly incomparable craftiness in this Antichrist persistently feigning virtues while in truth disguising vice, a vast passion, a savage audacity, an empty boasting, a Luciferian pride, a most impudent mendacity supported at every

---

[8] Quoted in Weinstein, *Savonarola and Venice*, p. 229.
[9] *Ibid.*, p. 239.

point with imprecations and oaths'.[10] Divine inspiration was now read as demonic possession. For often, as he spoke, Ficino tells us, 'he would suddenly cry out, take fire, and thunder forth, being carried away exactly like those possessed by demons'.[11]

The death of Savonarola failed to spell the end of Italian eschatological fervour. Towards the end of the year 1500, the preacher Martino di Brozzi, in ragged garments and with matted hair, appeared, predicting imminent doom and announcing that God 'was going to punish Italy, Rome, and Florence for the death of Savonarola'.[12] Around the same time, twenty of Savonarola's disciples founded a society and elected 'pope' an illiterate man, by the name of Pietro Benardino, who had nonetheless learnt the Bible almost by heart. The church, Benardino declared, had to be purified by the sword, since there was not one just man left on the earth.[13] In 1508, the hermit Hieronymus of Bergamo appeared in Florence, proclaiming that Italy would be devastated and Rome, Venice, and Milan destroyed.[14]

Five years later, and eschatological fervour in Florence had still not diminished. On 10 December 1513, Niccolò Machiavelli (1469–1527) told his patron, Francesco Vettori, that he had 'just composed a little work On Princedoms'. A week later, on 19 December, he

[10] Borelli and Passo (trans.), *Selected Writings of Girolamo Savonarola*, pp. 355–6.
[11] *Ibid.*, p. 356.
[12] Ludwig Pastor, *History of the Popes, from the Close of the Middle Ages…* *Vol. V* (London: Kegan Paul, Trench, Trübner, & Co., 1901), p. 213.
[13] *Ibid.*, p. 215.
[14] *Ibid.*, p. 217.

wrote to Vettori of a sermon preached the day before in the church of Santa Croce by a Franciscan apocalyptic preacher, Francesco da Montepulciano, that all Florence was talking about.[15] Francesco had prophesied that in the very near future there would be an unjust pope with his own false prophets and cardinals set up against a just pope. Francesco also predicted that the king of France would be annihilated, that Florence would be sacked and burned, that its churches would be abandoned and ruined, and that plague and famine would destroy its people. 'Blood will be everywhere', he declared. 'There will be blood in the streets, blood in the river; people will sail in boats through blood, lakes of blood, rivers of blood … two million devils are loosed from hell … because more evil has been committed in the past eighteen years than in the preceding five thousand.'[16] A contemporary of Francesco's noted that he was believed by many to be a saint and that 'Thousands of people followed after him.'[17]

By 1516, the Catholic authorities had had enough of apocalyptic sermonising and the capacity of radical preaching more generally to stir up the riff-raff. Thus, the eleventh session of the Fifth Lateran Council in December 1516 determined to bring prophetical, and especially apocalyptic, preaching under ecclesiastical control. It commanded that all preaching needed to be in agreement with the traditional exposition and interpretation of the Bible without any addition contrary to or in

[15] Allan Gilbert (trans.), *The Letters of Machiavelli: A Selection of His Letters* (New York: Capricorn Books, 1961), pp. 142, 147.
[16] Quoted in Weinstein, *Savonarola and Venice*, pp. 348–9.
[17] Quoted in Ottavia Niccoli in her *Prophecy and People in Renaissance Italy* (Princeton University Press, 1990), p. 101, n. 42.

conflict with its true meaning. In particular, those who were accredited to preach were

in no way to presume to teach or declare a fixed time for future evils, the coming of antichrist or the precise day of judgment; for truth says, it is not for us to know times or seasons which the Father has fixed by his own authority. Let it be known that those who have hitherto dared to declare such things are liars, and that because of them not a little authority has been taken away from those who preach the truth.[18]

It would seem that, as a consequence, while still predicting that God would bring calamities against the sinful, preachers took heed and went a bit quiet on the Antichrist and the Day of Judgement.[19]

The Magisterial Antichrist

Within a year, the church was to be under a new challenge when, as legend has it, a young Augustinian priest named Martin Luther (1483–1546) nailed his ninety-five theses to the door of the castle church in Wittenburg on 31 October 1517. And, with that act, the Reformation and a new chapter in the life of the Antichrist began. The Roman Catholic tradition, following the lead of Adso, continued to await a future individual Antichrist and, generally speaking, the further in the future the better.

[18] 'Fifth Lateran Council 1512–17 A.D.', *Papal Encyclicals Online*. Available at www.papalencyclicals.net/councils/ecum18.htm. See especially Nelson H. Minnich, 'Prophecy and the Fifth Lateran Council (1512–1517)', in Nelson H. Minnich (ed.), *Councils of the Catholic Reformation: Pisa 1 (1409) to Trent (1545–63)* (Aldershot: Ashgate Variorum, 2008), pp. 63–87.
[19] Niccoli, *Prophecy and People in Renaissance Italy*, p. 104.

The Protestant tradition, give or take a bit of toing and froing, knew that the Antichrist was already individually and collectively present, and was to be identified with the pope and the institution of the papacy. For the next 300 years, these different understandings of the Antichrist were to be deeply embedded in the confessional conflicts between Catholics and Protestants.

In December 1536, the Saxon elector John Frederick commissioned Luther to write a statement of his reform programme. Luther took his finished statement to a gathering of Lutheran princes in Smalcald, Hesse, and it was endorsed by most of the theologians present as a summary of their collective faith. Among the so-called Smalcald Articles was Luther's considered opinion on the Antichrist. The 'Fourth Article' begins by declaring that 'the pope is not the head of all Christendom "by divine right" or on the basis of God's Word, because that belongs only to the one who is called Jesus Christ. Instead, the pope is only bishop, or pastor, of the church at Rome.'[20] As a consequence, everything that the pope has done on the basis of 'such false, offensive, blasphemous, arrogant power was and still is a purely diabolical affair and business'.[21]

Luther was convinced that he was living in the end times. The result of this was that he was able to equate the final Antichrist and the papal Antichrist. All this shows overwhelmingly, he declared, 'that he [the pope] is the true endtimes [Endchrist] Antichrist [Widerchrist]

---

[20] Timothy Lull and William R. Russell (eds.), *Martin Luther's Basic Theological Writings* (Minneapolis: Fortress Press, 2012), p. 348.
[21] *Ibid.*

who has raised himself over and set himself against Christ'.[22] Moreover, the pope damns, slays, and plagues all Christians who refuse to exalt and honour him. Just as Christians would not worship the Devil as God, 'so we cannot allow his apostle the pope or Antichrist, to govern as our head or lord'.[23]

Nineteen years earlier, in late 1517, Luther's views on the relationship between the papacy and the Antichrist were already developing. Thus, for example, on 11 December 1517, he was flirting with the idea. 'I will send you my playful remarks', he wrote to fellow Augustinian Wenceslaus Link, 'so you may see, whether I am right in guessing, that the true Antichrist, according to Paul, reigns in the Roman Court: I think I am able to prove that he [the pope] is now worse than the Turks.'[24] A few months later, he was floating the idea to his friend Georg Spalatin. Between you and me, he wrote, 'I do not know whether the Pope is Antichrist himself, or his Apostle: so miserably is Christ (that is, truth) corrupted and crucified by him in the decrees'.[25]

The 'imperial papacy' was the consequence of the *Donation of Constantine*. This document, we recall, purported to record Emperor Constantine's bestowal of authority over Rome and the Western part of the Roman Empire to the pope and his successors.[26] In 1440, the Italian Humanist Lorenzo Valla (c. 1407–57) demonstrated in his *On the Donation of Constantine* that the *Donation of Constantine* was an eighth-century forgery.

---

[22] *Ibid.*, p. 349.   [23] *Ibid.*, p. 350.
[24] Henry O'Connor, S.J., *Luther's Own Statements concerning His Teaching and Its Results* (New York: Benziger Brothers, 1885), p. 9.
[25] *Ibid.*, p. 10.   [26] See Chapter 5 above.

Luther was reading Valla's work in February 1520. He wrote to Spalatin that he was staggered that 'such unauthentic, crass, impudent lies not only lived but prevailed for so many centuries'. It led him to his conviction that the pope was the Antichrist. 'I am in such a passion', he wrote, 'that I scarcely doubt that the Pope is the Antichrist expected by the world, so closely do their acts, lives, sayings and laws agree.'[27]

Luther was soon to go public with this new-found conviction. He was motivated to do so by an attack on his teachings by the Dominican Sylvester Prierias (c. 1456–1527), Luther's first Italian literary opponent, and Pope Leo X's (1475–1521) theological advisor and censor of books. In his *Epitome of a Response to Martin Luther* in 1519, Prierias had declared that a pope could not be judged or deposed even if his behaviour were so scandalous as to lead people with him into the possession of the Devil in hell. In June of 1520, in his *Address to the Christian Nobility*, Luther accused Prierias of being Rome's chief devil for saying that the pope could not be deposed. 'At Rome', he declared, 'they build on this accursed and devilish foundation, and think that we should let all the world go to the devil rather than resist their knavery … It is to be feared that this is a game of the Antichrist, or at any rate that his forerunner has appeared.'[28] Moreover, by accepting money to dissolve oaths, vows, and agreements, the pope was exalting himself above God:

[27] Preserved Smith, *The Life and Letters of Martin Luther* (Boston and New York: Houghton Mifflin, 1911), p. 73.
[28] Martin Luther, *To the Christian Nobility of the German Nation*, in Timothy J. Wenger (ed.), *The Annotated Luther, Vol. I* (Minneapolis: Augsburg Fortress, 2015), pp. 386–7.

If there were no other base trickery to prove that the pope is the true Antichrist, this one would be enough to prove it. Hear this, O pope, not of all men the holiest but of all men the most sinful! O that God from heaven would soon destroy your throne and sink it in the abyss of hell! ... Thus through your voice and pen the wicked Satan lies as he has never lied before. You force and twist the Scriptures to suit your fancy. O Christ, my Lord, look down; let the day of your judgment burst forth and destroy this nest of devils at Rome. There sits the man of whom St. Paul said, 'He shall exalt himself above you, sit in your church, and set himself up as God, that man of sin, the son of perdition' [2 Thessalonians 2.3–5]. What else is papal power but simply the teaching and increasing of sin and wickedness? Papal power serves only to lead souls into damnation in your name and, to all outward appearances, with your approval![29]

A few months later, in October of 1520, Luther appeared to broaden his attack from the pope as the Antichrist (see Plate 26) to the institution of the papacy. Thus, in *The Babylonian Captivity of the Church*, he declared that the papacy was 'truly the kingdom of Babylon and of the very Antichrist'.[30]

For his part, the pope was also upping the theological ante. On 10 December 1520, Luther received the papal bull *Exsurge Domine* condemning forty-one of his 'errors', exhorting him to recant, and calling for his books to be burned 'publicly and solemnly in the presence of

[29] *Ibid.*, pp. 441–2.
[30] Martin Luther, *The Babylonian Captivity of the Church*, in Paul W. Robinson (ed.), *The Annotated Luther, Vol. III* (Minneapolis: Augsburg Fortress, 2016), p. 75.

the clerics and people'.[31] Luther was quick to respond, in his *Defence and Explanation of All the Articles*. Luther's 'Antichrist' rhetoric now reached its heights. 'The Antichrist' and 'the pope' are now virtually synonymous:

Now burn and condemn books, pope. So shall God cast thee down and give thee up to madness, that thou mayst receive the reward thou has merited, because thou strives always against divine truth. Let him doubt who will that the pope, who spreads more than enough of these errors throughout the world and receives in return for it the wealth of the nations, is the true, chief, final Antichrist. Thank God, I know him.[32]

In his *Defense and Explanation* of 1521 Luther saw himself as part of a tradition of reform that went back to John Wycliff, John Hus, Jerome of Prague, and Girolamo Savonarola. Hus and Jerome, he wrote, were good Christians 'burned by heretics and apostates and antichristians, – the papists, – for the sake of the holy Gospel'.[33] Other good Christians such as Savonarola were burned 'according to the prophecy concerning Antichrist that he will cast Christians into the oven … That is the way the holy church of the papists doeth God service'.[34] From this position on the papal Antichrist, Luther was never to waver.

Luther's supporters were to follow suit. Thus, for example, the Lutheran reformer Andreas Osiander (1498–1552)

[31] *Exsurge Domine: Condemning the Errors of Martin Luther.* Available at www.papalencyclicals.net/leo10/l10exdom.ht
[32] *Works of Martin Luther, Translated with Introductions and Notes, Vol. III*, p. 48. Available at http://media.sabda.org/alkitab-8/LIBRARY/LUT_WRK3.PDF
[33] *Ibid.*, p. 91.   [34] *Ibid.*

openly preached on the papal Antichrist as early as 1524. 'I proved to my listeners, solely from the Holy Scriptures', he wrote, 'who this Antichrist is ... and did not need to give any additional comments on them ... When Constantine moved out of Rome, the Antichrist moved in.'[35] The aim of his *Coniectures of the Ende of the World* was to give a clear and brief exposition of Scripture 'concerning this last monarchy of Rome, the description and lively picture of that Antichristian horned whore, of her fall, and end of this world, shortly to come' (see Plate 27).[36]

For the better part of the sixteenth century, however, Europe had felt itself under threat from the Ottoman Turks. With the Turks at the gates of Vienna in 1529, Luther came to view them as a demonic army and a part of the Antichrist. 'Antichrist is the pope and the church together', he is reported to have said, 'a beast full of life must have a body and soul; the spirit or soul of antichrist is the pope, his flesh or body the Turk. The latter wastes and assails and persecutes God's church corporally; the former spiritually and corporally too, with hanging, burning, murdering, etc.'[37] Luther did believe that the Turks were part of the demonic forces that would engage in the final eschatological battle: 'Because the end of the world is at hand, the Devil must attack Christendom with both of his forces.'[38]

[35] Quoted in Le Roy Edwin Froom, *The Prophetic Faith of Our Fathers... Vol. II* (Washington, DC: Review and Herald, 1948), pp. 295–6.
[36] Andreas Osiander, *The Coniectures of the Ende of the World* (Antwerp, 1548), sigs. A.3.r–v. I have modernised the spelling in this citation.
[37] William Hazlitt (trans.), *The Table Talk of Martin Luther* (London: George Bell and Sons, 1909), no. 429, p. 193.
[38] Quoted in Adam S. Francisco, *Martin Luther and Islam: A Study in Sixteenth-Century Polemics and Apologetics* (Leiden: Brill, 2007), p. 84.

However, in his writings rather than in reports of his conversations, while recognising that both the papacy and the Turks were demonic, Luther seemed to pull up short of identifying the Turk with the Antichrist. Thus, for example, in his *On War against the Turk* in 1529, he declared,

The pope, as a true Antichrist, along with his followers, wages war, commits murder, and robs not only his enemies, but also burns, condemns, and persecutes the innocent, the pious, and the orthodox. And he does this while sitting in the temple of God [2 Thessalonians 2.4] as head of the church, something the Turk does not do. But just as the pope is the Antichrist, so the Turk is the very Devil incarnate. Our prayer, and the prayer of Christendom, is against both – that they would go down to hell, even though it may take the Last Day to send them there, a day which I hope will not be far off.[39]

Luther's position on the double Antichrist was sufficiently ambivalent for Lutherans to be divided on the issue. That the Turks were a part of the Antichrist probably correlated with the immediacy of any Ottoman military threat. It also aligned with the traditional views that the Antichrist would come from the East and that he would be a tyrant from outside the church. Martin Luther's friend and defender Nicholas von Amsdorf (1483–1565) was determined to emphasise the papal Antichrist alone. Against the possibility that the Turk was the Antichrist, he argued that the Antichrist

[39] Martin Luther, *On War against the Turk*, in Hans J. Hillerbrand (ed.), *The Annotated Luther, Vol. V* (Minneapolis: Augsburg Fortress, 2017), pp. 363–4.

will be revealed and come to naught before the last day, so that every man shall comprehend and recognise that the pope is the real, true Antichrist and not the vicar of Christ ... Therefore those who consider the pope and his bishops as Christian shepherds are deeply in error, but even more so are those who believe that the Turk is the Antichrist.[40]

Amsdorf rejected the Adsonian Antichrist. The Antichrist was the hidden hypocrite within the church and not the open tyrant outside it. Thus, the Turk could not be the Antichrist: 'Because the Turk rules outside the church and does not sit in the holy place, nor does he seek to bear the name of Christ but is an open antagonist of Christ and his church. This does not need to be revealed, but it is clear and evident because he persecutes Christians openly and not as the pope does, secretly under the form of godliness.'[41]

That the papacy was the Antichrist was to be the default Lutheran position. It was to become dominant within Protestantism more generally. Like Luther, the French reformer John Calvin (1509–64) believed that the end of the world was at hand. But Calvin was clearer than Luther in his belief that Islam was part of the Antichrist. The Antichrist, according to Calvin, was not an individual. Rather, not only the Ottoman Turks but the religion of Islam from its beginnings, along with the institution of the papacy, was the Antichrist – a part of the 'falling away' and the revelation of the man of sin and the son of perdition that had to occur before Christ would come again (2 Thessalonians 2.1–3):

---

[40] Froom, *The Prophetic Faith*, p. 305.   [41] *Ibid.*

It was no better than an old wife's fable that was contrived respecting Nero, that he was carried up from the world, destined to return again to harass the Church by his tyranny; and yet the minds of the ancients were so bewitched, that they imagined that Nero would be Antichrist. Paul, however, does not speak of one individual, but of a kingdom, that was to be taken possession of by Satan, that he might set up a seat of abomination in the midst of God's temple – which we see accomplished in Popery. The revolt, it is true, has spread more widely, for Mahomet, as he was an apostate, turned away the Turks, his followers, from Christ ... Paul, however, when he has given warning that there would be such a scattering, that the greater part would revolt from Christ, adds something more serious – that there would be such a confusion, that the vicar of Satan would hold supreme power in the Church, and would preside there in the place of God.[42]

The papal Antichrist, with or without the 'Turks', was foundational for the Calvinist or Reformed tradition. Thus, for example, the Swiss reformer Ulrich Zwingli (1483–1531) declared, 'I know that in its works the might and power of the Devil, that is, of the Anti-Christ ... The Papacy has to be abolished.[43] Zwingli's successor, Heinrich Bullinger (1505–75), rejected the reading of the little horn of Daniel as Islam in favour of the papacy. 'By

[42] John Calvin, *Commentary on Philippians, Colossians, and Thessalonians* (Grand Rapids, Michigan: Christian Classics Ethereal Library, n.d.), pp. 297–8. Available at www.ccel.org/ccel/calvin/calcom42.pdf. See also John T. McNeill, *Calvin: Institutes of the Christian Religion, Vol. II* (Louisville, Kentucky: Westminster John Knox Press, 2006), 7.7.25, pp. 1144–5.

[43] Stephen J. Vicchio, *The Legend of the Antichrist: A History.* E-book (Kindle edition) (Eugene, Oregon: Wipf and Stock, 2009), location 4387.

the little horn', he declared, 'many understand the kingdom of Muhammed, of the Saracens and the Turks ... but when the apostolic prophecy in Second Thessalonians 2 is more carefully examined, it seems that the prophecy of the apostle belong more rightly to the kingdom of the Roman Pope.[44]

The identification of the papacy with the Antichrist crossed over to Scotland and England as Calvinism took a hold there. The leader of the Scottish Reformation, John Knox (1505–72), began his history of the Reformation in Scotland with the words:

It is not unknowen, Christeane Reader, that the same clud [cloud] of ignorance, that long darkened many realms under this accursed kingdome of that Romane Antichrist, hath also overcome this poore Realme ... But that same God that caused light to schyne out of darkness ... hath of long tyme opened the eis of some evin within this Realm, to see the vanitie of that which then was universally embrased for trew religioun.[45]

For his 'soft Calvinism', the English reformer Archbishop Thomas Cranmer (1489–1556) was burned at the stake by the Catholic Queen Mary. But before thrusting his hand into the fire that was to consume him, his last words were, 'And forasmuch as my hand offended in writing contrary to my heart, therefore my hand shall first be punished. For if I may come to the fire, it shall first be burned. And as for the Pope, I refuse him, as Christ's enemy and antichrist with all his false doctrine.[46]

---

[44] *Ibid.*, location 4387.
[45] David Laing (ed.), *The Works of John Knox: Volume First* (Edinburgh: James Thin, 1895), p. 3.
[46] 'Thomas Cranmer's Final Speech, before Burning (March 21, 1556).' Available at www.luminarium.org/renlit/cranmerspeech.htm

Revisiting the Book of Revelation

As we know, from the time of Irenaeus, the story of the Antichrist had been closely interwoven with the interpretation of the book of Revelation, even though there is no mention of the Antichrist within that book. Within the Reformation period, new readings of Revelation were to reinforce the judgement that the Antichrist was to be found in the institution of the papacy and had been present there since its inception.

The magisterial reformers, Luther and Calvin in particular, had serious reservations about the book of Revelation. Throughout his career, Calvin avoided writing a commentary on it. In his preface to the book in the 1522 edition of the Luther Bible, Luther declared, 'My mind cannot reconcile itself to this book and for me it is reason enough not to value his [the author's] mind when I see that Christ is neither taught nor recognized in this work.[47] Still, by the time of the 1530 preface to the same book, Luther had changed his mind. For he had recognised by then that, if it failed to teach Christ, Revelation seemed to have plenty to say about the Antichrist, and it provided grist for his antipapal mill.

The Antichrist had been identified with the papacy in any number of radical fourteenth- and fifteenth-century commentaries on Revelation. And it was when one of these came to light in Wittenberg in the 1520s – the anonymous *Commentarius in Apocalypsin ante centum annos aeditus* – that Luther realised that he was not alone in

---

[47] Irena Backus, *Reformation Readings of the Apocalypse: Geneva, Zurich, and Wittenberg* (Oxford University Press, 2000), p. 7. I am indebted to Backus for this discussion of Luther.

interpreting the papacy to mean the reign of Antichrist and wrote an enthusiastic preface to this effect. The key factor in this commentary was not only that it provided Luther with a schema that enabled him to identify the Antichrist with the papacy, but also that it did so in the context of an interpretative scheme that was to be the central feature of Protestant readings of Revelation.

This central feature was that Revelation was not to be read merely or only allegorically or spiritually, but historically in the broadest sense – as a book about the past, the present, and the future. As Luther put it in his 1530 preface to the book of Revelation, 'This book contains things that God revealed to John and that John revealed to the Church; it tells us how great are the tribulations that the Church suffered in its early days and suffers now and will suffer at the time of the Antichrist.[48]And what mattered to Luther was that Satan, who had been bound since the early days of the church, was about to be unleashed, that he was about to march across the earth with Gog and Magog (now identified with the Turks), and that the Last Judgement was to follow shortly afterwards. Thus, within Protestantism, as within Joachite readings of Revelation, it became a text that, correctly decoded, could enable readers to understand their past, pinpoint their present in the history of salvation, and predict their future.

In the context of Protestant apocalypticism, then, the book of Revelation assumed an importance it had not had previously. As the English bishop John Bale (1495–1563) put it in 1545, in his commentary on the book *The Image of Both Churches*:

[48] Quoted in *ibid.*, p. 9.

Not one necessary point of belief is in all the other Scriptures, that is not here also in one place or another. The very complete sum and whole knitting up is this heavenly book of the universal verities of the bible ... He that knoweth not this book, knoweth not what the Church is whereof he is a member. For herein is the estate thereof from Christ's ascension to the end of the world.[49]

Bale's book was an encyclopaedia of apocalyptic sources – from Irenaeus and Hippolytus to Joachim, Wycliff, Valla, and Savonarola, and thence to Luther and Calvin. And it was littered with references to the papal Antichrist.[50] Thus, for example, of 'the beast of the bottomless pit' (Revelation 11.7), he wrote, 'The beast of the bottomless pit is the cruel, crafty, and cursed generation of antichrist, the pope with his bishops, prelates, priests, and religious in Europe, Mahomet with his doting dousepers [douze pers, twelve peers] in Africa, and so forth in Asia and India; all beastly, carnal and wicked in their doings.'[51] The murder of the two witnesses (Revelation 11.7–8) now became the tormenting of the Protestant reformers and their followers when 'they [papists] hate them, curse them, blaspheme them, and persecute them'.[52] In short, the book of Revelation had become the Protestant manifesto against the Catholic intolerance of reform.

John Napier's (1550–1617) commentary, *A Plaine Discovery of the whole Revelation of Saint John*, first published in 1593, was anything but plain. But it had a similarly political edge. The immediate reason for the

---

[49] Henry Christmas (ed.), *Select Works of John Bale, D.D.* (Cambridge University Press, 1849), p. 252.
[50] By my count, some eighty-three references.
[51] Christmas (ed.), *Select Works of John Bale*, p. 392.   [52] *Ibid.*

publication of the work, in a hurry and in English rather than the Latin originally planned, was the so-called affair of the Spanish blanks in 1592. The discovery of letters and blank documents showed that several Catholic nobles (among them Napier's father-in-law) were conspiring with Spain to overthrow King James VI (1566–1625) of Scotland (also James I of England from 1603). Napier was no doubt keen to indicate that, unlike his wife's father, he was loyal to his Protestant ruler. The work was dedicated to King James and the 'Epistle Dedicatory', reading Revelation as a book about kingdoms for kings, makes no bones about the fact that the king needed to clear his own house, family, and court of all those not passionately of the Protestant persuasion:

Let it be your M. continuall study ... to reforme the universall enormities of your country, and first ... to begin at your M. owne house, familie and court, and purge the same of all suspicion of Papists, and Atheists or Newtrals, whereof this Revelation foretelleth, that the number shall greatly increase in these latter daies. For shall any Prince be able to be one of the destroiers of that great seate, and a purger of the world from Antichristianisme, who purgeth not his own countrie? Shal he purge his whole country, who purgeth not his owne house? Or shal hee purge his house who is not purged himselfe by priuate meditations with his God?[53]

---

[53] John Napier, *A Plaine Discovery of the whole Revelation of Saint John: set down in two Treatises: the one searching and proving the true Interpretation thereof: the other applying the same paraphrastically and historically to the text* (Edinburgh: Robert Waldegrave, 1593), sigs. A.3.v–A.4.r. Napier is most remembered today as the inventor of algorithms. On Napier, see Philip C. Almond, 'John Napier and the Mathematics of the "Middle Future" Apocalypse', *Scottish Journal of Theology* 63 (2010), 54–69.

Napier, of course, knew full well that James had (notionally anyway) already done his own bit of personal purging in his work on Revelation in his *Ane fruitfull Meditatioun* (on Revelation 20.7–10) in 1588. And he knew that the king had claimed a divine right authoritatively to interpret the text. Napier knew too that the king would be sympathetic to his reading of it. For James, like other Protestant readers, saw Revelation as a 'speciall cannon against the Hereticall wall of our common adversaries the Papists'.[54] So Napier's work was not an injunction to passively await the end, imminent as that might be, but an incitement to Christian kings to continue the work of the reformers and purge the world of the Antichrist.

For Napier, the papacy was identical with the Antichrist. He would reign for 1,260 years, beginning in the year 300 at the earliest or 316 at the latest, this being the time in which the church became a tolerated religion and the power of the papacy was established. In this calculation, the reign of the Antichrist was therefore ending around 1560 (the year in which, not coincidentally we might say, Scotland declared itself 'Reformed') to 1576. Napier also held that Satan was bound at the same time as the Antichrist took power in Rome. So God was seen as cleverly balancing, as it were, the amount of evil in the world by binding Satan while simultaneously allowing the reign of the Antichrist in the persons of the popes. Satan was then loosed around the year 1300 to stir up the armies of Gog and Magog – the 'Papistical and Mahometicke' armies – at that time.

[54] James I, King of England, *The Workes of the most high and mightie Prince, James by the Grace of God, King of Great Britaine, France and Ireland* (London, 1616), p. 2.

In Napier's own eyes, he was living in the good times. The complete time for revelation and knowledge had now come. And he was living in the Last Days, with the end perhaps only a hundred years away. So there was, in Napier's reading of Revelation, no sense that the world needed radical social and political reform. On the contrary, as his commentary showed, God was working his purposes out, the reign of Antichrist was over, and the true church in a true society could and would now come to the fore.

This was a vision of hope rather than doom. The end was close – knowledge, wisdom, and truth were increasing. But it was not so close that everyone could down tools and passively await it. Nor should the time be hastened by turning the world upside down. Napier's importance lies in his reading of Revelation in terms of a monarchical conservatism. His was a socially and politically moderate vision of the end times. But it was still a socially active one. To spread the gospel, to bring in Reformed religion, and to fight the Antichrist were eschatological obligations. And they were laid upon both king and people.

The Empire Strikes Back

Not surprisingly, the Roman Catholic church retaliated against the Protestant claim that the papacy was the Antichrist. It did this by re-reading the book of Revelation to distance it from the present. And it did this in two quite different ways. On the one hand, it read Revelation as a text that covered the first few centuries of the Christian era only, although some place was occasionally left for the last three and a half years of history (preterism). On the other hand, it read it as a text relevant mostly to the last three and a half years of the Antichrist, preceding the end of the world (futurism).[55]

The former of these was exemplified in the Jesuit Luis de Alcazar's (1554–1613) 900-page commentary on Revelation entitled *Vestigatio Arcani Sensus in Apocalypsi* (*An Investigation into the Hidden Sense of the Apocalypse*). According to Alcazar, the prophecies of Revelation described the victory of the early church, as fulfilled in the downfall of the Jewish nation and the overthrow of pagan Rome. In this scenario, the Antichrist was equated with the original Emperor Nero.[56] For those preterists steeped in the Adsonian tradition, this was a bridge too far. A place needed to be found for a future Antichrist. Thus, for example, although the French Catholic bishop Jacques Bossuet (1627–1704) found the first nineteen chapters of Revelation fulfilled in the early church, he still found a place for the future Antichrist who would arise at the end of the world in Revelation 20.9–17. Similarly, the French Benedictine monk Augustin Calmet (1672–1757) held that 'the greater part of the book of Revelation must be regarded as having had its accomplishment in the earlier centuries of the church'.[57] He admitted that Antiochus Epiphanes and Nero were so many Antichrists in the sense of being forerunners of the Antichrist. But he defined the Antichrist as a future individual – 'that Man of Sin who is expected to precede the second coming of our

---

[55] See Kenneth G. C. Newport, *Apocalypse and Millennium: Studies in Biblical Eisegesis* (Cambridge University Press, 2000), ch. 1.
[56] See Froom, *The Prophetic Faith*, pp. 506–9.
[57] Charles Taylor (ed.), *Calmet's Dictionary of the Holy Bible* (Boston: Crocker and Brewster, 1832), p. 80.

Saviour'.[58] This preterist position was to have a limited influence in Protestantism as a result of its adoption by the Dutch historian and theologian Hugo Grotius (1583–1645) and his English follower Henry Hammond (1605–60).[59] Grotius was clearly attempting some rapprochement between Catholics and Protestants, but Catholics viewed him as little more than a Protestant puppet.

As we recall, there is no specific mention of the Antichrist in the book of Revelation. But from the time of Irenaeus in the second century, the Antichrist had been read into it as a key player in the Christian eschatological drama. So those inclined towards a strongly preterist reading of Revelation like Alcazar's were reading very much against the dominant Antichrist tradition, one informed not only by the prevalent reading of Revelation until the time of the Reformation, but reinforced from the end of the first millennium by Adso's biography of the Antichrist. So it is not perhaps surprising that, in its pushback against the Protestant papal Antichrist, Catholic interpreters of the book looked to a futurist reading and to an Antichrist outside the church.

Of these futurist interpreters, the most influential was the Italian Jesuit cardinal Robert Bellarmine (1542–1621). He is most remembered for his conflict with Galileo over the issue of the sun-centred cosmos.[60] But his critique of the idea of a papal Antichrist was part of his *Lectures on*

---

[58] *Ibid.*, p. 70.
[59] On Grotius and Hammond, see Froom, *The Prophetic Faith*, pp. 521–4 and 524–5.
[60] See Richard J. Blackwell, 'Galileo Galilei', in Gary B. Ferngren (ed.), *Science & Religion: A Historical Introduction* (Baltimore and London: The Johns Hopkins University Press, 2002), pp. 105–16.

Controversies of the Christian Faith against the Heretics of This Time (1581–93), a work that was to become a standard for contemporary Roman Catholic doctrine. It was a vehement reassertion of the Adsonian Antichrist.

His basic strategy was simple. A close examination of the Scriptures read in the light of the early church fathers, together with a detailed critique of the particular Protestant arguments on the papacy as the Antichrist, could not but show that the Antichrist could not be the papacy either in the past or in the present. Rather, he would be a single individual who would only reign for the three and a half years right before the end of the world. The consensus of the fathers, he declared, was that the Antichrist would reign until the end of the world. Hence,

if the world is going to end immediately after the death of Antichrist and Antichrist will not be alive three and a half years after he appears, then it is clear that he will not appear or begin to reign except for three and a half years before the end of the world. But the Pope now, according to our adversaries, has reigned with both swords for more than five hundred years but still the world still endures.[61]

Bellarmine reinforced this key argument by declaring that a number of the essential components of the times before and during the time of the Antichrist were not yet in evidence – the desolation of the Roman Empire, the arrival of Enoch and Elijah, persecutions by the Antichrist, the three and a half years of the Antichrist's reign, and the imminence of the end of the world. As for

---

[61] Ryan Grant (trans.), *Antichrist: St. Robert Bellarmine, S.J.* E-book (Kindle edition) (Post Falls, Idaho: Mediatrix Press, 2016), location 894.

the number of the beast and the name of the Antichrist, 'the truest opinion of this matter is of those who confess their ignorance and say that they still do not know the name of Antichrist'.[62]

From the details woven into Bellarmine's text, we can construct his life of the Antichrist, one that proceeds essentially along Adsonian lines. He was not the Devil himself, nor the Devil incarnate, nor would he be born of a virgin by a work of the Devil as Christ was born of a virgin by a work of the Holy Spirit. Nor was he Nero, either resurrected or reappearing. It is probable, he declared, that the Antichrist would be born from a woman by fornication. It is exceedingly probable that he would be born as a Jew from the tribe of Dan and be circumcised. It is also probable that he would come on account of the Jews and be received by them as if he were the Messiah. He would rule over the Jews by fraud and treachery. Far from Rome being the seat of the Antichrist, he would rule in Jerusalem, on the throne of David in the temple of Solomon.

When the Antichrist came, he would deny that Jesus was the Christ and oppose all the things that Christ established – baptism, confirmation, and so on. He would teach that the Sabbath, circumcision, and other ceremonies of the old law were still valid. He would also assert that he was the true Christ, would declare that he was God, and would demand to be worshipped as such. He would also perform such miracles as raising the dead and healing the sick, but these would be the illusions of demons.

[62] *Ibid.*, location 979.

He would engage in warfare against the kings of Egypt, Libya, and Ethiopia, and eventually kill them and occupy their kingdoms. The remaining seven kings would be subjected to him, and he would rule over them all. Eventually there would be the last battle of the Antichrist (Gog) and his army (Magog) against the church. The church would gain the victory in this final battle. Christ would defeat the Antichrist and God the Devil.

Bellarmine gave no indication of when all this might happen. He had no interest in apocalyptic arithmetic and criticised those who did have.[63] That said, he was sympathetic to the idea that the world would last for 6,000 years from its creation around 4000 BCE, and that it therefore had 400 years yet to run. Nevertheless, he wrote, 'St. Augustine bitterly rebuked those who asserted that the world is going to end at a certain time, when the Lord said: "It is not for us to know the time and the hour which the Father has placed in his power".'[64] This was no doubt a deliberate strategy. The stability of the Roman Catholic church depended on minimising expectations that the end of the world was at hand and on pushing it well into the future. Only thus could the imminent Antichrist of the Protestant radicals be intellectually restrained.

The Antichrist of the Radical Reformation

Luther and Calvin were reformers, not revolutionaries. They were unsympathetic to those groups of radical dissenters within the Reformation that were to become

---

[63] See *ibid*., location 309.   [64] *Ibid*.

known as the Radical Reformation.[65] The Radical Reformation was to broaden the Protestant understanding of the Antichrist. For the Radicals, the Antichrist was a collective term for all those who, since the days of the apostles, had persecuted the church. Thus, for example, Sebastian Franck (c. 1499–c. 1542) considered the Antichrist as that which ruined the work of Christ and his apostles immediately after their time. Since then, the true church had been concealed in heaven. 'Therefore, I believe', he wrote in a letter in 1531 to the Lutheran radical John Campanus, 'that the outward church of Christ ... because of the breaking in and laying waste by Antichrist right after the death of the apostles, went up into heaven and lies concealed in the Spirit and in truth. I am thus quite certain that for fourteen hundred years now there has existed no gathered church nor any sacrament.'[66] In short, the history of Christianity was really the history of *Antichristianity.*

Perhaps not surprisingly, and following the magisterial reformers, the institution of the papacy was included in the Antichrist by the Radical reformers. So also were the followers of Muhammad. But when the Radicals were opposed by the magisterial reformers, they included them also in the Antichrist. Thus, for example, Conrad Grebel (c. 1498–1526) identified Ulrich Zwingli with the beast of Revelation 13 and the Antichrist. Caspar Schwenckfeld (c. 1489–1561) included the Lutherans as

[65] See George Huntston Williams, *The Radical Reformation* (Philadelphia: Westminster Press, 1962).
[66] George Huntston Williams (ed.), *Spiritual and Anabaptist Writers: Documents Illustrative of the Radical Reformation* (London: SCM Press Ltd, 1957), p. 149.

a part of the Antichrist.[67] Melchior Hoffman (c. 1495–c. 1543) divided the Christianity of his time into three divisions – the Roman church under its papal Antichrist, its Lutheran and Zwinglian accomplices, and the true spiritual Christians – himself and his followers.[68]

The tendency to use the term 'the Antichrist' in highly charged social, political, and theological contexts to describe all those in opposition reached its peak in the English Revolution in the 1640–50s. Thus, as Christopher Hill aptly notes, 'Orthodox divines saw the Pope as Antichrist. More radical Puritans came to regard bishops and indeed the whole church of England as antichristian, and the civil war as a crusade for Christ against Antichrist.'[69] The leader of the 'True Levellers' (aka 'the Diggers'), Gerrard Winstanley (1609–76), went one step further, viewing the holding of property as, in itself, 'Antichristian'. 'That government that gives liberty to the gentry', he wrote, 'to have all the earth, and shuts out the poor commons from enjoying any part … is the government of imaginary, self-seeking Antichrist.'[70] For Winstanley, Christ dwelt only among the poor and downtrodden. The rest were the Antichrist.

'The Antichrist' thus became a term to describe any kind of power – that of the church, local and national government, the monarchy, the bishops, the clergy, and

---

[67] See Walter Klaassen, *Living at the End of the Ages: Apocalyptic Expectations in the Radical Reformation* (Lanham, Maryland: University Press of America, 1992), pp. 58–9.
[68] See McGinn, *Antichrist*, pp. 214–15.
[69] Christopher Hill, *The World Turned Upside Down* (Harmondsworth: Penguin, 1975), pp. 148–9.
[70] Quoted in *ibid.*, p. 149.

those who supported them, the king, Oliver Cromwell, and so on. The Radicals also had 'anti-intellectual' inclinations. Learning in general and the universities in particular were the Antichrist. This was a familiar criticism of learning made by both European and English Radicals, although not often, as with the Cambridge clergyman William Dell (c. 1607–69), master of Gonville and Caius College, from the inside. It is evident, he declared, 'that this practice of Universities and Colledges in giving men Degrees in Divinity, as they call it, and Titles, Habits, and Dignities accordingly, is contrary to the express command of Jesus Christ, and so is a meer Invention of Antichrist, to put Honour and Reputation on his Ministers.'[71]

So, in effect, 'the Antichrist' or 'Antichrist' or 'Antichristian' became terms of abuse rhetorically available to everyone to use against whomever they disliked. Nothing is so familiar these days, said Archbishop James Ussher (1581–1656), 'as to father upon Antichrist, whatsoever in church matters we do not find to suit with our own humours'.[72] Similarly, Joseph Sedgwick (fl. 1650s), fellow of Christ's College, Cambridge, heartily desired that the

encroaching term of *Antichrist* and *Antichristian* had its unlimited bounds once somewhat fixt by assigning a Conception that might tell us wherein the nature of Antichristianisme consists. It seems to me one of those words that have worn out all their

[71] William Dell, *A Testimony from the Word against Divinity Degrees in the University* (London, 1653), p. 3.
[72] Charles Richard Elrington, *The Whole Works of the Most Rev. James Ussher... Vol. VII* (Dublin: Hodges, Smith, and Co., 1864), p. 45.

signification by frequency of being: or else onely a nickname to reproach any opposer of our private opinions or designes.

Everything, he went on to say, 'is Antichristian in some or others mouths'.[73]

Sedgwick's plea fell on deaf ears. The Radicals continued to see the conservatives as the Antichrist. And vice versa. The Radicals also turned on each other. Lodowick Muggleton (1609–98), for example, saw the Ranter John Robins (who modestly claimed that he was God the Father and that his wife was carrying Christ) as that last great Antichrist or Man of Sin. Later, he added the Quakers to the list. The founder of the Quakers, George Fox (1624–91), thought that the (Radical) Fifth Monarchy men, 'fighters with carnal weapons', were servants of the beast and whore.[74] His wife, Margaret Fell (1614–1702), called the teaching of the Ranters 'the Beast which hath seven heads and ten horns'.[75]

Ever inventive, the English Radicals had another innovation. The Antichrist was not only within the world outside, but within each individual. The activist politics of the Antichrist as the enemy without was here counterpointed by the quietist mysticism of the Antichrist as the enemy within. Thus, for example, the Radical Ranter Joseph Salmon (fl. 1647–56), in his *Antichrist in*

[73] Joseph Sedgwick, *Episkopos Didaskalos: Learnings Necessity to an Able Minister of the Gospel* (London, 1653), p. 39.
[74] The Society of Friends (ed.), *The Journal of George Fox* (London: Headley Brothers, 1902), vol. I, p. 517.
[75] Quoted in Christopher Hill, *Antichrist in Seventeenth-Century England* (London: Verso, 1990), p. 133. I use the term 'Ranter' here, aware that the existence of such a group has been recently called into question.

Man, remarking on the controversy there had been about the identity of 'this great *Whore*, that spirit of *Antichrist*', wrote:

[S]ome there are that affirm this great whore to be the Pope; some the Presbyter, some the Episcopacy ... Know therefore, O man, whoever thou art! That judgest the Whore by these carnal conceptions of her, that thou art far deceived by her, in her fleshly appearances to thee ... Know first then O man! That this great whore is in thee, whil'st thou seekest to behold her without thee, whil'st thou beholdest her in other men, she is in the mean time acting in a *mystery* in thee ... Now then looking upon this whore spiritually, not carnally; *in us*, and not out of us; in the mystery, and not in the history: once more let us take inquisition after her, and endeavour to find her out in all her subtile and close corners.[76]

With the restoration of the English monarchy in 1660 and the decline in Radical sectarianism, the Antichrist went into something of a decline. This was no doubt because, with the end of civil war, 'Antichrist' rhetoric was no longer needed. In part, too, the term had lost intellectual purchase. When the Antichrist was here, there, and everywhere, both within and without, it was easy to see him as nowhere in particular.

Moreover, apocalypticism generally was becoming intellectually old hat. While elite apocalypticism in the manner of Joseph Mede (1586–1638) continued to have some scholarly heft, for many it stank of unwashed *hoi polloi*. The Cambridge philosopher Henry More (1614–87) was following in the footsteps of Joseph Mede. But he

---

[76] Joseph Salmon, *Antichrist in Man* (London, 1649), pp. 1–3.

recognised that, in his own time, apocalypticism was no longer 'socially' quite the thing.[77] Thus, he had to begin his consideration of 'the true idea of Antichristianism' by defending himself against those who thought it

ignoble, inglorious and ungentile, thus to tincture your style and soil your pen with the names of Antichrist and Antichristianism, of which the breath of the rude and ignorant vulgar usually smells as strong as of onions and garlick, and have so fouled these words by their unmannerly mouthing them without all aime, that they have made them now unfit to pass the lips of any civil person.[78]

In short, if the idea of the Antichrist was to be sustained, apocalypticism had to regain its intellectual integrity. And if apocalypticism was to have any credibility, it had to be rescued from a world turned upside down and made compatible with the possibility of a stable and long-lasting religious polity. It needed social respectability. And it needed the intellectual wherewithal to fit with the 'new science'.

[77] See Philip C. Almond, 'Henry More and the Apocalypse', *Journal of the History of Ideas* 54 (1993), 189–200.
[78] Henry More, *A Modest Enquiry into the Mystery of Iniquity* (London, 1664), sig. A.3.v.

7

Antichrists – Papal, Philosophical, Imperial

~

Many shall run to and fro and knowledge shall be increased.

Daniel 12.4 (KJV)

The 'Scientific' Antichrist

With the rise of modern experimental science in the latter half of the seventeenth century, there was a consciousness of living in a new age. For the Cambridge Platonist
Henry More, this was to be expected. The prophet Daniel
had predicted it:

> That which some have noted, if not complained of … that
> the Age we live in is Seculum Philosophicum, a Searching,
> Inquisitive, Rational and Philosophical Age, is a truth so plain
> that it cannot be hid; but was foreseen many and many years
> agoe by the Prophet *Daniel* or rather foretold him by that glo-
> rious Angel that appeared unto him on the banks of the great
> River *Hiddekel, That many shall run to and fro, and knowledge shall
> be increased*: That this should happen *at the time of the End*. And
> I think it is manifest that we are even at the end of that time.[1]

During the seventeenth century, apocalypticism and
the advancement of learning in general, and science in
particular, went hand in hand. As Charles Webster has
suggested, apocalypticism 'induced an increased confidence in the capacity of the human intellect; spectacular
advances could be anticipated in all fields of learning',

[1] More, *A Modest Enquiry into the Mystery of Iniquity*, p. 482.

236

and this on the basis of the text quoted by More in the above passage, namely, Daniel 12.4.[2]

More, then, was an heir of the expectation of a radical increase in knowledge as a presage of the end times. His apocalyptic writings were dominated by the quest for a rational and 'scientific' key to the unlocking of the secrets of the books of Daniel and Revelation. For More, the prophecies of Daniel and Revelation were powerful because of their role among radicals during the period of the English Revolution (1642–60). But they were powerful too precisely because they were *prophetic*. When properly analysed, declared More, prophecy 'is one of the most irrefragable Arguments for Natural Religion, viz., for the existence of God, and of Angels, and for Divine Providence over the affairs of men, and a reward after this life'.[3] As the new science was suggestive of the regularity of nature, so prophecy implied the regularity of history. Thus, for More, the book of Revelation, like the book of Nature, could be read by using the same methods.

As we have noted in the last chapter, the key to the Protestant reading of Revelation lay in determining the future by locating the present through a systematic interpretation of the past. More sat squarely in this tradition. That said, he was never overly concerned with precise dates, believing that the author of Revelation provided only approximate ones. More was nonetheless certain that the church had not become 'Antichristian' until around the year 400. This was the time when the 'two witnesses' (Revelation 11.7) were killed. More was then able to

---

[2] Charles Webster, *The Great Instauration: Science, Medicine, and Reform* (London: Duckworth, 1975), p. 8.
[3] Henry More, *Paralipomena Prophetica* (London, 1685), p. 3.

calculate that the resurrection of the two witnesses happened three and a half days (Revelation 11.12), or twelve
hundred and sixty years, later.[4] This enabled him to identify the resurrection of the two witnesses precisely with
the restoration of the monarchy and episcopacy in 1660
(and more generally with the English Reformation).

Twelve hundred and sixty years was also the period of
the rule of the Antichrist (the papacy) that began around
the same time: 'a kind of *Paganochristianity* instead of
pure Christianity shall visibly domineer for forty and
two months of years, that is 1260 years'.[5] In 1681, More
confessed that his purpose in interpreting Daniel and
Revelation was an anti-Catholic one: 'Nor have I out
of any curiosity of prying into hard and obscure things
medled with either the *Apocalypse* or *Daniel*, but merely for
more full satisfaction in the great Controversy betwixt us
and the Papists, who leave no stone unturned to pervert
souls, and to bring them over to their Idolatrous Church.'[6]

The defeat of the papal Antichrist was therefore imminent. So too was the thousand-year reign of Christ with
the saints (Revelation 20.4). This, however, would be in
heaven and not on earth. The course of history on earth
would continue as normal. The world could not expect
its end until a thousand years into the future. Only then
would the final judgement happen. Those souls already
in heaven reigning with Christ would be exempt from

---

[4] Three and a half days equals three and a half years equals forty
months equals forty-two × thirty years of days equals twelve hundred
and sixty years.

[5] Henry More, *Apocalypsis Apocalypseos; or the Revelation of St John the
Divine Unveiled* (London, 1680), p. 102.

[6] Henry More, *A Plain and Continued Exposition of the several Prophecies
or Divine Visions of the Prophet Daniel* (London, 1681), pp. 267–8.

the conflagration. The righteous would be rescued, while the wicked would be eternally tormented on a fiery earth:

For who can imagine the horror, the stench, the confusion, the crackling of Flames of Fire, those loud murmurs and bellowings of the troubled Seas working and smoking like seething Water in a Caldron, the fearfull howlings and direfull grones of those rebellious Ghosts ... in that day shall all the Faithful renew their strength, and shall mount up with Wings as Eagles, and be carried far above the reach of this dismal Fate; that is, they shall ascend up in those *Heavenly Chariots* or *Ethereal Vehicles* ... and so enter into Immortality and Eternal rest.[7]

Like his friend Henry More, Isaac Newton saw his method for interpreting the apocalyptic texts as a scientific one, seeking both simplicity and harmony.[8] As in nature, so in the prophetic texts:

Truth is ever to be found in simplicity, and not in the multiplicity & confusion of things. As the world, which to the naked eye exhibits the greatest variety of objects, appears very simple in its internall constitution when surveyed by a philosophic understanding, and so much the simpler by how much the better it is understood, so it is in these visions. It is the perfection of God's works that they are all done with the greatest simplicity. He is the God of order and not of confusion. And therefore as they that would understand the frame of the world must indeavour to reduce their knowledg to all possible simplicity, so it must be in seeking to understand these visions.[9]

---

[7] Henry More, *An Explanation of the Grand Mystery of Godliness* (London, 1660), p. 41.
[8] See Rob Iliffe, *Priest of Nature: The Religious Worlds of Isaac Newton* (Oxford University Press, 2017), ch. 7.
[9] Manuel, *The Religion of Isaac Newton*, appendix A, p. 120.

Importantly, to understand prophecy it was necessary to recognise the Antichrist. If God was angry with the Jews for not searching diligently into the prophecies by which they could recognise Christ, Newton inquired, 'why should we think he will excuse us for not searching into the Prophecies which he hath given us to know Antichrist by? ... And therefore it is as much our duty to indeavour to be able to know him that we may avoyd him, as it was theirs to know Christ that they might follow him.'[10] So, for Newton, understanding the apocalyptic texts was both a moral duty and a religious obligation. 'Wherefore it concerns thee', he declared, 'to look about thee narrowly least thou shouldest in so degenerate an age be dangerously seduced and not know it. Antichrist was to seduce the whole Christian world and therefore he may easily seduce thee if thou beest not well prepared to discern him.'[11]

Newton was in agreement with More that the end times would begin when the 1,260 years of the rule of the Antichrist ended. Like More, he then expected the thousand-year rule of the saints, although (following Joseph Mede) on earth and not in heaven. He also agreed with More that the 1,260 years began when the church or the papacy attained worldly power and dominion.

And now being arrived at a temporal dominion, and a power above all human judicature, he [the pope] reigned *with a look more stout than his fellows*, and *times* and *laws* were henceforward *given into his hands, for a time times and half a time*, or three times and a half; that is for 1,260 solar years, reckoning a time for a Calendar of 360 days, and a day for a solar year. After

---

[10] *Ibid.*, appendix A, p. 109.   [11] Quoted in *ibid.*, p. 89.

which *the judgment is to fit, and they shall take away his dominion*, not at once, but by degrees, *to consume, and to destroy it unto the end.*[12]

But Newton was never particularly clear as to when this date was. At its earliest, it was in the early part of the fourth century, when Constantine legitimised Christianity and a flood of insincere converts from paganism entered the church. From then on, Newton believed, the church was progressively corrupted: 'then did the honour, riches, power & temporal advantages of this religion begin to tempt the heathens dayly to turn Christians; & in such converts who for temporall interest thus flowed into the Church the Devil now came amongst the Christian people of the Eastern & Western Empires called the inhabitants of the earth and sea.'[13] At its latest, it was 841.[14] But he also variously suggested 381, 607, 609, 788, and 800.

Generally speaking, Newton was unhappy with setting dates for the end times. 'The folly of Interpreters has been', he declared, 'to foretell times and things by this Prophecy, as if God designed to make them Prophets. By this rashness they have not only exposed themselves, but brought the Prophecy also into contempt.'[15] Information about the time of the end could only be gained when the

[12] Isaac Newton, *Observations upon the Prophecies of Daniel, and the Apocalypse of St. John* (London, 1733), pp. 113–14.
[13] Isaac Newton, *Yahuda Ms. 18*, 1r. Available at www.newtonproject .ox.ac.uk/view/texts/normalized/THEM00061
[14] See Stephen D. Snobelen, '"A Time and Times and the Dividing of Times": Isaac Newton, the Apocalypse, and 2060 A.D.', *Canadian Journal of History* 38 (2003), 537–51.
[15] Isaac Newton, *Observations upon the Prophecies of Daniel*, p. 251.

end was upon us. In short, the prophecies could be read backwards but not forwards. God gave men the prophecies 'not to gratify men's curiosities by enabling them to foreknow things, but that after they were fulfilled they might be interpreted by the event, and his own Providence, not the Interpreters, be then manifested to the world'.[16] In sum, interpreting the books of Daniel and Revelation was a rather complicated way of doing history.

William Whiston (1667–1752) was Isaac Newton's successor as Professor of Mathematics at the University of Cambridge. He followed Newton in his 'scientific' approach to the book of Revelation. His approach to the matter of prophecy, he wrote in 1725, 'was intimated first to me, when I was Young, and was in the common Opinion, by a very Great Man [i.e. Newton], who had very exactly studied the sacred writings'.[17] But he was much less reluctant to make predictions about the future on the basis of apocalyptic calculations than Isaac Newton was, or, at least, not to project them into the far-distant future.

In keeping with standard Protestant moves, in his *An Essay on the Revelation of Saint John* in 1706, Whiston identified the papacy with the 'beast rising out of the sea' in Revelation 13. Here, declared Whiston, 'we have a plain account of the Rise of *Antichrist himself*, strictly so called; or of the *Pope of Rome, and his subordinate Hierarchy*'.[18] The pope may have the appearance of a lamb, but he

---

[16] *Ibid.*

[17] Quoted in James E. Force, *William Whiston: Honest Newtonian* (Cambridge University Press, 2002), p. 76.

[18] William Whiston, *An Essay on the Revelation of Saint John, So far as concerns the Past and Present Times* (Cambridge, 1706), p. 243.

speaks like a dragon, 'exalting himself above all that is called God; Excommunicating and Destroying Princes; Absolving Subjects from their allegiance; Introducing new, false, and pernicious doctrines and practices; Commanding Idolatry in the worship of Angels, Saints, Images and Reliques; Tyrannizing over the Consciences of Men; and Anathematizing all who will not submit to his ungodly doings'.[19]

For the time of the rise of the Antichrist, Whiston looked to the book of Daniel, identifying the papal 'beast from the sea' with 'the little horn' that came up among the ten horns (Daniel 7.8). This occurred in the year 606, when Pope Boniface III took the titles 'Head of the Church' and 'Universal Bishop'. Thus began the epoch of the popes' 'Ecclesiastical Tyranny'.[20] As for how long the Antichrist would reign, Whiston came up with a unique reading of 'a time and times and the dividing of time' (Daniel 7.25, KJV): 'Thus, also *Time, Times, and a division or part* of *time, i.e.* three years, and a division or part of a year, must signify *three years and a month*, because the most eminent and remarkable division, or part of a year, is a *Month.*'[21] This was then taken as a period of 37 months at 30 days per month, or 1,110 years.

Whiston was a supporter of the view that, from the creation of the world until its end would be some 6,000 years. Granted that he took the creation of the world to be some 4,000 years BCE, he expected its end to be some 300 years into the future, around 2000. But the reign of the Antichrist would end in the *immediate* future, in 1,110 years from 606, that is, in 1716:

[19] *Ibid.*   [20] *Ibid.*, p. 245.   [21] *Ibid.*, p. 4.

[S]o at this *Epocha* A.D. 606. His Power was advanc'd to a height abundantly sufficient to begin the Date of his overbearing Dominion and Tyranny over the Christian Church: which being so, and his Duration but 1110 years ... we have great reason to expect the Period of his *Grandeur* and *Tyranny*, at the period of those 1110 years *i.e.* at the same time with that of the ten kings *A.D.* 1716, and his utter Destruction, with that of the whole *Roman* Empire, at our Saviour's coming.[22]

All that said, like many failed prophets before him, Whiston appeared to remain undaunted when 1716 passed by with no notable change in the established order of things.

Sceptics and Believers

As we know, there is no mention of the Antichrist within the book of Revelation. He was 'back-written' into it by Irenaeus in the second century. From that time on, the history of the Antichrist and that of the book of Revelation was interwoven in a myriad complex ways. By virtue of this interweaving, the fate of the Antichrist depended upon the ongoing credibility of Revelation as a source for events that were to unfold in the future and that had been fulfilled in the past. The bishop of Bristol, Thomas Newton (1704–82), in his *Dissertations on the Prophecies* (1754), like others before him (and many after him), recognised the inherent difficulties in interpreting a book as obscure as Revelation. This was a work, he wrote, that is 'so wrapped and involved in figures and

---

[22] *Ibid.*, p. 248. See also pp. 270–2 for a full list by Whiston of grounds for the year 1716.

allegories, is so wild and visionary, is so dark and obscure, that any thing or nothing, at least nothing clear and certain, can be proved and collected from it'.[23]

But what had been once seen as a challenge to interpretation was now viewed as a ground for rejection. Thus, by the time Thomas Newton was publishing his thoughts and reasserting that the papacy was the Antichrist, change was in the air, at least among a burgeoning sceptical elite. And Thomas Newton knew it. He had read the essay of Voltaire (1694–1778) on Isaac Newton, and he referenced Voltaire's witticism on Newton's *Observations* to the effect that 'Sir Isaac Newton wrote his comment upon the Revelation, to console mankind for the great superiority that he had over them in other respects.'[24] In fact, Voltaire had made his comment in 1734, only a year after Isaac Newton's commentary had been posthumously published. At best, it was a comment on the fact that there was nothing particularly new in Isaac Newton's work. But it was also a recognition that, even by the 1730s, this kind of work had become a subject of ridicule, at least to some.

Whiston's expectations of the imminent end of the world had also become intellectually unfashionable and the subject of mockery among London wits. Thus, for example, around 1731–2, John Gay (1685–1732), a member of the satirists' Scriblerus Club, composed 'a True and Faithful Narrative of What pass'd in London during

---

[23] Thomas Newton, *Dissertations on the Prophecies, which have been remarkably fulfilled in the World* (London: J. F. Dove, 1825), p. 440.

[24] *Ibid.*, p. 440. See also William F. Fleming (trans.), *The Works of Voltaire: A Contemporary Version* (New York: Dingwall-Rock, 1927), pp. 19, 172–6. Available at www.k-state.edu/english/baker/english287/Voltaire-Newton.htm

the general Consternation of all Ranks and Degrees'. This 'reported' on a lecture supposedly held by William Whiston to an audience that had paid a shilling a piece to hear him lecture on a subject, only to discover that he had changed the topic of his discourse. After a short pause, as if lost in devotion and mental prayer, Whiston spoke:

Friends and Fellow-Citizens, all speculative Science is at an end; the Period of all things is at Hand; on *Friday* next this World shall be no more. Put not your confidence in me, Brethren for tomorrow Morning five Minutes after Five the Truth will be Evident; in that instant the Comet shall appear, of which I have heretofore warn'd you. As ye have heard, believe. Go hence, and prepare your Wives, Your Families and Friends, for the universal Change.[25]

The audience were astonished, although Whiston remained sufficiently calm to return a shilling to several youths disappointed that he had changed topics without notice.

Within two or three hours, the news had spread throughout the city. It rapidly became the subject matter of all conversations. Indeed, the belief was soon universal 'that the Day of Judgement was at hand'.[26] When the comet duly arrived, even the sceptics were convinced that the end would come in the predicted two days' time. But when the second day passed without the world's ending, scepticism inevitably kicked in:

---

[25] [Jonathan Swift and Alexander Pope], *Miscellanies: The Third Volume* (London, 1732), p. 241. On Whiston and the sceptics, see George Rousseau, '"Wicked Whiston" and the Scriblerians: Another Ancients–Modern Controversy', *Studies in Eighteenth-Century Culture* 17 (1987), 17–44.

[26] *Ibid.*, p. 246.

The subject of all Wit and Conversation was to ridicule the Prophecy, and railly each other. All the Quality and Gentry were *perfectly asham'd*, nay, some utterly disown'd that they had manifested any Signs of Religion. But the next day, even the Common People, as well as their Betters, appear'd in their usual state of Indifference. They Drank, they Whor'd, they Swore, they Ly'd, they Cheated, they Plunder'd, they Gam'd, they Quarrell'd, they Murder'd. In short, the World went on in the old Channel.[27]

The new experimental science was committed to the synthesis between God and nature on the one hand, and prophecy and history on the other. By the 1740s, however, rifts were appearing. William Stukeley (1687–1765), the Anglican antiquarian, was a friend to both Isaac Newton and Whiston. He bemoaned the fact that, with the election of Martin Folkes to the presidency of the Royal Society, the philistines were within the citadel. Folkes, he said, had 'a great deal of learning, philosophy, astronomy: but knows nothing of a future state, of the Scripture, of Revelation'.[28] In 1720, he went on, Folkes had set up an 'infidel Club' at his house, where those of 'the heathen stamp' assembled. From that time on, he declared, 'he has been propagating the infidel System with great assiduity, & made it even fashionable in the royal Society, so that when any mention is made of Moses, of the deluge, of religion, scriptures, &c., it generally is received with a loud laugh'.[29]

Whiston, along with some of the old guard, was not deterred by their having become the target of the wits.

[27] *Ibid.*, p. 260.
[28] Quoted in Force, *William Whiston*, p. 128. I am indebted to Force for this discussion.
[29] *Ibid.*

When two earthquakes rocked London on 8 February and 8 March 1750, he saw them as warnings of a greater quake to come. On 10 March, he devoted a public lecture to the topic, 'Of the horrid Wickedness of the present Age, highly deserving such terrible Judgments'. They were, in his view, signs of the end. A further earthquake predicted for 5 April by a guardsman named 'the military prophet' failed to materialise. One wit, writing as if it had, wrote of a 'Mr. W--n, the Astronomer, upon the first Beginning of the Trembling, set out on Foot for *Dover*, on his Way to *Jerusalem*, where he made an Appointment to meet the *Millennium:* It is thought, if he makes tolerable Haste, he will arrive there first.'[30]

Still, even if imminent expectations of the apocalypse had become the subject of satire and derision among a sceptical elite, there remained a market for more conservative readings of the book of Revelation. Thomas Newton's *Dissertations on the Prophecies* was in its twentieth edition by 1835. Over 120 books were published in English between 1750 and 1850 on Revelation or parts of it.[31]

As a result, the papal Antichrist remained on the Protestant theological agenda throughout this period.

---

[30] Anon., *A full and true account of the dreadful and melancholy Earthquake, which happened between twelve and one o'clock in the morning, on Thursday the fifth instant. With an exact list of such persons as have hitherto been found in the Rubbish* (London, 1750), p. 6.

[31] See the bibliography in C. A. Patrides and Joseph Wittreich (eds.), *The Apocalypse in English Renaissance Thought and Literature: Patterns, Antecedents and Repercussions* (Manchester University Press, 1984). It is a matter of surprise that, although Isaac Newton's work on the book of *Revelation* was often mentioned, apart from its inclusion in Samuel Horsley's *Opera Omnia* of Newton in the 1780s, the next edition was that of Sir William Whitla in 1922. I am indebted to Robert Iliffe for this note.

Thus, for example, the architect Matthew Habershon (1789–1852) in his *A Dissertation on the Prophetic Scriptures* (1834) saw himself in the tradition of Joseph Mede, Isaac Newton, and Thomas Newton. He identified the Antichrist with the papacy and also with 'Mohamedanism and Infidelity'.[32] These were all, as it were, successive Antichrists. To solve the problems of chronology concerning the 1,260 years, he proposed a double commencement in 533 and 583, and consequently a double termination of them in 1793 and 1843. The first termination of popery thus occurred when revolutionary France aimed 'the most deadly blows at that superstition which Voltaire and other Atheistical writers had long held up to the scorn and derision of the world'.[33] The final downfall of the papacy would occur in 1843, and the Ottoman Empire soon after.

At the end of the day, Habershon's work was, perhaps, nothing more than another addition to what was by then 300 years of Protestant polemics against the papal Antichrist. The historical importance of Matthew Habershon's work lies in the influence it was to have on a young English naturalist by the name of Philip Gosse (1810–88). In June 1842, Habershon sent him a copy of his *A Dissertation on the Prophetic Scriptures.* He began to read it one afternoon, 'eagerly devouring the pages', and finished the book before darkness set in. It was to change his life:

---

[32] M. Habershon, *A Dissertation on the Prophetic Scriptures, chiefly those of a Chronological Character* (London: James Nisbet and B. Wertheim, 1834), p. 368.

[33] *Ibid.*, p. 334.

Of the Restoration of the Jews [to Israel], I had received some dim inkling already, perhaps from Croly's *Salathiel*; but of the destruction of the Papacy, the end of Gentilism, the kingdom of God, the resurrection and rapture of the Church at the personal descent of the Lord, and the imminency of this, – all came to me that evening like a flash of lightning. My heart drank it in with joy; I found no shrinking from the nearness of Jesus.[34]

Interpreting the book of Revelation was to be a never-ending source of joy for Philip Gosse and his wife, Emily. His son, Edmund Gosse (1849–1928), wrote that his father remarked in his later years that no small element in his wedded happiness had been the fact that he and his wife were of one mind in the interpretation of sacred prophecy. Interpreting Revelation was almost their only relaxation, taking the place of cards or the piano in more profane families:

When they read of seals broken and of vials poured forth, of the star which was called Wormwood that fell from Heaven, and of men whose hair was as the hair of women and their teeth as the teeth of lions, they did not admit for a moment that these vivid mental pictures were of a poetic character, but they regarded them as positive statements, in guarded language, describing events which were to happen, and could be recognized when they did happen.[35]

---

[34] Edmund Gosse, *The Life of Philip Henry Gosse F.R.S.* (London: Kegan Paul, Trench, Trübner & Co., Ltd, 1890), pp. 375–6. The reference to Croly is to George Croly, *Salathiel: The Wandering Jew, a Story of the Past, Present, and Future* (London: H. Colburn, 1828).

[35] Edmund Gosse, *Father and Son: A Study of Two Temperaments* (Boston: Houghton Mifflin, 1965), pp. 49–50.

They read Revelation with the works of the Newtons and Habershon to hand. This helped them to recognise 'in wild Oriental visions' direct statements regarding Napoleon III, Pope Pius IX, and the king of Piedmont 'under the names of denizens of Babylon and companions of the Wild Beast'.[36]

Edmund and his father would also study the book of Revelation together, and they 'chased the phantom of Popery through its fuliginous pages'.[37] Together, they investigated the number of the beast. They inspected the nations to see if they had the mark of Babylon upon their heads. They hunted the Scarlet Woman through the 1850s. His father could not have desired 'a pupil more docile or more ardent than I was in my flaming denunciations of the Papacy'.[38]

When Edmund Gosse's mother was dying of cancer, the 8-year-old Edmund read to her aloud Edward Bishop Elliott's *Horae Apocalypticae* (1844). At 2,500 pages of exhaustive (and exhausting) commentary and references to some 10,000 sources, ancient and modern, it was the most comprehensive work ever produced on the book of Revelation. For Gosse, it was a labour of love. 'When my Mother could endure nothing else', he poignantly wrote,

the arguments of this book took her thoughts away from her pain and lifted her spirits. Elliott saw 'the queenly arrogance of Popery' everywhere, and believed that the very Last Days of Babylon the Great were come. Lest I say what may be thought extravagant, let me quote what my Father wrote in his diary at the time of my Mother's death. He said that the thought that Rome was doomed (as seemed not impossible in 1857) so

[36] *Ibid.*, p. 50.   [37] *Ibid.*, p. 66.   [38] *Ibid.*

affected my Mother that it 'irradiated' her dying hours with an assurance that was like 'the light of the Morning Star, the harbinger of the rising sun'.[39]

French Antichrists

In the first half of the nineteenth century, new Antichrists were on the eastern horizon – over the channel in France. At first, the French Revolution of 1789–99 was viewed favourably by English apocalypticists. The revolution-aries had attacked the Catholic church. This was after all, happily, an attack on the Roman Antichrist. This positive take on the Revolution was soon to change. Revolutionary France itself came to be seen, along with the papacy and Islam, as the Antichrist. It is a sign of how deeply disturbing the English Anglican establish-ment, at least those of an apocalyptic bent, found the French Revolution.

In the case of the Anglican clergyman Henry Kett (1761–1825), the critique of the Revolution went along with a more general anti-Enlightenment narrative. Thus, to the Antichrist of the papacy and Islam, 'the parents of infidelity' as he called them, Kett added the Antichrist of the French Enlightenment. Just as English Protestant identity was forged over against the Antichrist of the papacy, so British national identity was now constructed over against the Antichrist of the French *philosophes*.

Kett was inclined to let English Enlightenment think-ers off the hook. At the least, they had kept their rad-ical thoughts to themselves. The French *philosophes*, on

[39] *Ibid.*, pp. 50–1.

the other hand, had made their radical philosophising available to the masses. And, God forbid, they thought that liberty was an idea applicable to all. Thus, in pursuit of an Antichristian atheism, they had made a fundamental mistake 'by *misrepresenting* the nature of *Liberty*, and asserting the *right* of *every* man to think for himself upon *all* subjects, and the duty of every man to *act* according to his own sentiments – by throwing *ridicule* upon the most serious subjects; and employing slander, invective, and falsehood, *whenever* and *wherever* it seemed likely to forward their purpose'.[40]

In short, the aim of the French Enlightenment and the Revolution that it incited had been to abolish Christianity. It was, according to Kett, a conspiracy begun by Voltaire in France in 1720, aided and abetted by the 'Illuminati' in Bavaria in 1776.[41] The ideas of infidelity had been around for a long time. But they were 'first embodied', he declared, 'into *a practical system of wickedness* by Voltaire, d'Alembert, Frederick II. King of Prussia, Diderot, and their confederates in iniquity … At no other period of the world could this system have been formed, or this power created … *the present reign of the Infidel Antichrist* has been expressly *foretold*.[42]

---

[40] Henry Kett, *History the Interpreter of Prophecy, or, a View of Scriptural Prophecies and their Accomplishment* (Oxford University Press, 1799), vol. II, p. 140.

[41] See *ibid.*, vol. II, p. 122. Kett was here up on the latest conspiracy theory. In the late 1790s, Augustin Barruel and John Robison claimed that the Bavarian society of the Illuminati (thought to have connections to Jesuits and Freemasons) were behind the French Revolution. See Terry Melanson, *Perfectibilists: The 18th Century Bavarian Order of the Illuminati* (Chicago: Trine Day, 2011).

[42] Kett, *History the Interpreter of Prophecy*, vol. II, pp. 122–3.

Although Kett had extended the Antichrist from the papacy and Islam to the contemporary French, the Anglican bishop Samuel Horsley (1733–1806) was to make a more radical move. As an Anglican 'High Churchman', Horsley was committed to the historical continuity of the church of England with the Catholic tradition. So he moved the Antichrist from Rome to Paris and replaced the papacy with 'the atheistical democracy of France'. 'The French democracy', he declared in 1799, 'from its infancy to the present moment, has been a conspicuous and principal branch at least of the western Antichrist.[43] He traced the rise of the Antichrist in the West from the apostolic age to French philosophy, Jacobinism, and Bavarian Illuminationism. But it was in the French Revolution that he saw 'the *adolescence* of that man of sin, or rather of lawlessness, who is to throw off all the restraints of religion, morality, and custom, and undo the bands of civil society'.[44] If a French corporate Antichrist was already present, the final Antichrist would be a wilful king, 'neither a Protestant, nor a Papist; neither Christian, Jew, nor Heathen' but one who would 'claim divine honours to himself exclusively'.[45] Taking on almost 300 years of Protestant identification of the Antichrist, the Man of Sin, the Son of Iniquity, and the beast with the papacy was brave stuff. Those who saw English identity as forged in the fires of anti-Catholicism were outraged.[46]

---

[43] Samuel Horsley, *Critical Disquisitions on the Eighteenth Chapter of Isaiah* (Philadelphia: James Humphrey, 1800), p. 94.

[44] *Ibid.*, p. 98.   [45] *Ibid.*, pp. 98–9.

[46] See Andrew Robinson, 'Identifying the Beast: Samuel Horsley and the Problem of Papal AntiChrist', *Journal of Ecclesiastical History* 43 (1992), 592–607.

Samuel Horsley's critique of the notion of the papal Antichrist was broadened in his posthumously published 'Letters to the Author of Antichrist in the French Convention'. In a move redolent of late medieval Franciscan apocalypticism, Horsley was to add an Eastern to his Western Antichrist. 'I have a strong suspicion', he wrote in April 1797, 'that the genuine Antichrist, St. Paul's man of sin, in the utmost height and horror of his character, is to rise out of a strange coalition between the French democracy and the Turk.[47] The thought of it sent shivers down Horsley's spine, not least because of the decay in sexual morality. 'Good God!', he declared,

What a monster will this be! – The Turk fraternized by the French Democracy! united in the nefarious project of exterminating the Christian religion; and for that purpose, studiously corrupting the morals of their subjects, by releasing them from the constraints of matrimony! A business in which the French, at present, far outdo the Turk; but the Turk, I dare say, will be an apt scholar.[48]

In the fifth letter, in July 1797, Horsley gave his own account of the end times:

The Church of God on earth will be greatly reduced … in its apparent numbers, in the times of AntiChrist, by the open desertion of the powers of the world. This desertion will begin in a professed indifference to any particular form of Christianity, under the pretence of universal toleration; which

[47] Samuel Horsley, 'Manuscript Letters of Bishop Horsley: Letter 1', *The British Magazine* 5 (1834), 134.
[48] Samuel Horsley, 'Manuscript Letters of Bishop Horsley: Letter 6', *The British Magazine* 5 (1834), 12. This is actually a continuation of Letter 5.

toleration will proceed from no true spirit of charity and for-
bearance, but from a design to undermine Christianity by
multiplying and encouraging sectaries. The pretended toleration will go far beyond a just toleration, even as it regards the
different sects of Christians. For governments will pretend to
an indifference to all, and will give a protection in preference
to none. All establishments will be set aside. From the toleration of the most pestilent heresies, they will proceed to the
toleration of Mahometanism, atheism, and at last to a positive
persecution of the truth of Christianity ... The merely nomi-
nal Christians will all desert the profession of the truth, when
the powers of the world desert it.[49]

The scene of the Antichrist's last exploits and of his final
destruction when Christ returned would be the East,
perhaps the Holy Land, or even Jerusalem.

The rise of Napoleon to the position of emperor of
the French Empire in 1804 created a new problem. Was
Napoleon the expected final Antichrist? Many in England
thought so (see Plate 28). Samuel Johnson's friend, Hester
Piozzi (1740–1821), the first Englishwoman to write a history of the world, concluded that the French Revolution
was a sign of the impending end of days. When Napoleon
took control of the French government, she began to
wonder if he was the expected Antichrist. She noted in
her diary that many were saying that Napoleon was the
'Devil Incarnate, the Appolyon [the Destroyer] mentioned in Scripture' [Revelation 9.11]'.[50] Piozzi's ingenious

[49] Samuel Horsley, 'Manuscript Letters of Bishop Horsley: Letter 5',
The British Magazine 5 (1834), 520.
[50] Quoted in Clarke Garrett, *Respectable Folly: Millenarians and the
French Revolution in England* (Baltimore and London: The Johns
Hopkins University Press, 1975), p. 211.

correlation of Napoleon and Appolyon arose from her study of the Corsican dialect. 'His name is Apollonio pronounced according to the Corsican Dialect *N'Apollione*', she declared, 'and he does come forwards followed by a cloud of devouring Locusts from ye bottomless Pit – whose Stings are in their *Tails*.'[51] Elsewhere, she provided three solutions to the number of the beast, two in Greek characters, spelling out 'Mahomet' and 'Napoleon', and the third 'copied from a *Spanish* Adaptation of the Mystic Number to the name of Buonaparte'.[52]

The theologian Lewis Mayer (1738–1849) informed his English readers that Napoleon was 'The Beast that arose out of the Earth, with Two Horns like a Lamb, and spake as a Dragon, whose number is 666.'[53] In an original take on the number of the beast, Napoleon, according to Lewis, was number 666 in a line of emperors, popes, and heads of state alluded to by the biblical prophetic texts. While the beast that arose from the sea (Revelation 13.1) represented the empire first established by Charlemagne, the beast that arose out of the earth (Revelation 13.11) 'is only applicable to Bonaparte, who is called the False Prophet that deceived the kings of the earth, to gather them together to the battle of that great day of God Almighty'.[54] Any reader persuaded by any of this would,

[51] Katherine C. Balderston (ed.), *Thraliana: The Diary of Mrs. Hester Lynch Hale, 1776–1809* (Oxford: Clarendon Press, 1951), vol. II, p. 1003.

[52] Quoted in Orianne Smith, *Romantic Women Writers, Revolution, and Prophecy: Rebellious Daughters, 1786–1826* (Cambridge University Press, 2013), p. 89.

[53] L. Mayer, *The Prophetic Mirror; Or, a Hint to England* (London: Williams and Smith et al., 1806), subtitle.

[54] *Ibid.*, p. 54.

no doubt, be comforted by Lewis' reassurance that, since the British nation did not form part of Charlemagne's empire, it would be 'exempt from the tyrannical power of France'.[55]

That Napoleon was a candidate for the position of the Antichrist went well beyond England. Leo Tolstoy's *War and Peace* opens with words from the St Petersburg society hostess Anna Pavlovna Scherer to Prince Vasili Kuragin:

> Well, Prince, so Genoa and Lucca are now just family estates of the Buonapartes. But I warn you, if you don't tell me that this means war, if you still try to defend the infamies and horrors perpetrated by that Antichrist – I really believe he is Antichrist – I will have nothing more to do with you and you are no longer my friend.[56]

Later in the same book, with the French emperor threatening Moscow itself, Pierre notes that 'Writing the words L'Empereur Napoleon in numbers, it appears that the sum of them is 666, and that Napoleon was therefore the beast foretold in the Apocalypse.' That Napoleon was the Antichrist was a common opinion in early nineteenth-century Russia. As early as 1806, the Russian Orthodox church had sent a letter to the faithful indicating why the struggle against Napoleon was an apocalyptic one, demonstrating that the French emperor was the Antichrist and urging believers to resist him.[57] As a

---

[55] *Ibid.*, p. 55.

[56] Louise and Aylmer Maude (trans.), *War and Peace by Leo Tolstoy* (Minneapolis: First Avenue Editions, 2016), p. 15.

[57] See Michael A. Pesenson, 'Napoleon Bonaparte and Apocalyptic Discourse in Early Nineteenth-Century Russia', *The Russian Review* 65 (2006), 382.

result, the Russian destruction of Napoleon became an essential prelude to the return of Christ. Czar Alexander I, his close friend Prince Alexander Golitsyn recalled, was so obsessed with reading the book of Revelation 'that, in the sovereign's words, he could not read it enough'.[58] In this scenario, Czar Alexander I took on the persona of the Last Roman Emperor whose role was to rid the Continent of the Gallic Beast.

American apocalypticists were similarly convinced. The title of an anonymous pamphlet published in New York in 1809 is emblematic – *The Identity of Napoleon and Antechrist; Completely Demonstrated or a Commentary on the Chapters of the Scripture which relate to Antechrist: Where all the Passages are Shown to Apply to Napoleon in the Most Striking Manner and where especially the prophetic number 666 is found in his name, with perfect exactness, in two different manners.* Here, Napoleon born on Corsica in the Mediterranean Sea is the beast rising out of the sea (Revelation 13.1). He leaves his mark on the foreheads of his soldiers (their hat cockades) and on their right hand (their swords) (Revelation 13.16). He makes war and gains power over all tongues and nations (Revelation 13.7). Both arrogant and boastful, he exalts himself above God. The title of Napoleon, with the Corsican spelling for his name ('L'empereur Napoleone'), adds up to 666, as does his true title – 'Le roi impie Napoleon'. 'It is the *Sovereign, Emperor or King of France*, which we have before us in all that is said of the Antichrist', he declared.[59]

---

[58] Quoted in *ibid.*, 381.

[59] Anon., *The Identity of Napoleon and Antechrist; Completely Demonstrated or a Commentary on the Chapters of the Scripture which relate to Antechrist* (New York: Sargeant, 1809), p. 22.

The independent Presbyterian William C. Davis (1760–1831) of South Carolina also saw Napoleon's birthplace in Corsica as the domain of the beast. Like Hester Piozzi, he lined up 'Napoleon' with 'Apollyon'. The Muslims (the locusts of Revelation 9) would eventually have ruling over them a king by the name of Apollyon (the destroyer), a variation on the name of the French emperor: 'With the addition of N', or Ne, which shows that he was born for this purpose, this is the name of the Emperor of Gaul, who has carried his dominions to the very confines of Turkey.'[60]

Apocalypticists were not necessarily discouraged when the eschatological predictions around Napoleon Bonaparte came to nothing. Napoleon III (1808–52) was a worthy substitute when he became emperor in 1852. Thus, for example, the English missionary preacher Michael Paget Baxter (1834–1910) detailed ten reasons, with biblical support, why Napoleon III was the final Antichrist. Among these were Napoleon III's persecution of Christians, his warlike prowess, insatiable ambition, vast military power, and rule over the original Roman Empire, not to mention his Grecian extraction, his sphinx-like countenance, and his addiction to spiritualism. Although the spiritualists were yet to do so, 'yet it is certain', he predicted, 'that the miracle-working spirits will soon instruct them to accept Napoleon as their political and ecclesiastical Head, and ultimately to worship him as their God'.[61] Napoleon III not only fulfilled the

[60] William C. Davis, *The Millennium, or, A Short Sketch on the Rise and Fall of Antichrist* (Salisbury: Coupee and Crider, 1811), p. 42.
[61] M. Baxter, *Louis Napoleon: The Destined Monarch of the World* (Philadelphia: James S. Claxton, 1867), p. 34.

prophecy that his name should be Apollyon (or Apoleon) in Greek, but also that it should be numerically equal to the number 666.[62] 'Satan was but experimenting', he concluded, 'when he raised up the first Napoleon as a Great Destroyer, but he has taxed his powers to the utmost to produce his most finished masterpiece, the Third Napoleon, who will be unapproachably the Greatest of all Destroyers.'[63] As for the pope, the best he could hope for, in the three and a half years before the end of all things, would be the role of vice-president 'of the inquisitorial tribunals of this Antichristian Reign of Terror over all kindreds and tongues and nations'.[64]

In spite of all these Napoleonic enthusiasms, Samuel Horsley was not persuaded that Napoleon Bonaparte was the final Antichrist, not least because he was expecting the end of the world later rather than sooner, and Napoleon did not fit his apocalyptic timetable. In one of the most tortured versions of eschatological mathematics ever, he predicted the end of the Antichrist to begin in 1968.[65] And Napoleon (unless, as some thought, he were to rise from the dead like Nero) was unlikely to live that long. Still, whether Napoleon was the Antichrist or not, Horsley was convinced that his rise and fall were all part of the divine plan, one part of which was England's going to war against him. 'In the case of Antichrist in particular', he wrote in his final sermon of 1805, celebrating Nelson's victory at Trafalgar, 'prophecy is explicit. So clearly as it is foretold, that he shall raise himself to power

[62] *Ibid.*   [63] *Ibid.*, p. 59.   [64] *Ibid.*, p. 34.
[65] See Samuel Horsley, 'Of the Prophetical Periods', *The British Magazine* 4 (1833), pp. 717–41.

by successful War; so clearly it is foretold, that War, fierce and furious War, waged upon him by the faithful, shall be, in part, the means of his downfall.[66] At the very least then, if not *the* Antichrist, he was *an* Antichrist. Most crucially, however, Horsley had traded in the present papal Antichrist within the church for the vision of a future imperial Antichrist outside it.

The Anglican theologian George Stanley Faber (1773–1854) was perhaps the most prolific and controversial theologian of his period, the author of some forty-two volumes over a period of fifty-five years. From 1799 to 1853, he produced works from the book of Genesis to the book of Revelation. He was undoubtedly controversial. Faber looked to Horsley, his 'Master in Israel', as his inspiration.[67] Like many of his apocalyptic predecessors, Faber had often to revise his apocalyptic views to line them up with contemporary events, but his final thoughts were laid out in 1828 in his *Sacred Calendar of Prophecy*.

In this work, Faber's views on the Antichrist were part and parcel of his apocalyptic timetable. According to this, the 1,260 years until the end of the world were to begin from the time that the Byzantine emperor Phocas handed power to the Roman pope in 606 and Islam arose. The upshot of this was that Catholicism and Islam would

---

[66] Samuel Horsley, *The Watchers and the Holy Ones. A Sermon* (London: J. Matchard, 1806), p. 25.

[67] Quoted in S. W. Gilley, 'George Stanley Faber: No Popery and Prophecy', in P. J. Harland and C. T. R. Hayward, *New Heaven and New Earth: Prophecy and the New Millennium* (Leiden: Brill, 1999), p. 299. This essay provides an excellent overview of Faber's life and works.

survive until 1,260 years later, that is, until 1866, with Christ to return in the following year. That said, the papacy was not the Antichrist:

The donation of the name of *Antichrist* to the Pope is purely gratuitous. It rests upon no certain warrant of Scripture: and, indeed, it may rather be said to contradict it. The predicted Antichrist is an infidel and atheist ... Whatever, therefore, may have been the delinquent character of the Papacy, the character of the Antichrist belongs not to it.[68]

Unlike Samuel Horsley, whose Antichrist was an individual in the future, Faber's was a collective in the present. The Antichrist, he declared, 'was to be no *individual*, but a *power* or *nation* composed of individuals, who should profess and act up to the impious principles of *the atheistical scoffers*'.[69] 'The long-expected and late-revealed Antichrist', he went on to say, was 'a pandemonium of licentious anarchists and determined atheists.'[70] In short, he concluded, 'we can scarcely hesitate to pronounce him to be *revolutionary France*'.[71] Consequently, in principle, no one person could be a candidate for the Antichrist. 'It matters little', he wrote,

whether Robespierre, or Buonapartè, or any other ruffian of the same stamp, be for a season at the head of affairs; the *revolutionary government*, as contradistinguished from *that which*

---

[68] George Stanley Faber, *The Sacred Calendar of Prophecy: Or a Dissertation on the Prophecies* (London: C. and J. Rivington, 1828), vol. II, p. 209.

[69] George Stanley Faber, *A Dissertation on the Prophecies* (Boston: Andrews and Cummings, 1808), vol. I, p. 239.

[70] *Ibid.*   [71] *Ibid.*, vol. I, p. 240.

preceded it, is alone the subject of prophecy. So that, in my view of the question, if Buonapartè were slain tomorrow ... no event would have occurred which were worth prophetic notice.[72]

Back to the Futurists

The only limit on interpretations of the number of the beast was the imagination of apocalyptically inclined readers of the book of Revelation. In his survey of British interpretations of the number '666' between 1560 and 1830, David Brady identifies no fewer than 147 different identifications.[73] This was an open invitation to parody, one taken up by John Henry Newman (1801–90) in 1851, by then a convert from the church of England to Catholicism of some six years' standing. Queen Victoria, he had a Russian count Potemkin declare, had the number of the beast: 'You may recollect that number is 666; now, she came to the throne in the year thirty-seven [1837], at which date she was eighteen years old. Multiply then 37 by 18, and you have the very number 666, which is the mystical emblem of the lawless King!!!'[74]

---

[72] George Stanley Faber, *Remarks on the Effusion of the Fifth Apocalyptic Vial, and the Late Extraordinary Restoration of the Imperial Revolutionary Government of France* (London: F. C. and J. Rivington, 1815), p. 5.

[73] See David Brady, *The Contribution of British Writers between 1560 and 1830 to the Interpretation of Revelation 13: 16–18* (Tübingen: Mohr Siebeck, 1983).

[74] John Henry Newman, *Lectures on the Present Position of Catholics in England* (London: Longman, Green, and Co., 1892), p. 35. On Newman and the Antichrist, see especially Paul Misner, 'Newman and the Tradition concerning the Papal Antichrist', *Church History* 42 (1973), 377–95. I am indebted to Misner for this account. See also Vicchio, *The Legend of the Antichrist*, ch. 9, locations 6568–7316.

Along with Newman's conversion to Catholicism from Anglicanism went another – from the papacy as a present Antichrist to an individual Antichrist yet to come. Until 1843, he wrote in his *Apologia pro Vita Sua* (1864), his imagination 'remained stained' by the idea that the pope was the Antichrist. He had read Thomas Newton's *Dissertations on the Prophecies* in 1816 when he was 15 years old and in consequence 'became most firmly convinced that the Pope was the Antichrist predicted by Daniel, St. Paul, and St. John'.[75]

By the early 1830s, however, Newman was moving away from the evangelical 'low' church wing of the church of England towards the 'high' church wing that saw Anglicanism as a middle way between Catholic Rome and Calvinist Geneva. Anglicanism, for him, was better termed 'Anglo-catholicism'. Consequently, his views on the papal Antichrist were softening. Thus, for example, in a sermon of 27 May 1832, he spoke generally of 'the spirit of Antichrist', 'the chief Antichrists who have, in these last times, occupied the scene of the world', and 'anti-Christian power'.[76] Again, in 1833 in his first major work, *The Arians of the Fourth Century*, he wrote only of 'the spirit of Antichrist'.[77] And, whereas in 1816 he had dated the papal Antichrist from Pope Gregory the Great, around 600, he now saw the 'papal apostasy' as having

[75] John Henry Newman, *Apologia Pro Vita Sua: Being a Reply to a Pamphlet entitled 'What, then, does Dr. Newman mean?'* (London: Longman, Green, Longman, Roberts, and Green, 1864), pp. 62–3.

[76] John Henry Newman, *Fifteen Sermons Preached before the University of Oxford* (London: Rivingtons, 1872), pp. 120, 126, 135.

[77] John Henry Newman, *The Arians of the Fourth Century* (London: E. Lumley, 1871), pp. 3, 478 n.

only begun with the Council of Trent in the mid sixteenth century.

Five years later, in 1838, he directly rejected the
notion that the church of Rome, whether before or after
Trent, was ever the Antichrist.[78] His most telling argument, and one that indicated that his bonds to the church
of England were loosening significantly, was that all the
criticisms of the Roman church were equally applicable
to its English counterpart:

> If Rome has committed fornication with the kings of the earth,
> what must be said of the Church of England with her temporal
> power, her Bishops in the House of Lords, her dignified clergy,
> her prerogatives, her pluralities, her buying and selling of pre-
> ferments, her patronage, her corruptions, and her abuses? If
> Rome's teaching be a deadly heresy, what is our Church's,
> which 'destroys more souls than it saves?' … We cannot prove
> her the enchantress of the Apocalyptic Vision, without incur-
> ring our share in its application.[79]

He had also turned against his apocalyptic mentor,
Thomas Newton, whom he still saw as the main source
of the view that the papacy was the Antichrist. At the
best, his savaging of Newton's personality was a sign of
the ongoing influence of Newton's reading of the papal
Antichrist. At the worst, Newman could be accused of
the opposite of the kindness and amiability that he purported to find in Newton:

---

[78] See John Henry Newman, *A Letter to the Rev. Godfrey Faussett, D.D.
Margaret Professor of Divinity* (Oxford: John Henry Parker, 1838),
p. 16. The claim in the first edition of *The Arians of the Fourth Century*
that the papal apostasy began only with the Council of Trent
was dropped from the third edition in 1871.

[79] *Ibid.*, pp. 32–3.

Now we are going to commit what may seem an invidious act, to appeal to the private life of a respectable and amiable man. His Dissertations on the Prophecies, however, are the main source, we suppose, of that anti-Roman opinion on the subject of Antichrist, now afloat among us, as far as men have an opinion; and if we venture to speak hardly against him, it is only to prevent his being believed, when he speaks hardly of his betters ... of Newton's kindness of heart and amiableness we have no doubt at all; but a man so idolatrous of comfort, so liquorish of preferment, whose most fervent aspiration apparently was that he might ride in a carriage and sleep on down, whose keenest sorrow that he could not get a second appointment without relinquishing the first, who cast a regretful look back upon his dinner while he was at supper, and anticipated his morning chocolate in his evening muffins, who will say that this is the man, not merely to unchurch, but to smite, to ban, to wither the whole of Christendom for many centuries, and the greater part of it even in his own day, if not, as we shall presently show to be the case, indirectly his own branch also.[80]

Newman had developed his alternative to the papal Antichrist in 1833 in four sermons he had then preached. Although derived from the early church fathers, this was a declaration of a future Antichrist in the Adsonian tradition and a rejection of the Joachite. The Antichrist, declared Newman, was still to come. He was neither a power nor a kingdom, but 'one man, an individual'.[81] That it would be some one person was made likely by the

[80] John Henry Newman, *Essays Critical and Historical* (London: Longman, Green, and Co., 1907), vol. II, pp. 134–9.
[81] Members of the University of Oxford, *Tracts for the Times: Vol. V. for 1838–40* (London: J. G. F. & J. Rivington, 1840), p. 7.

historical anticipations of the final Antichrist – Antiochus Epiphanes, Julian the Apostate, Muhammad the prophet, and (although he doesn't name him, he clearly intends him) Napoleon.

According to Newman, the Antichrist would only arrive immediately before Christ. He would appear in a time of apostasy, 'a very awful and unparalleled outbreak of evil'.[82] He would be an open blasphemer, opposing himself to every existing worship, and a persecutor. When he arrived, Newman believed, the Jews would support him. 'It was the judicial punishment of the Jews, as of all unbelievers in one way or another, that having rejected the true Christ, they should take up with a false one.'[83] He would be a Jew, restore Jewish worship, and observe the Jewish rites. He would also be the creator of a new form of worship, in the style of the French Revolution, in which the spirit of Antichrist was already present. The Antichrist would be supported by a display of apparent miracles. He would appear at the very end of the Roman Empire (the present framework of society) and rule for three and a half years. This would be a time of great tribulation for the church, far greater than anything it had known before. It would only end when Christ came in judgement.

Without putting too fine a point on it, Newman was essentially reproducing the sixteenth-century Catholic futurist readings of the Antichrist exemplified in the work of Cardinal Bellarmine.[84] But there is no sign in Newman's sermons on the Antichrist that he is drawing

[82] *Ibid.*, p. 10.   [83] *Ibid.*, p. 18.   [84] See Chapter 6 above.

directly on any of these. Rather, the most direct influence is probably his Anglican contemporary Samuel R. Maitland (1792–1866), priest and librarian to the archbishop of Canterbury. Maitland was the first Protestant to accept the Catholic futurist pushback against the papal Antichrist. In his *An Attempt to Elucidate the Prophecies concerning Antichrist* in 1830, he summed up the key differences between the position held by all Christians concerning the Antichrist until the twelfth century and those held by Protestants from the time of the Reformation to the present day. These were, first, that the early church did not expect 'the Apostacy' to take place until three and a half years before the return of Christ, in contrast to the Protestant belief that it took place more than a thousand years ago. Second, while the early church expected an individual Antichrist, who would be an infidel blasphemer, giving honour to no God and expecting to be himself worshipped, Protestant writers supposed a succession of individuals, each of whom in turn became part of an Antichrist composed of the whole series. The leader of this corporate Antichrist has been, and is, the Roman pope. He found the position of the early church to be the correct Scriptural position. Thus, he declared:

It will be obvious therefore, that I do not find in the Scripture anything about the ten Gothic kingdoms, or the delusions of Mahomet, the overthrow of the French monarchy, or the Turkish Empire. I believe that the prophetic Scriptures do not (unless it may be incidentally) throw any light on the state of things, either in the Church or in the world, previous to the breaking out of the Apostacy. The main subject I believe to be, the great and final struggle between the God of this world, and the God of Heaven – between the Destroyer, and the Redeemer of man – between Christ, and Antichrist.[85]

Deconstructing the Antichrist

After his conversion to Catholicism in 1845 Newman made little of the Antichrist who was to come. But among apocalyptic Catholics in the nineteenth century the Adsonian take on the Antichrist remained dominant. As 'anti-Popery' in England came off the boil in the mid nineteenth century, so also the 'papal Antichrist' lost some of its social and political purchase among Protestants. An intellectual space was thereby opened up, following the lead of Samuel Maitland, for the return of the Adsonian Antichrist to English Protestantism, whence it was to migrate to North America. From that time to the present, within conservative Protestant circles, the fortunes of both the Adsonian and the papal Antichrist have waxed and waned.[86] Ironically however, within the Anglophone Protestant world, from the middle of the nineteenth century the Adsonian image of the tyrannical Antichrist, whether present or future, has dominated the theological landscape.

That said, from the middle of the nineteenth century, within both mainstream Catholic and Protestant theology, 'the Antichrist' became more muted. Above all, this was the consequence of the rise of the historical criticism (or higher criticism) of the Bible and of the prophetic

---

[85] S. R. Maitland, *An Attempt to Elucidate the Prophecies concerning Antichrist* (London: C. J. G. and F. Rivington, 1830), p. 3.
[86] See Robert Fuller, *Naming the Antichrist: The History of an American Obsession* (New York: Oxford University Press, 1996).

books, Daniel and Revelation, in particular. The key principle of historical criticism was to treat the Bible like any other ancient text. The consequence of this was that the relationship between the prophetic texts and history collapsed. The connection between prophetic prediction and historical fulfilment was broken. And the criss-crossing between sacred and profane history was ended.

The year 1860 saw the publication of *Essays and Reviews*, a collection of seven essays by six Anglican clergymen and one layman. It summed up the nineteenth-century challenges to the Bible from historical criticism, geology, and biology. It appeared four months after Charles Darwin's *On the Origin of Species*. It sold 22,000 copies in two years, more than Darwin's *Origin* in its first twenty years. It was, as Josef L. Altholz puts it, to provoke 'a crisis of faith contemporary with that provoked by Darwin's *Origin of Species* but more central to the religious mind'.[87] The controversy was as heated as it was not so much because of the quality or originality of the essays, but because the essays highlighted a challenge to 'the Church' from 'the University'. Academic freedom was pitted against religious faith.

This was particularly reflected in the final essay in the collection, 'On the Interpretation of Scripture', by Benjamin Jowett (1817–93), then Regius Professor of Greek at the University of Oxford.[88] On the face of it,

---

[87] Josef L. Altholz, 'The Mind of Victorian Orthodoxy: Anglican Responses to "Essays and Reviews", 1860–1864', *Church History* 51 (1982), 186.

[88] Jowett was the subject of a Balliol rhyme: 'Here come I, my name is Jowett. / All there is to know I know it. / I am Master of this College, / What I don't know isn't knowledge!'

his argument was a simple one: 'Interpret the Scripture like any other book.'[89] For Jowett, this meant that there was only one meaning, and this was the original one, 'the meaning, that is, of the words as they first struck on the ears of or flashed before the eyes of those who read and heard them'.[90] So the 'original meaning' of the Bible is neither a written source behind the text, nor is it the events or circumstances that lie behind the text. Rather, it is the Bible itself that 'remains as at the first unchanged amid the changing interpretations of it'.[91] If we remain focused on the text itself, he believed, its true meaning would reveal itself. This did not mean, for Jowett, that the Bible had no more authority than other ancient texts. Rather, the Bible will still remain unlike any other book: 'its beauty will be freshly seen, as of a picture which is restored after many ages to its original state'.[92]

In sum, the true interpreter needed imaginatively to travel around the history of the interpretations of the Bible to the Bible itself. In effect, in the history of Christianity, the historical interpretations were not 'interpretations' of Scripture so much as merely 'applications' of it. If we apply Scripture under the pretence of interpreting it, he wrote, then 'the language of Scripture becomes only a mode of expressing the public feeling or opinion of our own day. Any passing phase of politics or art, or spurious philanthropy, may have a kind of scriptural authority.'[93] The task of the critical interpreter of Scripture, then, is to be a corrective influence on its historical and popular

[89] [John William Parker (ed.)], *Essays and Reviews* (London: John W. Parker and Son, 1860), p. 377. See also pp. 338, 375, 404.
[90] *Ibid.*, p. 338. [91] *Ibid.*, pp. 337–8. [92] *Ibid.*, p. 375.
[93] *Ibid.*, pp. 407–8.

use. Until such time as the critical approach to the Bible becomes determinative,

[t]he Protestant and Catholic, the Unitarian and Trinitarian will continue to fight their battle on the ground of the New Testament. The Preterists and Futurists, those who maintain that the roll of prophecies is completed in past history, or in the apostolical age; those who look forward to a long series of events which are yet to come ... may alike claim the authority of Daniel, or the Revelation. Apparent coincidences will always be discovered by those who want them.[94]

It is the critical approach to the Bible, he declared, that is leading Protestants to doubt whether the Reformation doctrine that the Pope is Antichrist is discoverable in Scripture.[95]

Five years earlier, in 1855, Jowett had applied his method to the Antichrist in the guise of 'The Man of Sin' in his commentary on the Second Epistle to the Thessalonians (2.3). In this work, 1,800 years of speculation on the identity of the Antichrist were gently and quietly laid to rest. He reminded his readers that, at this period of his life, St Paul himself expected 'to remain and be alive' (1 Thessalonians 4.17) in the Day of the Lord. When the coming of Christ was to be preceded by Antichrist, he told them, it was clear that the vision of the future had to be confined within the next ten, twenty, or thirty years at the utmost, if it were not the case that the acts of the drama had already or were soon to begin.[96] There was an advantage, he declared, in excluding from

[94] *Ibid.*, p. 371.　[95] See *ibid.*, p. 411.
[96] Benjamin Jowett, *The Epistles of St. Paul to the Thessalonians, Galatians, Romans. With Critical Notes and Dissertations* (London: John Murray, 1859), p. 178.

the consideration of 'the Man of Sin' all those topics from which it had, in the past, derived its interest. 'We shall run no risk', he wrote,

of attributing an exaggerated importance to the history of our own time. We shall be under no temptation to point the words of St. Paul against an ancient enemy … We may hope to escape the charge which has been brought upon writers on these subjects, that they explain 'history by prophecy'. There will be no fear of our forging weapons of persecution for one body or party of Christians against another. *We shall be in no danger of losing the simplicity of the Gospel in Apocalyptic fantasies.*[97]

The Floating Signifier

The intellectual viability of 'the Antichrist' was closely tied to that of prophetic history. Where prophetic history continued to thrive, as it did during the twentieth century in American conservative evangelical Protestantism, so too did the Antichrist. But with the decline in prophetic history from the middle of the nineteenth century among more liberal forms of the Christian tradition, the Antichrist lost his place in the intellectual furniture of the Western mind. But he didn't disappear. Far from it. Rather like Simon Magus, he became a 'signifier' floating freely above the earth. We might say that he has shifted from the apocalyptic to become available for a much more general cultural critique of the evil present in the world and in others. 'The Antichrist' has now become a general category available for application to multiple references as the demonic 'other'.

[97] Fuller, *Naming the Antichrist*, p. 180 (my italics).

This has enabled the proliferation of Antichrist candidates. Granted the tradition of the papal Antichrist, Pope Francis is not unexpectedly high on the list (but any pope will do). That said, the tyrant outside the church is more present than the deceiver within. Among the most popular 'tyrants', Mussolini and Hitler top the list. Ronald Wilson Reagan (each of whose names has six letters), John F. Kennedy, and Barack Obama are favourites among American presidents. As I write, Donald Trump is rapidly gaining in popularity as a worthy candidate. Charles Prince of Wales and King Juan Carlos of Spain deserve honorary mentions. Henry Kissinger, secretary of state for both the Nixon and Ford administrations, was toppled from his high ranking by the Russian leader Mikhail Gorbachev. In spite of a female, in principle, not being a possible candidate for the Antichrist, Hillary Clinton is, to the best of my knowledge, the only woman to be accused of being so. Among notable Muslim leaders, we should include Saddam Hussein of Iraq, Mu'ammar Gaddafi of Libya, Yasser Arafat, Anwar Sadat, the Ayatollah Khomeini, and Osama bin Laden.

As we recall, the Antichrist can be a collective as well as an individual. Recent collectives named as Antichrist candidates have included New Age religion, rock music culture, the United Nations (sign of an impending 'new world order'), socialism, secular humanism, American Democrats, and modern technology (computers, microchips, fibre optics, zip codes, and supermarket bar codes). 'Progressive' social movements also feature strongly: feminism, the gay movement, advocates for abortion, and environmentalism. Islam and Catholicism have maintained their traditional high status as the Antichrist among conservative Protestants. But ecumenical multi-denominational Christian organisations have not been immune from criticism. Of the American Federal Council of Churches, the southern preacher J. Harold Smith leaves us in little doubt of what he thought: 'The Federal Council of Churches of the Anti-Christ would make prostitutes of your daughters and libertines of your sons … Leave this atheistic, communistic, Bible-ridiculing, blood-despising, name-calling, sex-manacled gang of green-eyed monsters and hell-bound devils before God's judgement is poured out on them.'[98]

The 'free-floating' Antichrist has also appeared in other guises in film and literature.[99] The most significant film culturally was *Rosemary's Baby* (1968), from the book of the same name by Ira Levin. This was not a story of overt evil, but of evil behind the picket fences of the everyday or, in this case, behind the Gothic brownstone apartment building. The relation to the Antichrist lies in the idea that Rosemary's baby is the consequence of her having been raped by the Devil and hence the child being the son of Satan (see Plate 29). Although we never see the child, 'He has his father's eyes', we are told after his birth. When Rosemary replies that her husband's eyes are normal, it is explained that

[98] Quoted in *ibid.*, p. 163.
[99] I have selected a number of 'Antichrists' in film and literature on several criteria: first, that the Antichrist figure has a 'real' and not merely 'arbitrary' relation to the Antichrist of history; second, that it can be said to have a general cultural importance and significance. For a full list, see the 'List of fictional Antichrists' available at www.artandpopularculture.com/List_of_fictional_Antichrists

Satan is his father, not Guy. He came up from Hell and begat a son of mortal woman … Satan is his father and his name is Adrian. He shall overthrow the mighty and lay waste their temples. He shall redeem the despised and wreak vengeance in the name of the burned and the tortured. Hail, Adrian! Hail, hail, Satan! Hail, Satan!

In *The Omen* series (1976–81), a box-office if not a critical success, it is the life and death of the Antichrist, as well as his birth, that was in play. Here, the Antichrist appeared as Damien Thorn, born on the sixth of the sixth month at 6.00 in the morning, and with a birthmark reading 666. Although he was born of a female jackal who died giving birth to him, he was fathered by Satan. By the third film in the series, *Omen III: The Final Conflict*, Damien has become American ambassador to Great Britain, where he expects that the second coming of Christ, as an infant, will re-occur. At his orders, his followers kill every male English newborn on the morning of 24 March, the day of the alignment of stars in the Cassiopeia constellation that generate a second star of Bethlehem. Christ eludes Damien's followers, before Damien is stabbed in the back by his follower, Kate Reynolds, with one of the seven daggers of Megiddo, the only weapons that can kill the Antichrist (see Plate 30). A vision of Christ appears in an archway, and Damien berates Christ for thinking that he has won. 'Nazarene', says Damien, 'you have won … nothing.'

The 'virtue' of the television series *Point Pleasant* (2005) lies in its rare female Antichrist figure, although the gender of the Antichrist figure seems here to have no 'deep' meaning. A young woman is rescued from a storm off Point Pleasant, New Jersey, a town we later learn is named in ancient signs and texts as 'home to the greatest coming of evil since the angels fell from heaven'. Christina (a near anagram of Antichrist) Nickson is taken in by a local family, the Kramers. Christina is the daughter of Satan, with the mark of the beast on the iris of one eye, and destined to destroy the world. 'She's the child of darkness', we are told, 'and she's under his protection. She's his daughter.' Tormented by visions of death and destruction, Christina is riven by the conflict between good and evil within her. At the end of the series, the audience is left unsure whether the good or the evil within wins the battle for her soul when she leaves Point Pleasant as it is engulfed by apocalyptic chaos.

With the eschatological tyrant in the *Left Behind* series of books (1995–2007) by Tim LaHaye and Jerry B. Jenkins, we return to more familiar territory. With over 80 million copies sold and the series adapted into four films, the Antichrist as the authoritarian tyrant has clearly resonated with modern audiences. That said, unlike the world, which ends eventually, this series of books seems to go on forever. The series is based on the futurist eschatology of John Nelson Darby (1800–82), founder of the Plymouth Brethren.[100] Its distinctive feature concerns the rapture into heaven by Christ of the faithful prior to the seven-year period on earth during which the Antichrist will rule before the eventual return of Christ. The core of the story concerns the fate of the chaotic world after the rapture. In these troubled times, a Romanian politician called Nicolae Carpathia becomes

[100] On the historical background of 'Left-Behind' theology, see David Malcolm Bennett. *The Origins of Left-Behind Eschatology* (Maitland, Florida: Xulon Press, 2010).

secretary-general of the United Nations with the promise of restoring order to the world. Carpathia is, in fact, the Antichrist, with a genealogy that goes back to ancient Rome.

From the position of secretary-general, Carpathia converts the United Nations into the Global Community, appointing himself as the Supreme Potentate. After three and a half years in power, Carpathia is murdered by an Israeli by the name of Chaim Rosenzweig. After three days, his body is possessed by Satan and he appears to rise from the dead. Carpathia creates the One World Unity Army, the mission of which is to take over Jerusalem and make it the capital of the new world. He gathers the armies in the valley of Armageddon for the final battle with Jesus and his army at the end of seven years after the rapture. Defeated by Christ, and with Satan exorcised from him, Carpathia kneels before Christ and declares him Lord before being sent into the lake of fire for eternity.

However nuanced, the Antichrist figure places the everyday against a cosmic background. Evil does not merely lie on the surface of things. Rather, to the evil inherent in human individuals and human collectives there are metaphysical depths. As Robert Fuller neatly puts it, 'Human history is thereby transformed into a drama of universal proportions … It is … a strategic battleground in the universal struggle between God and Satan, Christ and Antichrist.'[101] This is the central theme in 'A Short Story of the Antichrist' (appended to his *Three Conversations*) by the Russian philosopher Vladimir Solovyev (1853–1900). This is Nietzsche's 'superman'

---

[101] Fuller, *Naming the Antichrist*, p. 167.

(*Übermensch*) gone Adsonian apocalyptic. For Solovyev, the question of the Antichrist was part of the larger question of evil more generally. 'Is *evil* only a natural defect, an imperfection disappearing of itself with the growth of good, or is it a real *power*, possessing our world by means of temptations [deceptions], so that for fighting it successfully, assistance must be found in another sphere of being?'[102] For Solovyev, the problem of evil could only be solved supernaturally, and not naturally.

Solovyev's discussion of the nature of evil is contained within a series of conversations between a politician, Prince, Lady, General, and a Mr Z (Solovyev). At the end of the third conversation, Mr Z recounts a story by Father Pansophius entitled 'A Short Story of the Antichrist'. The key to this story lies in the Antichrist's not being a denier of Christianity but a false version of it. Its aim is to reveal not only the true nature of evil, but the falsity of Tolstoyan passive resistance to it. The setting for Solovyev's tale is Europe in the twenty-first century, finally brought together as the United States of Europe after the overthrow of the Pan-Mongol hordes from the East who had conquered it during the twentieth century.

At that time, there appeared a brilliant young man whom many called a superman and who vaingloriously thought of himself as the real Messiah.

He believed in God', we read, 'but at the bottom of his heart he involuntarily and unconsciously preferred himself to Him … In a word, he considered himself to be what Christ in reality was … I come last at the end of history for the very reason

---

[102] Vladimir Solovyev, *War, Progress, and the End of History: Three Discussions* (London: University of London Press, 1915), p. xix.

that I am most perfect. I am the final saviour of the world, and Christ – is my precursor.[103]

With that, he settled down to wait for God to call upon him to begin the work of saving humankind. Three years pass without an unmistakable divine calling, and he begins to lose faith in his messianic destiny, sufficiently so to throw himself off a cliff. He is carried back to the top of the cliff by a strange figure (Satan), who promises to help him. 'I am thy god and father', he tells the super-man, 'I have no other son but thee. Thou art the sole, the only begotten one, the equal of myself.'[104]

The next day, the superman locked himself in his study and rapidly wrote his most famous work, *The Open Way to the Universal Peace and Well-being*. Whereas many of his previous works had met with criticism from the pious for their 'exceptional and excessive self-love', this book was met with universal acclaim: 'On every side it was accepted as the revelation of the all-complete truth.'[105] Soon after its publication, a congress of the United States of Europe was held in Berlin. The superman was elected president of the United States of Europe and given the title '[Last] Roman Emperor'. His imperial residence was transferred from Rome to Jerusalem. A time of peace and prosperity now ensued, the result of the implementation of Marxist principles: 'Everybody now received according to his tal-ents, and every talent according to its work and merit.'[106]

Having solved the political and social problems, the emperor turned his attention to religion. He called the leaders of the three major branches of Christianity – Pope

---

[103] *Ibid.*, pp. 188–9.   [104] *Ibid.*, p. 192.
[105] *Ibid.*, pp. 194, 195.   [106] *Ibid.*, p. 199.

Peter II from the Catholic tradition, Elder John from the Orthodox, and Professor Ernst Pauli representing Protestantism – to a great ecumenical congress in the temple in Jerusalem. There he announced his intention of uniting them all under his leadership. Peter, John, and Pauli refused to join with him unless he acknowledged his Christian faith. An immense black cloud could now be seen covering the sky outside. Elder John, staring at the face of the silent emperor, declared to Peter, Pauli, and their remaining followers, 'My dearest ones, it is Anti-Christ.'[107] With that, a great thunderbolt flashed into the temple and killed Elder John. 'I had no wish', declared the emperor, 'to take any man's life, but thus my Heavenly Father avenges His beloved Son. It is finished. Who will oppose the will of the Most High?'[108] Pope Peter reiterated Elder John's accusation and was also struck down dead. Thus perished the 'two witnesses' of Revelation 11, now Peter and John, rather than Enoch and Elijah as the Adsonian tradition had it.

The bodies of the two witnesses were publicly exhibited in 'the street of the Christians'. Pauli and the faithful remnant of Christians fled to the desert mountains of Jericho. Four days later, they re-entered Jerusalem by night to retrieve the bodies of Peter and John. But, having been put onto stretchers, the dead men revived, and Pauli held each by the hand. In this way, we read, 'the unification of the churches took place in the midst of a dark night, on a high and deserted spot'.[109] The night darkness was then illuminated with light, and a woman appeared in the heavens. This was the woman clothed in the sun

---

[107] *Ibid.*, p. 215.   [108] *Ibid.*   [109] *Ibid.*, p. 223.

with the moon beneath her feet, and a wreath of twelve stars upon her head (Revelation 12.1). For Solovyev, this was the divine Wisdom (Sophia). Pauli, Peter, and John, together with the crowd of faithful that remained, followed the apparition to Mount Sinai.

Mr Z then told his listeners that the manuscript of Father Pansophius was cut short there. But Pansophius had told him how the story ended. Under the rule of the Antichrist, Mr Z reported, evil spread across the earth: 'Communion of the living with the dead, and also of men with demons, became a matter of everyday occurrence, and new unheard-of forms of mystic lust and demonology began to spread among the people.'[110] When the Antichrist had moved his capital to Jerusalem, the Jews had proclaimed him as the Messiah. But when they discovered that he wasn't even circumcised, they rose up against him. The emperor then issued a decree sentencing all rebellious Jews and Christians to death. Tens of thousands were massacred. Nevertheless, an army of 1 million Jews took Jerusalem and bottled up the Antichrist in the Temple Mount. By magic, the Antichrist found his way through the besieging army to Syria at the head of his pagan army. But before the army of the Jews could engage with that of the Antichrist, fiery streams of lava from an erupting volcano swallowed up the Antichrist and his army. The Jews fled back towards Jerusalem, praying that God would deliver them from peril. Then Christ returns:

When the holy city was already in sight, a great lightning cut the sky open from east to west, and they saw Christ

[110] *Ibid.*, p. 224.

descending to them in kingly apparel, and with the wounds from the nails on His outstretched hands. At the same time a crowd of Christians, led by Peter, John, and Paul, were moving from Sinai to Sion, and other crowds, all seized with enthusiasm, came flocking from all sides. These were all the Jews and Christians executed by the Anti-Christ. They rose to life, and reigned with Christ for a thousand years.[111]

Thus, for Solovyev, evil was never to be overcome through the natural processes of human history. It required the coming, the glorification, and eventually the destruction of evil incarnate by the supernatural intervention of Christ. Only Christ could defeat the Antichrist. Only the perfectly good could overcome the unspeakably evil.

[111] *Ibid*, p. 226.

EPILOGUE

A Brief Meditation on History

≈

The outstanding element … out of which an interpretation
of history could arise at all, is the basic experience of evil and
suffering, and of man's quest for happiness.

Karl Löwith, *Meaning in History* (1949)

The story of the Antichrist who comes at the end of history is part of a larger Christian story, one that begins
with the creation of the angels, of the world, and then
of Adam and Eve and other living things. It is a story
in which evil is central – cosmic evil as a result of the
fall of the angels, human evil as a result of the Fall of
the first humans. As its solution to the problem of evil,
Christianity created a linear history in which present,
past, and future evils would be finally and decisively
overcome at the end of history. Thus, Christian history
proceeded from fall and condemnation at the beginning
of history to redemption and salvation at its end. In short,
far from being a series of happenstance events over time,
history had a deep meaning.

Within the Christian tradition, this story has been
configured in two interwoven but quite distinct ways – in
terms of providence on the one hand, and apocalypse on
the other, the former more optimistic about the meaning
of history, the latter more pessimistic.

In the first of these, in spite of the presence of evil in
the world, the consequence of the freely chosen acts of
both humans and evil angels, the process from Fall to

final salvation is a relatively smooth one. It is punctuated definitively by the life, death, and resurrection of Jesus Christ, who was God made man. On this account, the work of Jesus is a sacrifice to God that satisfied the debt that man owed towards God for his sins. Here, the end of history is oriented towards the salvation of the individual. Although evil, configured as sin, continues after the debt that Christ paid, God is providentially working his purposes out as year succeeds to year until the Kingdom of God, inaugurated in the life, death, and resurrection of Christ, is fully and finally realised.

This optimistic view of history enabled Christianity to absorb the Platonic view of evil not as a thing in itself, but rather as a *privatio boni* – an absence of good. Consequently, evil was not at the depth of things, but only at their surface, more appearance than reality. History was not so much a site of conflict between good and evil as an inevitable progress towards the good. The problem of evil would be resolved within and through the processes of history. This was a view that the French philosopher Voltaire (1694–1778) met with withering criticism:

This system of All is good represents the author of nature only as a powerful and maleficent king, who does not care, so long as he carries out his plan, that it costs four or five hundred thousand men their lives, and that the others drag out their days in want and in tears. So far from the notion of the best of possible worlds being consoling, it drives to despair the philosophers who embrace it. The problem of good and evil remains an inexplicable chaos for those who seek in good faith.[1]

---

[1] Theodore Besterman (trans. and ed.), *Philosophical Dictionary* (London: Penguin, 2004), pp. 73–4.

The providentialist account intended to deal with evil as providing a context for the good and, at the end of the final day, as outweighed by the good. But Voltaire's point went to the incapacity of providence to deal with the unspeakably and irredeemably evil. This points to evil at the depths of things, metaphysical evil – not the merely bad, but evil with a capital 'E', we might say. As Voltaire was suggesting, in the face of unspeakable and irredeemable evil, the providential view of history is always on the verge of atheism, or at least demanding a radical rethink in the nature of God from benevolent to maleficent.

Within modernity, this faith in providentialism has been transformed into a belief in secular progress. It is a providentialism without God or any other permanent foundation beyond this world. Like providentialism, secular progress is intended conceptually to manage evil. But in the face of the unspeakably and irredeemably evil, it is always on the verge of having to declare history not in progress, but in decay, with no ultimate meaning or purpose at all. In short, in the face of unspeakable evil, secular progress is always on the edge of cosmic nihilism, on the precipice of nothing at all left to believe in.

In contrast to the stories of progress or providence, in the apocalyptic story history is not a site of progress, but a domain of conflict. Since the time of creation and the fall of the angelic and the human immediately afterwards, history has been the place of a conflict between good and evil, personified in the cosmic struggle between God and Satan and, eventually, between Christ and the Antichrist. Here, both good and evil are at the depth of things. On this account, humanity had been taken hostage by the Devil in the form of a serpent in the Garden of Eden, the result of capitulating to his temptations. The death of Jesus, however, paid a ransom to the Devil, thus freeing humanity from his power. Evil was thus constrained, if not destroyed.[2] At the end of history, however, the evil at the depth of things would be comprehensively and decisively defeated.

On this apocalyptic account, the problem of evil could not be resolved through the imminent processes of history. This is why the apocalyptic story resists a secular version of itself or renders one impossible in principle. In the apocalyptic story, the solution to evil is transcendent and not imminent – of the sacred and not of the secular. History manifests this conflict, but it cannot resolve it. Resolution depends upon a transcendent event beyond the imminent realm, an event that is both outside, and also the end of, history. Thus, although after his defeat by Christ, Satan was imprisoned for a 'thousand years' and evil constrained, it was necessary for him to be eventually released. Only thus could cosmic evil be defeated in the victory of God over Satan at the end of time. Thus, too, at the end of history, human evil needed to be summed up in one man – the Antichrist. Only thus could human evil be finally defeated in the victory of Christ over the Antichrist. On the apocalyptic story, meaning in history was thus realised only outside history and at its completion.

I want to end where Karl Löwith in his *Meaning in History* began: 'To ask earnestly the question of the ultimate meaning of history', he declared, 'takes one's breath away; it transports us into a vacuum which only hope and

---

[2] See Almond, *The Devil*, ch. 3.

faith can fill.'³ Where, then, might ultimate meaning in history reside – in divine providence, or secular progress in history, in an apocalyptic battle at its end, or in no place at all? In the face of unspeakable and irredeemable evil, stories of divine providence or secular progress fail to be persuasive. Simply put, evil is too much and too often with us. The world does not seem to be becoming a better place. ''Tis all in peeces, all cohaerence gone', as John Donne eloquently put it. The final eschatological battle provides an ideal solution. It is how the conflict between good and evil ought to end. But, for many of us, it is no longer possible to believe that the problem of evil will be resolved in the defeat of Satan and the Antichrist at the end of history. Does this leave cosmic nihilism as the only remaining alternative? Well, perhaps!

But the acceptance of cosmic nihilism does not mean the endorsement of personal nihilism. That there may be no ultimate meaning in history does not entail that there is no meaning in our individual histories. That there is no meaning of life does not exclude the possibility that meaning can be found in our individual lives. Thus, the solution to the question of evil may be not so much a matter of cosmic as of personal meaning, a matter of how we comport ourselves as ethical subjects in the present and the future. Here lies the ultimate meaning of the story of the Antichrist. It is a story about the future that lays upon us the ethical imperative that we take evil seriously in the here and now, *as if* it has metaphysical depths. This is eschatology within the limits of the ethical alone.

³ Karl Löwith, *Meaning in History* (University of Chicago Press, 1949), p. 4.

Thus, the story of the Antichrist directs us towards 'the Christ within' rather than 'the Antichrist within', to the examination and regulation of the ethical self, to the cultivation of the good. It demands a personal spirituality that maximises good and minimises harm. It also requires an ethical commitment to progress towards the good and away from evil over the course of our lives. It entails that we pursue personal goodness in the hope that, at the end of our part in history, the world will be no worse, and perhaps a little better, for our having been in it.

BIBLIOGRAPHY

Abbreviations

ANF: Roberts, Alexander and James Donaldson (eds.),
revised by A. Cleveland Coxe, *Ante-Nicene Fathers*
(Peabody, Massachusetts: Hendrickson Publishers,
2004).

NPNF, first series: Schaff, Philip (ed.), *Nicene and Post-Nicene
Fathers, first series* (Peabody, Massachusetts: Hendrickson
Publishers, 2012).

NPNF, second series: Schaff Philip and Henry Wace (eds.),
Nicene and Post-Nicene Fathers, second series (Peabody,
Massachusetts: Hendrickson Publishers, 2012).

PL: Migne, Jacques Paul (ed.), *Patrologiae Cursus Completus,
Latina*.

Works Consulted

Alexander, Paul J. (ed. Dorothy deF. Abrahamse), *The
Byzantine Apocalyptic Tradition* (Berkeley: University of
California Press, 1985).

Allison, Dale C., Jr, 'The Eschatology of Jesus', in John J.
Collins (ed.), *The Encyclopedia of Apocalypticism: Vol. I, The
Origins of Apocalypticism in Judaism and Christianity* (New
York: Continuum, 1998), pp. 267–302.

Almond, Philip C., *Afterlife: A History of Life after Death*
(London and Ithaca: I. B. Tauris and Cornell University
Press, 2016).

The Devil: A New Biography (London and Ithaca: I. B.
Tauris and Cornell University Press, 2014).

God: A New Biography (London: I. B. Tauris, 2018).

'Henry More and the Apocalypse', *Journal of the History of
Ideas* 54 (1993), 189–200.

'John Napier and the Mathematics of the "Middle Future"
Apocalypse', *Scottish Journal of Theology* 63 (2010), 54–69.

A Priest of Mount Melleray (trans.), *St. Bernard's Sermons
on the Canticle of Canticles* (Dublin: Browne and Nolan,
Limited, 1920).

Altholz, Josef L., 'The Mind of Victorian Orthodoxy:
Anglican Responses to "Essays and Reviews", 1860–
1864', *Church History* 51 (1982), 186–97.

Anderson, Andrew Runni, *Alexander's Gate, Gog and Magog,
and the Inclosed Nations* (Cambridge, Massachusetts:
Medieval Academy of America, 1932).

Anon., *A full and true account of the dreadful and melancholy
Earthquake, which happened between twelve and one o'clock
in the morning, on Thursday the fifth instant. With an exact
list of such persons as have hitherto been found in the Rubbish*
(London, 1750).

*The Identity of Napoleon and Antechrist; Completely
Demonstrated or a Commentary on the Chapters of the
Scripture which relate to Antechrist* (New York: Sargeant,
1809).

Archer, Gleason L. (trans.), *St. Jerome, Commentary on Daniel,
7* in Roger Pearse (ed.), *Early Church Fathers – Additional
Texts*. Available at www.tertullian.org/fathers/index
.htm#JeromeChronicle

Armstrong, Regis J. et al., *Volume III of Francis of Assisi: Early
Documents* (New York: New City Press, 2001).

Babcock, William S. (trans.), *Tyconius: The Book of Rules*
(Atlanta, Georgia: Scholars Press, 1989).

Backus, Irena, *Reformation Readings of the Apocalypse: Geneva,
Zurich, and Wittenberg* (Oxford University Press, 2000).

Balderston, Katherine C. (ed.), *Thraliana: The Diary of Mrs.
Hester Lynch Hale, 1776–1809* (Oxford: Clarendon Press,
1951).

Bartusch, Mark W., *Understanding Dan: An Exegetical Study
of a Biblical City, Tribe and Ancestor* (London: Sheffield
Academic Press, 2003).

Bauckham, Richard, 'The List of Tribes in Revelation Again', *Journal for the Study of the New Testament* 42 (1991), 99–115.

Baxter, M., *Louis Napoleon: The Destined Monarch of the World* (Philadelphia: James S. Claxton, 1867).

Bennett, David Malcolm, *The Origins of Left-Behind Eschatology* (Maitland, Florida: Xulon Press, 2010).

Besterman, Theodore (trans. and ed.) *Philosophical Dictionary* (London: Penguin, 2004).

Birdsall, J. N., 'Irenaeus and the Number of the Beast: Revelation 13.18', in A. Denaux (ed.), *New Testament Textual Criticism and Exegesis* (Leuven University Press, 2002), pp. 349–59.

Blackwell, Richard J., 'Galileo Galilei', in Gary B. Ferngren (ed.), *Science & Religion: A Historical Introduction* (Baltimore and London: The Johns Hopkins University Press, 2002), pp. 105–16.

Bliss, James (trans.), *Morals on the Book of Job by St. Gregory the Great* (Oxford and London: John Henry Parker and J. Rivington, 1844). Available at www.lectionarycentral .com/gregorymoraliaindex.html

Blumenfeld-Kosinski, Renate, *Not of Woman Born: Representations of Caesarean Birth in Medieval and Renaissance Culture* (Ithaca: Cornell University Press, 1990).

Bonura, Christopher, 'When Did the Legend of the Last World Emperor Originate? A New Look at the Textual Relationship between *The Apocalypse of Pseudo-Methodius* and the *Tiburtine Sibyl*', *Viator* 47 (2016), 47–100.

Borelli, Anne and Maria Pastore Passo (trans.), *Selected Writings of Girolamo Savonarola: Religion and Politics, 1490–1498* (New Haven: Yale University Press, 2006).

Bostick, Curtis V., *The Antichrist and the Lollards: Apocalypticism in Late Medieval and Reformation England* (Leiden: Brill, 1998).

Boureau, Alain, *The Myth of Pope Joan* (University of Chicago Press, 2000).

Bousset, Wilhelm, *The Antichrist Legend; A Chapter in Christian and Jewish Folklore, Englished from the German of W. Bousset* (London: Hutchinson and Co., 1896).

Brady, David, *The Contribution of British Writers between 1560 and 1830 to the Interpretation of Revelation 13: 16–18* (Tübingen: Mohr Siebeck, 1983).

Budge, Ernest A. Wallis (trans.), *A Christian Legend concerning Alexander*, in Ernest A. Wallis Budge, *The History of Alexander the Great*.
The History of Alexander the Great, Being the Syriac Version of the Pseudo-Callisthenes (Cambridge University Press, 1889).

Burr, David, *Olivi's Peaceable Kingdom: A Reading of the Apocalypse Commentary* (Philadelphia: University of Pennsylvania Press, 1993).

Calvin, John, *Commentary on Philippians, Colossians, and Thessalonians* (Grand Rapids, Michigan: Christian Classics Ethereal Library, n.d.). Available at www.ccel .org/ccel/calvin/calcom42.pdf

Capes, William W. (ed.), *The Register of John Trefnant, Bishop of Hereford (A.D. 1389–1404)* (Hereford: Wilson and Phillips, 1914).

Cartwright, Steven R. and Kevin L. Hughes, *Second Thessalonians: Two Early Medieval Apocalyptic Commentaries* (Kalamazoo, Michigan: Medieval Institute Publications, 2001).

Catley, S. R. and J. Pratt (eds.), *The Acts and Monuments of John Foxe, Vol. III* (New York: AMS Press, 1965).

Chadwick, Henry (trans.), *Origen: Contra Celsum* (Cambridge University Press, 1953).

Charlesworth, James H. (ed.), *The Old Testament Pseudepigrapha, Vol. I* (New York: Doubleday, 1983).
The Old Testament Pseudepigrapha, Vol. II (New York: Doubleday, 1985).

Christmas, Henry (ed.), *Select Works of John Bale, D.D.* (Cambridge University Press, 1849).

Cohn, Norman, *The Pursuit of the Millennium* (London: Paladin, 1970).

Collins, John J., 'From Prophecy to Apocalypticism: The Expectation of the End', in John J. Collins (ed.), *The Encyclopedia of Apocalypticism: Vol. I, The Origins of Apocalypticism in Judaism and Christianity* (New York: Continuum, 1998), pp. 129–61.

Constable, Olivia Remie (ed.), *Medieval Iberia: Readings from Christian, Muslim, and Jewish Sources* (Philadelphia: University of Pennsylvania Press, 2012).

Cooper, James and Arthur John Maclean (trans.), *The Testament of Our Lord* (Edinburgh: T. & T. Clark, 1902).

Coulton, G. G., *From St. Francis to Dante: Translations from the Chronicle of the Franciscan Salimbene, 1221–1288* (Philadelphia: University of Pennsylvania Press, 1972).

'Council of Constance 1414–18', *Papal Encyclicals Online*. Available at www.papalencyclicals.net/councils/ecum16 .htm

Court, John M., *The Book of Revelation and the Johannine Apocalyptic Tradition* (Sheffield Academic Press, 2000).

Croly, George, *Salathiel: The Wandering Jew, a Story of the Past, Present, and Future* (London: H. Colburn, 1828).

Crouzet, Denis, 'Millennial Eschatologies in Italy, Germany, and France: 1500–1533', *Journal of Millennial Studies* 1 (1999), 1–8.

Cuthbert, Father, *The Friars and How They Came to England: Being a Translation of Thomas of Eccleston's De Adventu F.F. Minorum in Angliam* (London: Sands & Co., 1903).

Daley, Brian E., *The Hope of the Early Church: A Handbook of Patristic Eschatology* (Grand Rapids, Michigan: Baker Academic, 1991).

Davis, William C., *The Millennium, or, A Short Sketch on the Rise and Fall of Antichrist* (Salisbury: Coupee and Crider, 1811).

Dell, William, *A Testimony from the Word against Divinity Degrees in the University* (London, 1653).

DeVun, Leah, *Prophecy, Alchemy, and the End of Time: John of Rupescissa in the Late Middle Ages* (New York: Columbia University Press, 2014).

Dunbar, David, 'The Delay of the Parousia in Hippolytus',
    Vigiliae Christianae 37 (1983), 313–27.
  'The Eschatology of Hippolytus of Rome', PhD
    dissertation, Drew University, 1979.
Elliott, J. K. (ed.), *The Apocryphal New Testament* (Oxford:
    Clarendon Press, 1993).
Elrington, Charles Richard, *The Whole Works of the Most Rev.
    James Ussher... Vol. VII* (Dublin: Hodges, Smith, and
    Co., 1864).
Emerton, Ephraim (trans.), *The Correspondence of Pope Gregory
    VII* (New York: Columbia University Press, 1932).
  'Antichrist as Anti-saint: The Significance of Abbot Adso's
    Libellus de Antichristo', *The American Benedictine Review* 30
    (1979), 175–90.
Emmerson, Richard K., *Antichrist in the Middle Ages: A Study
    of Medieval Apocalypticism, Art, and Literature* (Seattle:
    University of Washington Press, 1981).
Evans, Elizabeth C., *Physiognomics in the Ancient World*
    (Philadelphia: The American Philosophical Society,
    1969).
Exsurge Domine: Condemning the Errors of Martin Luther.
    Available at www.papalencyclicals.net/leo10/l10exdom.ht
Faber, George Stanley, *A Dissertation on the Prophecies*
    (Boston: Andrews and Cummings, 1808)
  *Remarks on the Effusion of the Fifth Apocalyptic Vial, and the
    Late Extraordinary Restoration of the Imperial Revolutionary
    Government of France* (London: F. C. and J. Rivington,
    1815).
  *The Sacred Calendar of Prophecy: Or a Dissertation on the
    Prophecies* (London: C. and J. Rivington, 1828).
Falls, Thomas B. (trans.), *Dialogue with Trypho*, in Thomas B.
    Falls (trans.), *Saint Justin Martyr* (Washington, DC: The
    Catholic University of America Press, 2008).
Ferreiro, Alberto, 'Simon Magus: The Patristic-Medieval
    Traditions and Historiography', *Apocrypha* 7 (1996),
    147–65.

'Fifth Lateran Council 1512–17 A.D.', *Papal Encyclicals Online*. Available at www.papalencyclicals.net/councils/ecum1 8.htm

Fleming, William F. (trans.), *The Works of Voltaire: A Contemporary Version* (New York: Dingwall-Rock, 1927), 19.1, pp. 172–76. Available at www.k-state.edu/english/ baker/english287/Voltaire-Newton.htm

Forbes, Clarence A. (trans.), *Firmicus Maternus: The Error of the Pagan Religions* (New York: Newman Press, 1970).

Force, James E., *William Whiston: Honest Newtonian* (Cambridge University Press, 2002).

Ford, J. Massyngbaerde, 'The Physical Features of the Antichrist', *Journal for the Study of the Pseudepigrapha* 14 (1996), 23–41.

Fox, Matthew (ed.), *Hildegard of Bingen's Book of Divine Works with Letters and Songs* (Santa Fe, New Mexico: Bear and Company, 1987).

Francisco, Adam S., *Martin Luther and Islam: A Study in Sixteenth-Century Polemics and Apologetics* (Leiden: Brill, 2007).

Froom, Le Roy Edwin, *The Prophetic Faith of Our Fathers… Vol. II* (Washington, DC: Review and Herald, 1948).

Fudge, Thomas A., *Jerome of Prague and the Foundations of the Hussite Movement* (Oxford University Press, 2016).

Fuller, Robert, *Naming the Antichrist: The History of an American Obsession* (New York: Oxford University Press, 1996).

Garrett, Clarke, *Respectable Folly: Millenarians and the French Revolution in England* (Baltimore and London: The Johns Hopkins University Press, 1975).

Gilbert, Allan (trans.), *The Letters of Machiavelli: A Selection of His Letters* (New York: Capricorn Books, 1961).

Gilley, S. W., 'George Stanley Faber: No Popery and Prophecy', in P. J. Harland and C. T. R. Hayward, *New Heaven and New Earth: Prophecy and the New Millennium* (Leiden: Brill, 1999), pp. 287–304.

Glimm, Francis X. et al. (trans.), *The Apostolic Fathers* (Washington, DC: The Catholic University of America Press, 2010).

Gosse, Edmund, *Father and Son: A Study of Two Temperaments* (Boston: Houghton Mifflin, 1965).

The Life of Philip Henry Gosse F.R.S. (London: Kegan Paul, Trench, Trübner & Co., Ltd, 1890).

Grant, Ryan (trans.), *Antichrist: St. Robert Bellarmine, S.J.* E-book (Kindle edition) (Post Falls, Idaho: Mediatrix Press).

Gregory the Great, *Dialogues*. Available at www.tertullian .org/fathers/gregory_03_dialogues_book3.htm#C38

Gumerlock, Francis X. (trans.) and David C. Robinson (intro.), *Tyconius: Exposition of the Apocalypse* (Washington, DC: The Catholic University of America Press, 2017).

Haberkern, Philip N., *Patron Saint and Prophet: Jan Hus in the Bohemian and German Reformations* (Oxford University Press, 2016).

Habershon, M., *A Dissertation on the Prophetic Scriptures, chiefly those of a Chronological Character* (London: James Nisbet and B. Wertheim, 1834).

Halperin, David H., 'The Ibn Sayyad Traditions and the Legend of Al-Dajjāl', *Journal of the American Oriental Society* 96 (1976), 213–25.

Hart, Mother Columba and Jane Bishop, *Hildegard of Bingen, Scivias* (New York: Paulist Press, 1990).

Hazlitt, William (trans.), *The Table Talk of Martin Luther* (London: George Bell and Sons, 1909).

Heiser, Richard H., 'The Court of the Lionheart on Crusade, 1190–2', *Journal of Medieval History* 43 (2017), 505–22.

Hill, Christopher, *Antichrist in Seventeenth-Century England* (London: Verso, 1990).

The World Turned Upside Down (Harmondsworth: Penguin, 1975).

Horsley, Samuel, *Critical Disquisitions on the Eighteenth Chapter of Isaiah* (Philadelphia: James Humphrey, 1800).

'Manuscript Letters of Bishop Horsley: Letter 1', *The British Magazine* 5 (1834), 131–4.

'Manuscript Letters of Bishop Horsley: Letter 5', *The British Magazine* 5 (1834), 517–23.

'Manuscript Letters of Bishop Horsley: Letter 6', *The British Magazine* 5 (1834), 10–12.

'Of the Prophetical Periods', *The British Magazine* 4 (1833), 717–41.

The Watchers and the Holy Ones. A Sermon (London: J. Matchard, 1806).

Hughes, K. L., *Constructing Antichrist: Paul, Biblical Commentary, and the Development of Doctrine in the Early Middle Ages* (Washington, DC: The Catholic University of America Press, 2012).

Hughes, K. L. (ed. and trans.), 'Haimo of Auxerre: Exposition of the Second Letter to the Thessalonians', in Cartwright and Hughes, *Second Thessalonians*, pp. 21–34.

Iliffe, Rob, *Priest of Nature: The Religious Worlds of Isaac Newton* (Oxford University Press, 2017).

James, Bruno Scott (trans.), *The Letters of St. Bernard of Clairvaux* (Chicago: Henry Regnery Company, 1953).

James, I of England and VI of Scotland, *The Workes of the most high and mightie Prince, James by the Grace of God, King of Great Britaine, France and Ireland* (London, 1616).

Jenks, Gregory C., *The Origins and Early Development of the Antichrist Myth* (Berlin: Walter de Gruyter, 1991).

Jowett, Benjamin, *The Epistles of St. Paul to the Thessalonians, Galatians, Romans. With Critical Notes and Dissertations* (London: John Murray, 1859).

Jurkowski, Maureen, 'Who Was Walter Brut?', *The English Historical Review* 127 (2012), 285–302.

Kaminsky, Howard, *A History of the Hussite Revolution* (Berkeley and Los Angeles: University of California Press, 1967).

Kaminsky, Howard et al. (eds.), 'Master Nicholas of Dresden, The Old Color and the New: Selected Works

Contrasting the Primitive Church and the Roman Church', *Transactions of the American Philosophical Society* 55 (1965), 1–93.

Kantorowicz, Ernst, *Frederick the Second, 1194–1250* (New York: Frederick Ungar Publishing Co., 1957).

Kaup, Matthias, *John of Rupescissa's Vade Mecum in Tribulatione* (London: Routledge, 2017).

Kelly, J. N. D., *Jerome: His Life, Writings, and Controversies* (London: Duckworth, 1975).

Kett, Henry, *History the Interpreter of Prophecy, or, a View of Scriptural Prophecies and their Accomplishment* (Oxford University Press, 1799).

Klaassen, Walter, *Living at the End of the Ages: Apocalyptic Expectations in the Radical Reformation* (Lanham, Maryland: University Press of America, 1992).

Klein, Darius Matthias (trans.), 'Excerpt from Commodianus' *Carmen Apologeticum*'. Available at http://christianlatin .blogspot.com/2008/08/excerpt-from-commodianus-carmen.html

Kritzeck, James Aloysius, *Peter the Venerable and Islam* (Princeton University Press, 2016).

Laing, David (ed.), *The Works of John Knox: Volume First* (Edinburgh: James Thin, 1895).

Landes, Paula Frederiksen, 'Tyconius and the End of the World', *Revue d'études augustiniennes et patristiques* 28 (1982), 59–75.

Landes, Richard, 'Lest the Millennium Be Fulfilled: Apocalyptic Expectations and the Pattern of Western Chronography 100–800 CE', in Werner Verbeke et al., *The Use and Abuse of Eschatology in the Middle Ages* (Leuven University Press, 1988), pp. 137–211.

'The Fear of an Apocalyptic Year 1000: Augustinian Historiography, Medieval and Modern', in Richard Landes, Andrew Gow, and David C. van Meter (eds.), *The Apocalyptic Year 1000: Religious Expectation and Social Change, 950–1050* (New York: Oxford University Press, 2003), pp. 243–70.

Lawlor, H. J. (trans.), *St. Bernard of Clairvaux's Life of St. Malachy of Armagh* (London: Macmillan, 1920).

Lerner, Robert E., 'Antichrists and Antichrist in Joachim of Fiore', *Speculum* 60 (1985), 553–70.

'Frederick II, Alive, Aloft and Allayed, in Franciscan–Joachite Eschatology', in Werner Verbeke et al. (eds.), *The Use and Abuse of Eschatology in the Middle Ages* (Leuven University Press, 1988), pp. 359–84.

'Refreshment of the Saints: The Time after Antichrist as a Station for Earthly Progress in Medieval Thought', *Traditio* 32 (1976), 97–144.

Lewis, Warren (trans. and ed.), *Peter of John Olivi: Commentary on the Apocalypse* (New York: Franciscan Institute Publications, 2017).

Loserth, Johann (ed.), *Iohannis Wyclif: Operis Evangelici Liber Tertius et Quartus sive De Antichristo Liber Primus et Secundus* (London: Wyclif Society, 1896).

Löwith, Karl, *Meaning in History* (University of Chicago Press, 1949).

Lull, Timothy and William R. Russell (eds.), *Martin Luther's Basic Theological Writings* (Minneapolis: Fortress Press, 2012).

Luther, Martin, *The Babylonian Captivity of the Church*, in Paul W. Robinson (ed.), *The Annotated Luther, Vol. III* (Minneapolis: Augsburg Fortress, 2016).

On War against the Turk, in Hans J. Hillerbrand (ed.), *The Annotated Luther, Vol. V* (Minneapolis: Augsburg Fortress, 2017).

To the Christian Nobility of the German Nation, in Timothy J. Wengert (ed.), *The Annotated Luther, Vol. I* (Minneapolis: Augsburg Fortress, 2015).

Maitland, S. R., *An Attempt to Elucidate the Prophecies concerning Antichrist* (London: C. J. G. and F. Rivington, 1830).

Mandeville, John, *The Travels of Sir John Mandeville* (London: Macmillan, 1900).

Manuel, Frank E., *The Religion of Isaac Newton* (Oxford: Clarendon Press, 1974).

Martyn, John R. C. (trans.), *The Letters of Gregory the Great* (Toronto: Pontifical Institute of Mediaeval Studies, 2004).

Maude, Louise and Aylmer (trans.), *War and Peace by Leo Tolstoy* (Minneapolis: First Avenue Editions, 2016).

Mayer, L., *The Prophetic Mirror; Or, a Hint to England* (London: Williams and Smith et al., 1806).

McGinn, Bernard, 'Angel Pope and Papal Antichrist', *Church History* 47 (1978), 155–73.

Antichrist: Two Thousand Years of Fascination with Evil (San Francisco: Harper, 1994).

'Portraying Antichrist in the Middle Ages', in Werner Verbeke et al., *The Use and Abuse of Eschatology in the Middle Ages* (Leuven University Press, 1988), pp. 1–48.

'Saint Bernard and Eschatology', in M. Basil Pennington (ed.), *Bernard of Clairvaux: Studies Presented to Dom Jean Leclercq* (Washington, DC: Consortium Press, 1973), pp. 161–85.

(trans.), 'Adso of Montier-en-Der: Letter on the Origin and the Time of the Antichrist', in McGinn (trans. and ed.), *Apocalyptic Spirituality*, pp. 81–96.

(trans. and ed.), *Apocalyptic Spirituality* (London: SPCK, 1979).

(ed.), *Visions of the End: Apocalyptic Traditions in the Middle Ages* (New York: Columbia University Press, 1998).

McNeill, John T., *Calvin: Institutes of the Christian Religion, Vol. II* (Louisville, Kentucky: Westminster John Knox Press, 2006).

Medieval Sourcebook: Twelfth Ecumenical Council: Lateran IV 1215. Available at https://sourcebooks.fordham.edu/basis/lateran4.asp

Melanson, Terry, *Perfectibilists: The 18th Century Bavarian Order of the Illuminati* (Chicago: Trine Day, 2011).

Members of the University of Oxford, *Tracts for the Times: Vol. V for 1838–40* (London: J. G. F. & J. Rivington, 1840).

Minnich, Nelson H., 'Prophecy and the Fifth Lateran Council (1512–1517)', in Nelson H. Minnich (ed.),

Councils of the Catholic Reformation: Pisa 1 (1409) to Trent (1545–63) (Aldershot: Ashgate Variorum, 2008), pp. 63–87.

Minns, Denis, *Irenaeus: An Introduction* (London: Bloomsbury, 2010).

Misner, Paul, 'Newman and the Tradition concerning the Papal Antichrist', *Church History* 42 (1973), 377–95.

More, Henry, *A Modest Enquiry into the Mystery of Iniquity* (London, 1664).

An Explanation of the Grand Mystery of Godliness (London, 1660).

A Plain and Continued Exposition of the several Prophecies or Divine Visions of the Prophet Daniel (London, 1681).

Apocalypsis Apocalypseos; or the Revelation of St John the Divine Unveiled (London, 1680).

Paralipomena Prophetica (London, 1685).

Napier, John, *A Plaine Discovery of the whole Revelation of Saint John: set down in two Treatises: the one searching and proving the true Interpretation thereof: the other applying the same paraphrastically and historically to the text* (Edinburgh: Robert Waldegrave, 1593).

Newman, John Henry, *A Letter to the Rev. Godfrey Faussett, D.D. Margaret Professor of Divinity* (Oxford: John Henry Parker, 1838).

Apologia Pro Vita Sua: Being a Reply to a Pamphlet entitled 'What, then, does Dr. Newman mean?' (London: Longman, Green, Longman, Roberts, and Green, 1864).

The Arians of the Fourth Century (London: E. Lumley, 1871).

Essays Critical and Historical (London: Longman, Green, and Co., 1907).

Fifteen Sermons Preached before the University of Oxford (London: Rivingtons, 1872).

Lectures on the Present Position of Catholics in England (London: Longman, Green, and Co., 1892).

Newport, Kenneth G. C., *Apocalypse and Millennium: Studies in Biblical Eisegesis* (Cambridge University Press, 2000).

Newsom, Carol A. with Brennan W. Breed, *Daniel: A Commentary* (Louisville, Kentucky: Westminster John Knox Press, 2014).

Newton, Isaac, *Observations upon the Prophecies of Daniel, and the Apocalypse of St. John* (London, 1733). *Yahuda Ms. 18.* Available at www.newtonproject.ox.ac.uk/view/texts/normalized/THEM00061

Newton, Thomas, *Dissertations on the Prophecies, which have been remarkably fulfilled in the World* (London: J. F. Dove, 1825).

Niccoli, Ottavia, *Prophecy and People in Renaissance Italy* (Princeton University Press, 1990).

O'Connor, Henry, S.J., *Luther's Own Statements concerning His Teaching and Its Results* (New York: Benziger Brothers, 1885).

Olivi, Peter, 'On the Seven Periods of Church History'. Available at https://sourcebooks.fordham.edu/source/olivi.asp

Osiander, Andreas, *The Coniectures of the Ende of the World* (Antwerp, 1548).

Painter, John, 'Johannine Literature: The Gospel and Letters of John', in David E. Aune, *The Blackwell Companion to the New Testament* (Oxford: Blackwell, 2010), pp. 344–72.

[Parker, John William (ed.)], *Essays and Reviews* (London: John W. Parker and Son, 1860).

Pastor, Ludwig, *History of the Popes, from the Close of the Middle Ages...Vol. V* (London: Kegan Paul, Trench, Trübner, & Co., 1901).

Patai, Raphael, *The Messiah Texts: Jewish Legends of Three Thousand Years* (Detroit: Wayne University Press, 1988).

Patrides, C. A. and Joseph Wittreich (eds.), *The Apocalypse in English Renaissance Thought and Literature: Patterns, Antecedents and Repercussions* (Manchester University Press, 1984).

Pearse, Roger (ed.), *The Chronicle of St. Jerome*, in *Early Church Fathers – Additional Texts*. Available at www.tertullian .org/fathers/index.htm#JeromeChronicle

Peerbolte, L. J. Lietaert, *The Antecedents of Antichrist: A Traditio-Historical Study of the Earliest Christian Views on Eschatological Opponents* (Leiden: Brill, 1996).

Penman, Leigh T. I., 'A Seventeenth-Century Prophet Confronts His Failures: Paul Felgenhauer's *Speculum Poenitentiae, Buß-Spiegel* (1625)', in Clare Copeland and Jan Machielsen (eds.), *Angels of Light? Sanctity and the Discernment of Spirits in the Early Modern Period* (Leiden: Brill, 2013), pp. 169–200.

Pesenson, Michael A., 'Napoleon Bonaparte and Apocalyptic Discourse in Early Nineteenth-Century Russia', *The Russian Review* 65 (2006), 373–92.

Prideaux, Humphrey, *The True Nature of Imposture Fully Displayed in the Life of Mahomet* (London, 1697).

Reeves, John C., (trans.), 'Sermon of Pseudo-Ephraem on the End of the World' (unpublished manuscript).

Trajectories in Near Eastern Apocalypses: A Postrabbinic Jewish Apocalyptic Reader (Atlanta: Society of Biblical Literature, 2005).

Reeves, Marjorie, *The Influence of Prophecy in the Later Middle Ages* (Oxford: Clarendon Press, 1969).

Resnick, Irven M. (trans.), *Peter the Venerable: Writings against the Saracens* (Washington, DC: The Catholic University of America Press, 2016).

Riess, Jonathan B., *The Renaissance Antichrist* (Princeton University Press, 1995).

Riley, Henry T. (ed.), *The Annals of Roger de Hoveden: Comprising the History of England, and of other Countries of Europe from A.D. 732 to A.D. 1201* (London: H. G. Bohn, 1853).

Robinson, Andrew, 'Identifying the Beast: Samuel Horsley and the Problem of Papal AntiChrist', *Journal of Ecclesiastical History* 43 (1992), 592–607.

Rosenstiehl, J.–M., 'Le Portrait de l'Antichrist', in
    M. Philonenko et al. (eds.), *Pseudépigraphes de l'Ancien
    Testament et Manuscrits de la Mer Morte* (Paris: Presses
    Universitaires de France, 1967), pp. 45–60.
Rousseau, George, '"Wicked Whiston" and the Scriblerians:
    Another Ancients–Modern Controversy', *Studies in
    Eighteenth-Century Culture* 17 (1987), 17–44.
Rusconi, Robert, 'Antichrist and Antichrists', in Bernard
    McGinn (ed.), *The Encyclopedia of Apocalypticism: Vol. II*
    (New York: Continuum, 1998), pp. 287–325.
Sahih Bukhari. Available at www.sahih-bukhari.com
Salmon, Joseph, *Antichrist in Man* (London, 1649).
Saritoprak, Zeki, *Islam's Jesus* (Gainsville: University Press of
    Florida, 2014).
Schaff, David S. (trans.), *The Church by John Huss* (New York:
    Charles Scribner's Sons, 1915).
Scheck, P. (trans.), *Commentary on Matthew* (Washington,
    DC: The Catholic University of America Press, 2010).
Schwartz, Daniel L., 'Religious Violence and Eschatology
    in the Syriac Julian Romance', *Journal of Early Christian
    Studies* 19 (2011), 565–87.
Sedgwick, Joseph, *Episkopos Didaskalos: Learnings Necessity to
    an Able Minister of the Gospel* (London, 1653).
Siddiqi, Muhammad Zubayr, *Hadith Literature: Its Origin,
    Development and Special Features* (Cambridge: The
    Islamic Texts Society, 1993).
Siddiqui, Abdul Hamid, *Sahih Muslim: Being Traditions of the
    Sayings and Doings of the Prophet Muhammad* (Lahore: Sh.
    Muhammad Ashraf, 1976–81).
Smith, Orianne, *Romantic Women Writers, Revolution, and
    Prophecy: Rebellious Daughters, 1786–1826* (Cambridge
    University Press, 2013).
Smith, Preserved, *The Life and Letters of Martin Luther*
    (Boston and New York: Houghton Mifflin, 1911).
Snobelen, Stephen D., '"A Time and Times and the Dividing
    of Times": Isaac Newton, the Apocalypse, and 2060
    A.D.', *Canadian Journal of History* 38 (2003), 537–51.

Society of Friends, The (eds.), *The Journal of George Fox* (London: Headley Brothers, 1902).

Solovyev, Vladimir, *War, Progress, and the End of History: Three Discussions* (University of London Press, 1915).

[Swift, Jonathan and Alexander Pope], *Miscellanies: The Third Volume* (London, 1732).

Taylor, Charles (ed.), *Calmet's Dictionary of the Holy Bible* (Boston: Crocker and Brewster, 1832).

'Thomas Cranmer's Final Speech, before Burning (March 21, 1556)'. Available at www.luminarium.org/renlit/cranmerspeech.htm

Tolan, John V., *Saracens: Islam in the Medieval European Imagination* (New York: Columbia University Press, 2002).

Vicchio, Stephen J., *The Legend of the Antichrist: A History*. E-book (Kindle edition) (Eugene, Oregon: Wipf and Stock, 2009).

Wakefield, Walter L. and Austin P. Evans, *Heresies of the High Middle Ages: Selected Sources Translated and Annotated* (New York and London: Columbia University Press, 1969).

Wasilewski, Janna, 'The "Life of Muhammad" in Eulogius of Cordóba: Some Evidence for the Transmission of Greek Polemic to the Latin West', *Early Medieval Europe* 16 (2008), 333–53.

Webster, Charles, *The Great Instauration: Science, Medicine, and Reform* (London: Duckworth, 1975).

Weinstein, Donald, *Savonarola and Venice: Prophecy and Patriotism in the Renaissance* (Princeton University Press, 1970).

Whalen, Brett E., *Dominion of God: Christendom and Apocalypse in the Middle Ages* (Cambridge, Massachusetts: Harvard University Press, 2009).

Whiston, William, *An Essay on the Revelation of Saint John, So far as concerns the Past and Present Times* (Cambridge, 1706).

Wilhite, David E., *Ancient African Christianity* (London: Routledge, 2017).

Williams, George Huntston, *The Radical Reformation*
(Philadelphia: Westminster Press, 1962).
  (ed.), *Spiritual and Anabaptist Writers: Documents Illustrative
  of the Radical Reformation* (London: SCM Press Ltd,
  1957).
Williams, John Alden (ed.), *Themes of Islamic Civilization*
(Berkeley: University of California Press, 1971).
Wolf, Kenneth B., *'Eulogius of Córdoba and His Understanding
of Islam'*. Available at www.academia.edu/20312136/
Eulogius_of_C%C3%B3rdoba_and_His_
Understanding_of_Islam
Wolin, Richard, *Heidegger's Children: Karl Löwith, Hans Jonas,
and Herbert Marcuse* (Princeton University Press, 2001).
*Works of Martin Luther, Translated with Introductions and Notes,
Vol. III*. Available at http://media.sabda.org/alkitab-8/
LIBRARY/LUT_WRK3.PDF

INDEX

Abbo, abbot of Saint-Benoît-
  sur-Loire (c. 945–1004) 9
abomination of desolation 21–2,
  23–5, 38, 46, 79, 90, 150
Acts of the Apostles 100, 101
*Acts of the Holy Apostles Peter and
  Paul* 123
Adam and Eve 17
Adso of Montier-en-Der (d. 992)
  2, 104–5, 116, 120, 144, 145
  life of the Antichrist 9–14
  response to Queen Gerberga
    9–11
Adsonian (tyrannical) Antichrist
  270
  Catholic doctrine of 227
  return of 201–8
afterlife, versions of 39
*Against Heresies (Adversus
  Haereses)* 18, 41
age of the Father 176
age of the Holy Spirit (third age)
  162–4, 167, 176–7, 187
age of the Son 176
Ahmad ibn Hanbal (d. 855) 138
Alcazar, Luis de (1554–1613) 225
al-Dajjal (Antichrist of Islam) 5,
  132–9
Alembert, Jean-Baptiste le Rond
  d' 253
Alexander, Paul 105
Alexander I, Czar 259
Alexander II, Pope 147
Alexander VI, Pope (Rodrigo
  Borgia) 205
Alexander the Great (356–323
  BCE) 110–11, 113–19

Almaric of Bena (d. 1204–7)
  165–7
Altholz, Josef L. 271
Alvarus, Paul 128, 130
Ambrosiaster 67
American apocalypticists
  259–60
American Federal Council of
  Churches 276
Anacletus II, Pope 150–1
Ancient One (book of Daniel)
  28
Angelic Pope 186–9
Anglican church, view of the
  French Revolution 252–8
Anthony the anchorite, Saint
  176
Antichrist
  account of Irenaeus 41–7
  beast(s) of Revelation 25–31
  biblical and other influences
    incorporated into 4–5
  broad definition of the
    Radical Dissenters 229–35
  Catholic church ruling on
    preaching about 207–8
  coming of/reign of 46–7
  concept linked to prophetic
    history 274
  conception by an evil spirit 67
  dating the arrival of 49–50
  decline of interest in 234
  development of traditions in
    the first millennium 15–18
  emergence of the term 41–2
  features in the eschatology of
    Jesus 21–3

Antichrist*(cont.)*
  figures or institutions
    identified as 4
  floating signifier 274–84
  fluidity of the concept 3–4
  from the East 58–9
  fully human and responsible
    (Haimo) 122
  in popular culture 5–6
  Man of Lawlessness (Sin), Son
    of Perdition 23–5
  Martin Luther's papal
    Antichrist 209–18
  mirror of Christ 81–2
  parallels with Christ 68–9
  product of a Christian
    dilemma 2–3
  proliferation of modern
    candidates for 275–6
  Satan/the Devil 67–8
  Savonarola as 205–6
  signs of his coming 61–2
  Son of Satan 67–72
  traditions incorporated into
    40
  use as a term of abuse 231–4
  view of Savonarola 203–4
  within each individual 233–4
Antichrist mysticus 174–80
Antichurch 89–91
anti-Judaism in Christian
  eschatology 44, 82
Anti-Mary 154
Antiochus IV Epiphanes, King
  (c. 215–164 BCE) 11, 21–2,
  83
  as a type of Antichrist 83–4
apocalypse, account of John of
  Rupescissa 183–7, 188–90
Apocalypse of Daniel 72
*Apocalypse (or Revelationes) of
  Pseudo-Methodius* 105–12,
  113–17

apocalyptic account of history
  285, 287–8
apocalyptic prophecy, ruling of
  the Catholic church 207–8
apocalyptic worldview 145–53
apocalypticism
  decline of 234–5
  frame of crisis and judgement
    77–8
  of Savonarola 202–6
  Protestant view 220–4
  science and 236–44
  tradition in Christianity
    19–23
Apollinarius (c. 310–c. 390) 83
Apollyon (or Apoleon) 260, 261
Appolyon (the Destroyer),
  Napoleon as 256–7
Arafat, Yasser 275
Aristotelianism 177
Arius 131
Armilus, Antichrist of Judaism
  5, 139–42
arrival of the Antichrist
  imminence of 145–53
  signs of 14
  timing of 1–2
atheism 287
Augustine, Saint (354–430) 7–9,
  62, 92–6, 112–13, 125, 161,
  162, 229
Augustus Caesar 60
avaricious Antichrist 147
Ayatollah Khomeini 275

Babylon 123, 191
  as one of the four beasts 54
  association with the
    Antichrist 12
  whore of 176, 201
Bacon, Roger 188
Bale, John, bishop (1495–1563)
  220–1

Barbarossa, Emperor Frederick
  147
Baxter, Michael Paget
  (1834–1910) 260–1
beast from the abyss 26, 27
beast from the earth/land 4–5,
  28–31, 90, 178, 181
beast from the sea 4–5, 28–31,
  90, 161, 178, 181, 243
beast(s) of Revelation, Antichrist
  as 25–31
Behemoth 4–5, 28, 103–4
Beliar (Sammael, Satan) 38–9,
  59, 60
Belkira, false prophet 38
Bellarmine, Robert, Cardinal
  (1542–1621) 226–9, 268
Benardino, Pietro 206
Benedict XI, Pope 181
Beno, Cardinal 147
Bernard, bishop of Bayeux 143
Bernard of Clairvaux (1090–
  1153) 149–53
Beth-saida (city) 12, 115–16
Bible
  historical criticism of 270–4
  New Testament mentions of
    the Antichrist 15–18
  time of the New Testament
    writings 20
  traditions incorporated into
    the Antichrist 4–5
  see also specific books
biblical time 87
bin Laden, Osama 275
birth of the Antichrist 153–4,
  157–8, 159
birthplace of the Antichrist
  115–16
bloody Antichrist 147
Bonaparte, Napoleon see
  Napoleon Bonaparte,
  emperor

bonfire of the vanities 204–5
Boniface III, Pope 243
Boniface VIII, Pope 181, 188
Bonura, Christopher 106
Book of Figures (Liber figurarum)
  160
Book of Rules (Tyconius) 87–8
books about the Antichrist
  278–9
Bossuet, Jacques, bishop
  (1627–1704) 225
Bracciolini, Giovanni Francesco
  Poggio (1447–1522) 205
Brady, David 264
Brut, Walter (?–1402) 190–3
Bullinger, Heinrich (1505–75)
  217
Burr, David 179, 180

Caesarius of Heisterbach
  (c. 1180–c. 1240) 165
Cain 99–100
Calmet, Augustin (1672–1757)
  225–6
Calvin, John (1509–64) 216–17,
  229
  on the book of Revelation 219
Calvinism 216–18
Campanus, John 230
Capernaum (city) 115–16
Carolingian Empire (800–88)
  120
Catholic church
  prophecy and the Fifth
    Lateran Council 207–8
  retaliation against papal
    Antichrist claims 224–9
Catholicism as Antichrist 275–6
Celestine, Pope 188
Charlemagne 120, 176
Charles, Prince of Wales 275
Charles VIII, King of France
  203

Charles the Fat, Emperor 120
Chorazin (city) 115–16
Christ
  dating of the birth of 48–9
  defeat of two kings 161
  second and third returns 164
  see also Jesus
Christ within, the ethical self
  289–90
Christian empire 77–8
Christian tradition
  apocalypticism 19–23
  dilemma that resulted in the
    Antichrist 2–3
  history from the creation to
    the last judgement 17
  problem of good and evil
    285–90
  process from the Fall to final
    salvation 285–90
Christians, persecution of
  12–14, 40, 52–4, 57
church
  and Antichurch 89–91
  Antichrist outside and within
    3
  Antichrists within 94, 99
  battle both within and outside
    89–91
  corruption by sexuality 153–8
  Reformation and defeat of the
    Antichrist 148–9
  Reformation of 184
church history
  four ages of (Bernard of
    Clairvaux) 151–3
  seven stages (persecutions) of
    (Joachim of Fiore) 159–64
Clinton, Hillary
Commentary on Matthew
  (Jerome) 79
Commodian, eschatology of
  56–60

Constans, Emperor 67, 117–18
Constantine, Emperor 77, 107,
  147, 176, 194, 210, 241
Constantius, Emperor 67, 126
Córdoban martyrs 127–8
Corozain 12
cosmic nihilism 287, 289–90
Cranmer, Thomas (1489–1556)
  218
creation of the world 17
critical approach to the Bible
  270–4

Dan, king called 71
Dan, tribe of 11, 42–4, 50, 68,
  97, 115, 118, 123, 191, 228
Daniel, book of 1, 21–2, 28–9,
  34–37, 41, 44, 49, 54, 77,
  79, 82–4, 124, 130, 179, 191,
  236
Darby, John Nelson (1800–82)
  278
Darwin, Charles 271
Davis, William C. (1760–1831)
  260
Day of Judgement
  Catholic church ruling on
    preaching about 207–8
  date of 124–5
  scepticism about 245–7
death of the Antichrist 124, 154,
  156–7
  location of 84, 144
Deceiver of the world 32–3
deceiver within the church
  2, 3
Dell, William (c. 1607–69) 232
demonising the other as
  Antichrist 4, 93–4, 146–7,
  150–1, 274–84
desolating sacrilege *see*
  abomination of desolation
destroyer (Bible) 4–5

Deuteronomy, book of 50
Dialogue with Trypho 34–6
Diderot, Denis 253
Diocletian, Emperor 121
Dissertations on the Prophecies
     (Thomas Newton) 265
Dominican order 180
Domitian, Emperor (51–96 CE)
     11, 107
Donation of Constantine 194, 196,
     198, 210
Donatists 86, 89, 95
Donne, John 289
double Antichrists *see* dual
     Antichrists
dragon, Satan as 25–31
dual Antichrists 56–66, 132,
     174–80
dual-Messiah tradition in
     Judaism 140–2

Eastern Antichrist 185–6
Elijah, prophet 14, 26, 27, 52,
     57, 118, 121, 156, 186, 190,
     1–193
Elliott, Edward Bishop 251–2
Emmerson, Richard K. 10,
     105
empires, succession of 28–9
end of the world
     concerns towards the end of
          the first millennium 7–11
     expectation of 17, 77–85
     explanations for failure to
          arrive 40
     failed predictions about
          95–6
     imminent expectations of
          96–7
     scepticism about 245–7
     signs of 31–6, 96–7
     third age and 162–4
     timing of 8–11, 229

end times
     account of Augustine 62
     account of Commodian
          56–60
     account of Hippolytus of
          Rome 47–55
     account of Lactantius 62–6
     account of Sulpicius Severus
          60–2
     account of Tertullian 55
     appearance of the Dajjal
          137–9
     estimations of the date of
          240–2, 243–4
     events of 8
     false prophets and 16–17
     living in 157
     signs of 16–17, 73–4, 137–9
     viewed as having already
          begun 4
English Enlightenment 252
English Reformation 238
English Revolution (1640–60)
     231, 237
Enoch, prophet 14, 27, 52, 118,
     121, 156, 186, 190, 191
Epistle of Barnabas 36–7
eschatological tyrant
     account of Lactantius 63–6
     Antichrist as 3, 4
     Satan as 36–40
eschatology (doctrine of the last
     things) 17
     of Jesus 19–23
Essays and Reviews (1860) 271–4
Ethelbert, King 97
ethical imperative of personal
     goodness 289–90
Euanthas 46
Eulogius of Córdoba 129–30
Eusebius of Caesarea (c. 260–
     c. 340) 80, 83, 107
Evanthus 51

evil
  as an absence of good 286
  continuation after Jesus 2–3
  present, past, and future
      285–90
  within the church 103–4
Ezekiel, book of 114

Faber, George Stanley
    (1773–1854) 262–4
false bishops 90
false brethren within the church
    90–1
false Christ(s) 16, 33–4, 101, 127,
    228
false Messiahs 21, 34, 185, 228
false pope (pseudopontifex) 159,
    188
false prophets 4–5, 16–17, 21, 30,
    31–6, 61, 127, 160
  Belkira 38
  Simon Magus 100–4
false teachers within the church
    104
Fell, Margaret (1614–1702) 233
Ficino, Marsilio (1433–99)
    205–6
figures identified as the
    Antichrist 4
film portrayals of the Antichrist
    276–7
final Antichrist 148–9, 164,
    190–200, 209
final eschatological tyrant 22
final judgement 22–3
  account of Irenaeus 47
  timing of 84–5
  versions of 39
final trap 36
Firmicus Maternus, Julius
    67–8
floating signifier, Antichrist as
    274–84

Florence, as new Jerusalem
    202–3
Folkes, Martin 247
four beasts of Daniel 54–5
Fox, George (1624–91) 233
Francesco da Montepulciano
    207
Francis, Pope 275
Francis of Assisi, Saint 174
Franciscan Order
  influence of Joachism 168–9,
      173–4
  nature of poverty in their
      tradition 174–83
  revival of Joachism 174–83
  spiritual tradition 174–83
  tribulations 185
Franck, Sebastian (c. 199–
    c. 1542) 230
fraudulent Antichrist 147
Frederick, John 209
Frederick II, Emperor
    (1194–1250) 168–74
Frederick II, King of Prussia
    253
French Antichrists 252–64
French Empire under Napoleon
    256–64
French Enlightenment, as
    Antichrist 252–3
French Revolution (1789–99)
    252–64, 268
Fuller, Robert 279
future Antichrist 3, 15, 78–9,
    85–91, 264–70
futurism 225, 226–9

Gaddafi, Mu'ammar 275
Gaiseric, Vandal king 96
Gallileo Galilei (1564–1642) 226
Garden of Eden 17, 287
  serpent as Antichrist 68
Gay, John (1685–1732) 245–7

Gehenna 39
Genesis, book of 44, 50, 68, 97, 113, 115
Geoffrey of Chartres 149
Geoffrey of Loreto 150
Gerard, archbishop of Auxienne 143
Gerard of Angoulême 150
Gerberga, Queen 9–11, 104–5, 120
Gerhoh of Reichersburg 147–9
God, beneficent versus maleficent nature of 287
Gog and Magog 4–5, 31, 110, 112–19, 141, 163, 164, 174–80, 189, 190–200, 220, 223, 229
Golgotha 115
Golitsyn, Alexander, Prince 259
Gorbachev, Mikhail 275
Gosse, Edmund (1849–1928) 250–2
Gosse, Emily 250, 251–2
Gosse, Philip (1810–88) 249–52
Goths 57, 80
Great Antichrist (magnus antichristus) 160–4, 174–80
Great Deceiver, Antichrist as 51
Grebel, Conrad (c. 1498–1526) 230
Greece, as one of the four beasts 54
Greeks, king of 112
Gregory I, Pope (Gregory the Great) (c. 540–604) 96–100, 103–4, 147, 265
Gregory VII, Pope 146–7, 148
Gregory IX, Pope (c. 1170–1241) 170–1
Grotius, Hugo (1583–1645) 226
Guelf Joachism 169
Gui, Bernard 182

Habershon, Matthew (1789–1852) 249
Hadith literature 133–9
Haimo (monk of St Germain at Auxerre) (fl. c. 840–70) 120–5
Hammond, Henry (1605–60) 226
Harmagedon 30
Henry IV, Emperor 148
heresies 175, 181–2, 190–200
heretics 165
Herod 126
Hieronymous of Bergamo 206
Hilarianus, Quintus Julius 119
Hildebert, archbishop of Tours 150
Hildegard of Bingen, Benedictine nun (1098–1179) 153–7
Hill, Christopher 231
Hippolytus of Rome (c. 130–c. 236) 47–55, 68
historical criticism of the Bible 270–4
history
    apocalyptic account (domain of conflict) 285, 287–8
    Christian view of 285–90
    providential account 285–7
    site of progress 287
    ultimate meaning in 288–90
Hitler, Adolf 275
Hoffman, Melchior (c. 1495–c. 1543) 231
Holy Spirit, age of see age of the Holy Spirit
Horsley, Samuel, bishop (1733–1806) 254–6, 261–2
Hughes, Kevin 55, 77
human Antichrist 75–6

humans
  Antichrist within 3
  battle between good and evil
    within 5–6
Huns 113
Hus, Jan (John) (c. 1370–1415)
  195–7, 213
Hussein, Saddam
Hussite movement 197–200

imminent arrival of the
  Antichrist 85–91
imperial Antichrist 262
impure Antichrist 147
Infidel Antichrist 253
Innocent II, Pope 150–1
Innocent III, Pope 166
Innocent IV, Pope (c. 1195–
  1254) 171–2
Inquisition 182
institutions identified as the
  Antichrist 4
Irenaeus, bishop of Lyons
  (c. 130–c. 200) 18, 75, 244
  account of the Antichrist 41–7
Isaiah 84
Ishmaelites 106
Islam 106, 127–8
  al-Dajjal, the Deceiver 132–9
  Antichrist of 5, 132–9
  as Antichrist 275–6
  as the little horn of Daniel 217
  rise of 179, 262–3
  view of Calvin 216
  see also Muhammad
isopsephy (numbers assigned to
  Greek letters to generate
  words) 46
Italian Renaissance 199–200

Jacobus de Voragine 102
Jakoubek of Stříbro (c. 1370–
  1429) 198–9

James I, King of England 222–3
James VI, King of Scotland
  222–3
Jenkins, Jerry B. 278
Jeremiah, book of 43
Jerome, Saint (c. 342–420) 76,
  79–85, 113, 115
  commentary on Matthew 85
  commentary on the book of
    Daniel 82–4
Jerome of Prague (1379–1416)
  195, 213
Jerusalem 12
  coming down from heaven 59
Jesus
  as killer of the Antichrist 14
  as the Messiah 19–20
  denial of the divinity of 15
  description of the Antichrist
    73–4
  eschatology of 19–23
  killing Al-Dajjal 138, 139
  life, death, and resurrection
    286
  signs of the end of the world
    73–4
  see also Christ
Jewish Antichrist 11, 42–4, 51–2,
  61, 228
Jewish eschatology 19–23
Jews
  Antichrist for 58–9
  portrayed as supporters of
    the Antichrist 12, 44, 69,
    82, 268
  rejection of Christ 82, 123–4
  see also Judaism
Joachim of Fiore (c. 1135–1202)
  2, 126–7, 142–4, 159–64,
  187
Joachism 167–74
  revival in the thirteenth
    century 174–83

Job, book of 103
John, apostle 101
John, bishop of Evreaux 143
John, gospel of 196
1 John 15–18, 41, 78, 80, 88, 93, 99
2 John 16–18, 41
3 John 17–18
John XXII, Pope (1234–1334) 181–2
John Chrysostom, bishop of Constantinople (c. 347–407) 76
John of Patmos 25, 74
John of Rupescissa (c.1310–c.1368) 183–7, 188–90
John of Seville 128
John the Evangelist, Saint 126
Jovian, Emperor (332–64) 111
Jowett, Benjamin (1817–93) 271–4
Juan Carlos, King of Spain 275
Judaism
    Antichrist of 5
    Armilus the Jewish Antichrist 139–42
    two-Messiah tradition 140–2
Judas 99–100
Julian Romance (sixth century) 111
Julian the Apostate, Emperor (332–63) 111, 121
Justin, Greek theologian (c. 100–c. 165) 34–6

Kennedy, John F. 275
Kett, Henry (1761–1825) 252–3
killer of the Antichrist 14, 98, 145
Kingdom of God (fifth monarchy) 29
Kissinger, Henry 275
Knox, John 218

Lactantius (c. 240–c. 320) 62–6, 67
LaHaye, Tim 278
Landes, Richard 95
Last Days
    events preceding 22–3
    role of the Roman emperor 104–12
    tribulation 22–3
    uncertainty of timing 23
    see also end times; end of the world; eschatology
Last Roman Emperor 149, 173, 259
Last World Emperor 104–12, 114, 115, 117, 167, 188–9, 203
Lateinos 46
Lateinus 51
Left Behind series of books (1995–2007) 278–9
Leo X, Pope (1475–1521) 211
Leonardo da Fivizzano (c. 1450–1526) 205
Lerner, Robert E. 159, 164, 168, 169, 173–4
Leviathan 4–5, 28, 103–4
Levin, Ira 276
Licinius, Emperor 107
life of the Antichrist
    account of Adso 9–11–14
    account of Hildegard of Bingen 153–8
    literal/real Antichrist 3, 146
Little Apocalypse (Matthew) 20, 33
little horn of the fourth beast (Daniel) 28–9, 54, 76, 217, 243
Lollards 190
Lombards 96–7
Louis IV d'Outremer, King 104
Löwith, Karl 285, 288–90

Lucius III, Pope (c. 1100–85)
159
Luke, gospel of 20
Luther, Martin (1483–1546) 208,
229
on the book of Revelation
219–20
view on the papal Antichrist
209–18
Lutherans, as Antichrist 230

1 Maccabees, book of 21–2
Machiavelli, Niccolò 206–7
magic used by the Antichrist
123–4
magisterial Antichrist 208–18
magisterial reformers, as
Antichrist 230–1
magnus antichristus (Great
Antichrist) 160–4
Mahomet see Muhammad
Maitland, Samuel R. (1792–
1866) 269–70
Malachy of Armagh, Saint 153
Man of Apostasy 35–6
Man of Sin (Lawlessness) 23–5,
34–6, 55, 81, 90, 122, 233,
273–4
Manasseh, King 38
Mansuetus, Brother 172–3
mark of the beast 4–5, 29–30,
70, 100, 156, 186
Mark, gospel of 16, 20–3
Martin of Tours 60, 61–2, 67
Martino di Brozzi 206
Mary I, Queen of England
(Mary Tudor) 218
Matthew, gospel of 12, 13, 20,
33, 128, 147, 196
Commentary on Matthew
(Jerome) 79, 85
Mayer, Lewis (1738–1849) 257–8
McGinn, Bernard 96, 145, 187

Meaning in History (Löwith)
285–7, 288–90
meaning of life 289–90
Mede, Joseph (1586–1638) 234,
240, 249
Melsermut 126
Messiah
coming of the Messiah and
the Last Days 19–20
two-Messiah tradition in
Judaism 140–2
see also false Messiahs
Messiah ben David 140–2
Messiah ben Joseph (or
Ephraim) 140–2
Methodius (d. c. 311) 83
Michael, archangel 14, 27, 110,
118, 145
millennial eschatology 77
Hippolytus of Rome 48–50
miracles, Antichrist's ability to
perform 100–1
More, Henry (1614–87) 234–5,
236–9, 240
Moses, prophet 26, 27
movements as Antichrist
candidates 275–6
Muggleton, Lodowick (1609–
98) 233
Muhammad (Mahomet),
prophet (570–623) 106, 217,
257
as the Antichrist 126–32,
204
followers as Antichrist 230
lives of 128–32
on al-Dajjal, the Deceiver
133–9
Muslims
conflict with the Roman
Empire 108–10
defeat by the Last World
Emperor 114

future ruler called Apollyon
(the destroyer) 260
Mussolini, Benito 275
mystery of iniquity 90, 121–2,
168
mystical Antichrist 174–80
mystical Elijah 186
mystical Enoch 186

name of the beast/Antichrist
29–30, 46, 51, 228
Napier, John (1550–1617)
221–4
Napoleon III, emperor (1808–
52) 251, 260–1
Napoleon Bonaparte, emperor,
as final Antichrist 256–64
Nebuchadnezzar, King 44
Nelson, Horatio 261
Nero, Emperor (37–68 CE) 11,
107, 121–2, 126, 175
as Antichrist 204, 217
as resurrected Roman
Antichrist 56–66
story of Simon Magus
102–3
Newman, John Henry (1801–90)
264–9, 270
Newton, Isaac (1642–1727) 1,
239–42, 245, 249
Newton, Thomas, bishop of
Bristol (1704–82) 244–5,
248, 249, 265, 266–7
Nicholas of Dresden (fl. early
1400s) 197–8
Nietzsche, Friedrich 279
nihilism 289–90
Noah 44, 113
Norbert of Xanten (c. 1080–
1134) 149–50
number of the beast (666) 4–5,
29–30, 44–6, 70, 172, 179,
181, 228, 251, 257, 261

616 as alternative number 45
variety of interpretations 264
number symbolism 45–6

Obama, Barack 275
Oisander, Andreas (1498–1552)
213–14
Olivi, Peter 174–80
On Christian Doctrine
(Augustine) 95
On the End of the World (Pseudo-
Hippolytus) 68, 100–1
On the Origin of Species (Darwin)
271
Origen of Alexandria (c. 185–c.
254) 78–9
Otho, Emperor (32–69) 89
Ottoman Empire 249
Ottoman Turks see Turks

pagans, rejection of Christ
123–4
papacy as Antichrist 4, 132,
142–3, 161, 167, 171–2, 188,
190–200, 209, 230, 238, 255
Catholic futurist pushback
264–70
Protestant view 248–9
Protestant view of Revelation
219–24
scepticism about 245
view of Martin Luther 209–18
Paul, apostle 23–5, 57, 81, 99,
101–3, 120–2, 161, 210, 217,
273–4
Penman, Leigh 182–3
Perfectus (Christian priest)
127–8
Persia, as one of the four beasts
54
Persian Antichrist 56, 58–9
personal goodness and the
Christ within 289–90

Peter the Venerable, abbot of
    Cluny (c. 1092–1156) 131
Peter, apostle 57, 101–3
Philippians 27
Phocas, Byzantine emperor 262
physical attributes of the
    Antichrist 71-2–76
Piedmont, king of 251
Piozzi, Hester 256–7
Pius IX, Pope 251
Plato, view of evil 286
Plymouth Brethren 278
Point Pleasant (2005 television
    series) 277–8
Polycarp, bishop of Smyrna
    (c. 69–c. 155) 18
Porphyry, Neoplatonist
    philosopher (c. 232–303) 82–4
powers of the Antichrist 100–1,
    123–4, 155
Premonstratensian monastic
    order 149
present Antichrists 3, 15–17,
    78–9, 85–91, 99
preterism 225–6
Prideaux, Humphrey 132
Prierias, Sylvester (c. 1456–1527)
    211
Primasius, bishop of
    Hadrumetum (fl. mid sixth
    century) 91–2
Prince of Iniquity 118
prophecies, search for
    knowledge of the Antichrist
    1–2
prophetic history, link to the
    Antichrist concept 274
prophetic texts, effects of
    historical criticism 270–4
Protestant Reformation 208
Protestantism 132
  Adsonian (tyrannical)
    Antichrist 270

evangelical embrace of the
    Antichrist 274
papal Antichrist 209, 248–9
readings of Revelation
    219–24, 237
providentialism in Christianity
    2–3, 14, 98, 285–7
Psalm 91 151
Pseudo-Ephraem 110, 113,
    132
Pseudo-Hippolytus 68–71,
    100–1
Pseudo-Methodius 105–12,
    113–17, 132, 158
pseudo-pope 177–9
Puritans 231

Quakers 233
Quodvulteus, bishop of
    Carthage (d. c. 450) 96
Qur'an 133

radical Antichrist 190–200
Radical Reformation, view of
    the Antichrist 229–35
Ralph of Namur 167
Ranters 233–4
rapture into heaven 278
Reagan, Ronald Wilson 275
recapitulation, doctrine of 42
Reeves, John C. 132
Reeves, Marjorie 200
Reformation 208
  new readings of the book of
    Revelation 219–24
refreshment of the saints 54
regal Antichrist 168–74
reign of the Antichrist 50–4,
    69–71, 84
religions as Antichrist
    candidates 275–6
Restorer Pope (Angelic Pope)
    186–9

Revelation, book of 1, 7, 8,
25–31, 41, 43–4, 49, 112,
124, 126, 165
Antichrist not mentioned in
226, 244
commentary by Tyconius
86–91
interpretation of Henry More
236–9
interpretation of Joachim of
Fiore 126–7, 142–4, 159–64
interpretation of John Napier
221–4
interpretation of John of
Rupescissa 183–7, 188–90
interpretation of Peter Olivi
174–80
interpretation of the Catholic
church 224–9
interpretation of the Gosse
family 249–52
new readings in the
Reformation period
219–24
number and range of
interpretations 264–70
seven-headed dragon 160
whore of Babylon 201
rhetorical Antichrist 4
Richard I (Lionheart), King of
England 126–7, 142–4
rise of the Antichrist 71
Robins, John (Ranter) 233
Robinson, David C. 86
Roger de Hoveden (fl. 1174–
1201) 126, 143–5
Roman Antichrist, Nero
resurrected as 56–66
Roman Empire
adoption of Christianity
77–8
as one of the four beasts 54
conflict with Muslims 108–10

fall and appearance of the
Antichrist 120–2
restraining the Antichrist 55,
80–1
role within Christian
eschatology 104–12
Roman origin of the Antichrist
51–2
Rosemary's Baby (film, 1968)
276–7
Royal Society 247
Rudolf of Saxony, Brother 168
Russian Orthodox church 258

Sadat, Anwar 275
saints, thousand-year reign on
earth 85
Saladin 126, 160
Salimbene, Franciscan abbot
(1221–88) 168–70, 173–4
Salmon, Joseph (fl. 1647–56)
(Ranter) 233–4
Satan (the dragon)
binding for a thousand years
7, 161–2
eschatological tyrant
36–40
imprisoning of 66, 189
release at the end time 8
release from hell after a
thousand years 66
release of 161–2, 179
thrown into the pit for a
thousand years 31
Savonarola, Girolamo
(1452–98) 202–6, 213
Scarlet Woman 251
scepticism about the papacy as
the Antichrist 245
Schwenckfeld, Caspar
(c. 1489–1561) 230
'scientific' Antichrist 236–44
Scottish Reformation 218, 223

Scriblerus Club 245
second coming (Parousia of
    Christ)
    date of 2–3, 48–9
    forerunners of 52–4
    timing of 46–7
secular progress 287
Sedgwick, Joseph (fl. 1650s)
    232–3
Sefer Zerubbabel 140–1
Sermon on the End of the World
    (Pseudo-Ephraem) 110,
    113
seventh king, Antichrist as
    159–64
Severus, Sulpicius (c. 363–c.
    420) 60–2
sexuality, corruption of the
    church by 153–8
Shadrach, Meshach, and
    Abednego 44
Sibyl of Babylon 60
Sibylline Oracles 60, 117
Signorelli, Luca 201–2
Simon Magus 99–100–104, 123
Smith, J. Harold 276
Solovyev, Vladimir (1853–1900)
    279–84
Son of Perdition (damnation)
    23–5, 36–40, 108, 115, 118,
    122, 155
Son of Satan, Antichrist as
    67–72
sons of Ismael 108–10
sons of Japheth 113
Spalatin, Georg 210, 211
Spanish blanks affair (1592) 222
spiritual Antichrist 3, 146
Stephen, stoning of 175
Stukeley, William (1687–1765)
    247
Synoptic Apocalypse 20
Syriac Antichrist accounts 132

Teitan 46, 51
television portrayals of the
    Antichrist 277–8
Temple in Jerusalem 46
    destruction of 20–1
    profanation of *see*
        abomination of desolation
    rebuilding by the Antichrist
        70
temple of Solomon, raising of 13
Tertullian (c. 160–c. 220) 55,
    107
Testament of Hezekiah 37–9,
    59
testicles of the Antichrist 103–4
*The Acts of the Apostles Peter and
    Paul* 101–3
The Annals of Roger de Hoveden
    143–5
The Apocalypse of Elijah 73, 74
The Apocalypse of Ezra 73, 75–6
The Apocalypse of Peter 33–4
The Apocalypse of Pseudo-John
    73, 74
The Ascension of Isaiah 37
The Didache or *The Teaching of
    the Apostles* 32–3
The Omen series of films
    (1976–81) 277
'The Sermon and Deeds of the
    Antichrist' (fresco) 201–2
The Testament of Our Lord 73–4
*The Travels of Sir John
    Mandeville* 116
Theodoret, bishop of Cyrrhus
    (c. 393–c. 458/466) 67
Theodosius I, Emperor 77, 107
1 Thessalonians 273
2 Thessalonians 23–5, 41, 55, 62,
    67, 81, 99, 120–2–123, 124,
    161, 216, 218, 273
Thietland of Einsiedeln
    (fl. 943–65) 124–5

Index

(text)

Thomas of Eccleston 172–3
Tiburtine Oracle 117–18
Tolan, John 130
Tolstoy, Leo 258
Trafalgar, battle of 261
Treatise on Christ and the Antichrist 48
Trefnant, John, bishop of Hereford 190
tribe of Dan *see* Dan, tribe of
tribe of Judah 50
tribulation of the end time 13–14
True Levellers (aka 'the Diggers') 231
true pope (orthopontifex) 188
Trump, Donald 275
Trypho 34–6
Turks
 as demonic 214–16
 association with the Antichrist 255
two witnesses (Revelation) 25–7, 52, 186
Tyconius (d. c. 400) 86–91
 commentary on Revelation 91–100
 types of Antichrist 83–4, 89
 Cain 99–100
 Judas 99–100
 Simon Magus 99–100–104
 Muhammad 127–32
tyrannical Antichrist (Adso) 2, 270

Ubertino of Casale (1259–after 1325) 180–1, 188
Ussher, James, Archbishop (1581–1656) 232

Vade mecum in tribulatione (Walk with Me in the Tribulation) 183–7
Valla, Lorenzo (c. 1407–57) 210, 211
Vettori, Francesco 206–7
Victoria, Queen 264
violence by Christians 111
virginity, attack by the Antichrist 155
Voltaire (1694–1778) 245, 249, 253, 286–7
von Amsdorf, Nicholas (1483–1565) 215–16

Walter de Coutances, archbishop of Rouen and Apamia 143
Walther, Rudolph (1519–86) 1
War and Peace (Tolstoy) 258
Webster, Charles 236–7
Western Antichrist 186
Whiston, William (1667–1752) 242–4
 end of the world prophesy 245–7–248
whore of Babylon 176, 201
Wibert (or Guibert) of Ravenna 146
William Aurifex (the goldsmith) 165–8
Winstanley, Gerrard (1609–76) 231
Wycliffe, John (c. 1329–84) 190, 193–5, 213

Zwingli, Ulrich (1483–1531) 217
 as Antichrist 230

323